Virtuous Giving

PHILANTHROPIC STUDIES

Robert L. Payton and Dwight F. Burlingame, *general editors*

VIRTUOUS GIVING

*Philanthropy, Voluntary Service,
and Caring*

Mike W. Martin

Indiana University Press

Bloomington & Indianapolis

The paper used in this publication meets the minimum requirements of American
National Standard for Information Sciences—Permanence of Paper for Printed
Library Materials, ANSI Z39.48-1984.

Manufactured in the United States of America

∞™

Library of Congress Cataloging-in-Publication Data

Martin, Mike W., date
Virtuous giving : philanthropy, voluntary service, and
caring / Mike W. Martin.
p.   cm.—(Philanthropic studies)
Includes bibliographical references and index.
ISBN 0-253-33677-5 (cloth)
1. Philanthropists. 2. Charity. 3. Voluntarism. 4. Caring.
I. Title. II. Series.
HV25.M37   1994
361.7′4—dc20
93-8027

1 2 3 4 5 99 98 97 96 95 94

For Shannon and for my mother,
and in memory of Theodore R. Martin,
Pearl Rector, and Martin C. Nalder

Contents

Preface

To do philosophy is to explore one's own temperament, and yet at the same time to attempt to discover the truth.
—Iris Murdoch

Voluntary acts of compassion and acts of community are always needed, in all societies, and always will be.
—Robert L. Payton

IN THIS BOOK I explore some of the ways philanthropy contributes to morally desirable relationships when we give with care—with good will and good judgment, with responsible moral concern.[1] In doing so I discuss a variety of moral issues: the role of the virtues in philanthropy, responsibilities to help others, distortions in helping, mixed motives in giving, and how voluntary service contributes to self-fulfillment.

After providing an overview of the philosophy of philanthropy, Chapter 1 develops a definition of philanthropy as voluntary private giving for public purposes. This definition is value-neutral and draws together the enormous variety of voluntary service for study without normative blinkers. It avoids assumptions about whether philanthropy has good motives, aims, or results, and it leaves open the question of whether philanthropy can be a moral responsibility. Sometimes philanthropy has a bad name; more often it has no name at all or else the emotionally clouded name of "charity." While it is less commonly used in everyday discourse than it was in the nineteenth century, the word "philanthropy" is currently undergoing a rebirth as a general term referring to both volunteering and monetary giving, whether for humanitarian or cultural purposes. "Voluntary service" is a good two-word equivalent, and I use it as a synonym, mindful that service comes in the form of money as well as time.

Chapter 1 also develops a framework for connecting desirable forms of philanthropy with the virtues. Most philanthropic giving occurs as participation in social practices, such as donating blood, contributing to public television, sheltering the homeless, paying tithing, and volunteering in museums or hospitals. These are practices in the colloquial sense: patterns of conduct engaged in by many people and continuing over time. They are also practices in Alasdair MacIntyre's technical sense: complex cooperative human endeavors which, when pursued virtuously, promote the good of individuals and communities. Philanthropy makes possible a variety of benefits to recipients and benefactors, especially the caring relationships it fosters.

Philanthropy is not itself a virtue; it is an activity which may be good or bad. Nor are any virtues unique to philanthropy. Instead, all major virtues play a role in philanthropic giving: obviously generosity and compassion, but also courage and conscientiousness, faith and fairness, gratitude and good judgment, honesty and humility, integrity and inspiration, love and loyalty, pride and perseverence, responsible authority and respect for others, self-knowledge and self-respect, wisdom and moral creativity. Chapter 2 discusses some thirty virtues relevant to philanthropy, sorting them into two general categories: participation virtues, which are especially important in motivating philanthropy, and enabling virtues, which tend to make philanthropy effective. Elucidating these virtues with examples helps sharpen our moral understanding of philanthropy and philanthropists.

Much philanthropy is morally optional—desirable or at least permissible, but not obligatory. In certain contexts there are also responsibilities to engage in philanthropy, as I argue in Chapter 3. Some of them derive from the obligation of mutual aid in assisting people in life-threatening situations. Others derive from the obligation of reciprocity to do our fair share in communities and practices from which we benefit. These two general obligations apply to everyone, though their precise requirements vary greatly according to circumstances. I also set forth a conception of "supererogatory responsibilities"—obligations transcending the call of duty incumbent on everyone, and whose origin lies in highly personal commitments to optional moral ideals. The responsibilities of professionals to engage in *pro bono publico* work (offering services at reduced or no fee) are often supererogatory but sometimes a professional requirement. All philanthropic responsibilities, both general and supererogatory ones, leave considerable room for discretion in deciding how to meet them. Whether optional or obligatory, philanthropy is primarily a forum for personal moral expression.

Philanthropy goes awry for many reasons besides bad luck. Attempts to help are self-defeating when they are based upon naiveté, stupidity, lack of imagination, insensitivity, arrogance, or any number of other character flaws. An especially egregious fault, one recurringly inveighed against in the history of philanthropy, is the failure to respect individual autonomy, that is, the right and the ability to competently pursue one's interests and values. In Chapter 4 I discuss several instances involving degrading attitudes toward recipients, abuses in fundraising, exploitation of volunteers, and harm to third parties. In a related vein, I examine circumstances in which incentives for volunteering are coercive, an issue that has surfaced in recent debates over tying financial aid for college students to volunteering for national service. Special attention is devoted to how sexism threatens the autonomy of women volunteers. With this chapter, I attempt to provide balanced attention to the gloomy and morally ambiguous side of philanthropy without allowing it to eclipse the brighter side, as it so easily does.[2]

Motives for philanthropy interest us because they reveal what a person is genuinely committed to. Unfortunately, we are eager to criticize the motives of philanthropists (other than ourselves). The first whiff of self-interest evokes charges of hypocrisy. Indeed, cynicism about philanthropy is a fashionable sign of sophistication, as well as a rationalization for moral complacency. In Chapter 5 I argue that "mixed motives," which combine self-concern with altruism, are as typical in philanthropy as anywhere else in life. Philanthropy can be highly admirable without being purely selfless, and mixed motives can even be desirable when they intensify philanthrophic endeavors. A challenge to this tolerance of mixed motives is psychological egoism, the view that we are all exclusively self-seeking. Formulated by Thomas Hobbes in the seventeenth century, this outlook on human life has been endorsed by many social scientists, not to mention authors of self-help books. It is almost unanimously rejected by philosophers, and I present the reasons why. I also comment on cynicism, the view that our motives are generally selfish or unsavory in other ways. And I argue against consequentialism, the view that only results are morally important, not motives.

Philanthropy breeds paradoxes, several of which are discussed in Chapter 6. Thus, it is said that selflessness promotes self-fulfillment; in giving we receive; we find ourselves by losing ourselves (in service to others); self-surrender (to good causes) is liberating; the way to get happiness is to forget it (while promoting the happiness of other people); faith is self-fulfilling. These conundrums are easily abused when they become rationalizations for exploiting people on behalf of immoral causes. Yet they also convey important insights as they apply to morally concerned individuals. Philanthropy offers numerous avenues for self-fulfilling service, at least when a match is found between personal interests and philanthropic opportunities, and even though altruism takes many other directions as well.

Acknowledgments

THIS BOOK BEGAN as a dialogue with students and later overflowed the classroom. My interdisciplinary course, "A Life of Service," was one of fourteen liberal arts courses funded as part of the 1986–1991 Program on Studying Philanthropy. I am grateful to the Association of American Colleges, which sponsored the program, for a course-development grant and a research grant.

I benefited from the insights of other participants in the project who met for conferences in Philadelphia and Chicago during 1989 and 1991. I especially wish to thank Thomas Jeavons (the project director), Albert Anderson, William Brandon, John Chandler, James Ferris, Fritz Fleischmann, Maurice G. Gurin, Virginia Hodgkinson, Craig Kennedy, Mary Oates, Joel Orosz, Susan A. Ostrander, Robert Payton, Richard Sundeen, Ivor Thomas, and Jon Van Til.

My students provided an invaluable stimulus. So did many colleagues and friends who guest-lectured, shared insights, and offered encouragement. I am grateful to Judie Argyros, Richard J. Arneson, Robert Audi, Earl Babbie, Tom and Martha Beck, Kurt Bergel, Arthur W. Blaser, Paul Delp, Dave Dodson, James Doti, Michele T. Dumont, Herbert Fingarette, Arthur C. Frantzreb, Craig Kei Ihara, Kathie Jenni, Olivia Johnson, Greg Kavka, Ken King, A. I. Melden, Jay Moseley, Barbara Mulch, Peter Muth, Robert Pralle, Joseph and Jean Runzo, Roland and Jane Schinzinger, Susan Schlaeger, Dennis Short, Cameron Sinclair, G. T. (Buck) and Joni Smith, Tim Stanton, Anita Storck, Vern Ummel, Judy Weissberg-Ortiz, Virginia Warren, Barbara West, Bert C. Williams, and Kenji Yoshida. I was helped by a sabbatical leave and a Hua-Cheng Wang Fellowship from Chapman University.

Most of all I am grateful to my wife, Shannon Snow Martin, and my mother, Ruth Lochhead Martin, for their support, inspiration, and love.

1

Giving with Care

The epithets *sociable, good-natured, humane, merciful, grateful, friendly, generous, beneficent*, or their equivalents, are known in all languages, and universally express the highest merit, which *human nature* is capable of attaining.

—David Hume

When I give I give myself.

—Walt Whitman

WE ARE ALL philanthropists on some occasions. Each of us has contributed beyond our circle of family and friends and work. We have donated money, time, talent, energy, blood, or clothing. We have volunteered to help a community, church, political organization, social cause, sports team, or scout troop. Put simply, philanthropy is voluntary giving for public ends. More fully, philanthropy is voluntary private (nongovernment) giving for public purposes, whether gifts are large or small, money or time, local or international in scope, for purposes which are humanitarian, cultural, religious, civic, environmental, or of mutual aid.[1]

At its best, philanthropy unites individuals in caring relationships that enrich giver and receiver alike. Often it is heroic and inspiring: witness the lives of Moses, Jesus, Muhammad, Susan B. Anthony, Jane Addams, Martin Luther King, Jr., and Mother Teresa of Calcutta. But philanthropy can also be harmful.[2] At its worst, it is divisive and demeaning to everyone involved, as in contributing to hate groups such as the Ku Klux Klan. Too often philanthropy squanders precious resources on misguided groups such as those promoting astrology and those more concerned with self-seeking than with helping others. In between the clearly good and the obviously bad, much philanthropy is morally ambiguous, combining good intentions with bad results, or bad intentions with good results, or good and bad motives with good and bad consequences.

Philanthropy, then, is morally complex, in theory as well as in practice. While luck plays a role, much turns on whether we give with care—with caring and carefulness, with good will and good judgment.

Philosophy of Philanthropy

Philanthropy raises important moral issues in at least four main areas. (1) Social and political philosophy is concerned with the overall impact of philanthropy on society, as well as with the role of government in regulating and supporting it, for example with tax deductions for gifts to charities. (2) Professional ethics studies the responsibilities of development officers (fundraisers), foundation officials, and other professionals involved in philanthropic organizations. (3) The ethics of recipients deals with the responsibilities of beneficiaries, such as honesty in writing grant proposals, fidelity to donors' intentions, and avoiding harmful forms of dependency (pauperism). (4) The ethics of philanthropic giving focuses on the ideals, virtues, and responsibilities of philanthropists.

In this book I focus on the ethics of philanthropic giving, only occasionally touching on the other areas. The topics discussed concern each of us as (actual or potential) donors and volunteers. Foundation and corporation philanthropy will be mentioned only as they bear on giving by individuals.

When ethicists have discussed philanthropy, typically under the name of charity, it has usually been in connection with particular topics such as giving to alleviate world hunger and volunteering to promote environmental causes. Yet some issues require more systematic reflection. When and why is philanthropy valuable? How does it contribute to meaningful life? What does it have to do with being a good person? In which ways does it promote desirable communities? What should be our priorities in choosing which of the innumerable good causes to support with our limited resources?

In addition to these general questions, or rather as my way of approaching them, I will ask six more focused questions, one in each of the chapters. (1) How should philanthropy be defined and understood for the purposes of moral inquiry? (2) Which virtues guide giving? (3) Are there any responsibilities to engage in philanthropy, and if so, how much should we give and to whom? (4) When is philanthropy morally damaging, and what does it mean for gifts to be coerced or coercive? (5) Should philanthropy be motivated by pure altruism, that is, unselfish concern for others, or is it all right for self-interest to be mixed with altruism? (6) How should we understand the paradox that selflessness contributes to self-fulfillment?

These are large topics. They can be approached from many perspectives and with the tools of many disciplines. While my research has been interdisciplinary, my framework is philosophical. I hope to show how philosophical ethics increases our moral understanding of philanthropy and to encourage others to do further work in this area.

Ethicists (moral philosophers, philosophers of morality) have neglected philanthropy, largely relinquishing the topic to social scientists. Philosophers' contributions have tended to be written for technical journals which are inaccessible to a wider audience, including a collection of essays which, remarkably, is the only contemporary philosophical book on philanthropy.[3] Apart from that collection, most philosophical essays have been narrowly focused on such special topics as world hunger, thereby missing the benefits of more systematic approaches. (Is it obvious, without argument, that world hunger should have priority over all other philanthropic giving?) Others are presented in the midst of developing an abstract ethical theory, more as illustrations than with an eye to practical implications.

This is a work in applied ethics, in three respects. First, the focus is on moral topics arising in a particular area of our lives, rather than on general issues in ethical theory. The topics are at once public and personal, delightful and disturbing, important and intriguing. They deserve to become an area of specialization in philosophy, alongside medical ethics, business ethics, engineering ethics, environmental ethics, and philosophy of women, to mention only a few areas of applied philosophy which have emerged in recent decades.

Second, this book is a philosophical response to practical moral needs. Rather than dwelling on abstruse intellectual puzzles, the book is rooted in practical interests. Nevertheless, those interests lead naturally into intellectually challenging tasks: to clarify the moral concepts used as tools in making philanthropic decisions, to explore philanthropy's contribution to community and character, and to develop a unifying perspective on philanthropic values.

Third, because I am convinced that the lifeblood of philosophy is its contribution to public discourse,[4] I have written for a wide audience of students, interdisciplinary scholars, social activists, and concerned citizens, as well as for professional philosophers. I have also tried to heed Molière's counsel to "humanize your talk, and speak to be understood."[5]

My approach is applied, then, in terms of focus, relevance, and audience. It is not, however, applied in the sense of embracing a general theory about the foundation of moral values and applying it to philanthropy (or other topics). The three theories which have been most influential in recent centuries have attempted to state the foundational principles of right (and wrong) action. Thus, according to Immanuel Kant's duty-ethics, right acts are those required by a set of duties which would be embraced by fully rational moral agents. According to John Locke's rights-ethics, right acts are those which respect human rights. And according to utilitarians such as Jeremy Bentham and John Stuart Mill, right acts are those which produce the most good for the most people, or which fall under rules producing the most overall good.

Why not select one of these theories and simply apply it to philanthropy?

For one thing, it is not clear which theory to select. All the theories come in different versions, and all of them are highly controversial. Defending any one of them would immerse us in theoretical disputes, effectively suspending applied inquiry. For another thing, these theories focus on rules about right and wrong action; they devote little attention to questions about higher ideals of character and community which are crucial in thinking about philanthropy.

Most important, we should be more impressed by the similarities than by the differences among the three theories.[6] Each theory is an abstract framework which can be filled out in many directions. Each emerged as an attempt to provide a clear and comprehensive overview of morality, and hence each must remain in line with our most carefully considered moral convictions. Since defenders of all the theories struggle to make those alignments, it matters relatively little whether the final appeal is to duties or rights or overall good. What matters is how principles of duties are formulated and weighed, how rights are understood, and how good consequences are measured and tallied. To be sure, there are fundamental disagreements among reasonable people, even in the moral judgments they are most certain about. Those differences, however, are reflected in different versions of each type of ethical theory, as well as in disputes over which type is preferable.

Accordingly, I draw freely upon ideas from all the theories, acknowledging that the ideas will be developed in different ways within different theoretical frameworks. For example, I draw upon the concept of rights, knowing that rights-ethicists will take them as morally fundamental, duty-ethicists will derive them from duties, and utilitarians will construe them as benefits and liberties whose recognition produces the most good for the most people. I also rely on principles that virtually all the theories endorse: for example, that we should do our fair share when we benefit from cooperative practices, and that we should help people whose lives are endangered when we can do so at little risk to ourselves.

One other ethical theory, virtue-ethics, will play a more prominent role. Virtue-ethics emphasizes good and bad character more than principles of right and wrong conduct. This ancient theory, which has attracted renewed interest during the past decade, has sometimes been viewed as an alternative to theories about right and wrong conduct. That is a mistake. Good character and right conduct are complementary ideas, not competing ones. An adequate ethical theory will integrate them rather than attempt to derive one from the other. Hence I am not claiming that virtue-ethics is a sufficient theory of morality, or that virtues are more theoretically fundamental than right action.[7] As an applied ethicist, my interest is in exploring specific virtues and other aspects of character which contribute to understanding philanthropy. I explore good character in all its dimensions: responsible conduct, sensible reasoning, justifiable attitudes, praiseworthy motives, desirable relationships, worthy ideals.

Virtues are admirable traits of character, manifested in valuable patterns of emotions, attitudes, reasoning, desires, intentions, conduct, commitments, and relationships. They are linked to ideals which structure the shared or overlapping moral understanding we use in joining our lives with mutual respect and caring. Even in this age of moral uncertainty, as we debate endlessly over how to formulate moral principles and resolve moral dilemmas, can we doubt the importance of compassion and courage, of honesty and integrity?

"Virtuous giving" may have a somewhat old-fashioned ring. That is all right, assuming we see a point in putting new wine in old bottles, and assuming we renounce any images of stuffiness and self-righteousness the expression conjures up. Virtues are not private merit badges smugly gleaned from hypocritical exercises in character building. They are morally desirable ways of relating to people, practices, and communities. The virtues center on caring for others, as well as for oneself, and self-righteousness is merely one of the many distortions of caring. At the same time, I will explore how caring for others, for their sake, indirectly contributes to our own self-fulfillment.

My central thesis, or rather theme, is that virtuous philanthropy fosters valuable caring relationships. As a result, philanthropy is a vital dimension of most good lives. Not all good lives, however, for individuals may emphasize other avenues for caring, such as family, friendship, and professions. I am not claiming that philanthropy is the primary mark of all caring people, but instead that virtuous philanthropy adds meaning to the lives of morally concerned individuals. Philosophical inquiry should help make that contribution perspicuous.

Philosophy begins in wonder (Aristotle) and love (Plato), develops by confronting perplexity (Wittgenstein), and culminates by enhancing meaningful life (Socrates). To study ethics is to scrutinize our own moral values, in philanthropy as elsewhere. Such is the heritage of Socrates, that remarkable philanthropist who engaged in philosophy as a voluntary service to his community, as well as a search for self-understanding.

Philosophy integrates personal vision and public argument. Like science, it seeks truth; like art, it seeks to convey an individual perspective which makes contact with interpersonal values. As Wittgenstein aptly suggested, philosophy is much like architecture.[8] In both disciplines, structures stand or fall because of realities independent of us. In both, much of the work is done on oneself, on one's interpretation of the world, on one's way of seeing and living.

The overall tone of this book is positive. In part that is because my primary interest is in how philanthropy contributes to valuable caring relationships. In part it reflects my conviction that philanthropy evokes some of our noblest impulses and does far more good than bad. Nevertheless, or rather because of this positive tone, three caveats are necessary.

First, my faith that philanthropy does far more good than bad is just that—a faith. Defending it would require a different kind of book.[9] In this book the focus is on the practical moral interests of individual givers. Defending claims about the overall effects of philanthropy would require a book that moved away from personal ethics and toward social and political philosophy centered on nonprofit organizations, foundations, governments, and the cumulative impact of philanthropy on society. For the purposes of this book, what matters is that *much* good is done through philanthropy, and that is not so much a faith as it is common knowledge.

The social-political approach would ask, for example: Are social services best provided by the federal government, state governments, nonprofit organizations, or some combination thereof? Should the arts and humanities be heavily subsidized by tax revenues or left to philanthropic patronage? To what extent should government regulate the activities of philanthropic organizations? Which gifts ought to be tax deductible? How should philanthropic organizations be structured and managed? Do predominant patterns of philanthropy in the United States benefit the rich more than the poor, men more than women, the arts more than malnourished children? My study of virtuous giving complements, but cannot replace, inquiry into these questions.

Second, I am not writing as an apologist for the Nonprofit Sector. It has become fashionable, if not altogether illuminating, to divide the public economy into three sectors: business (for-profit companies), government, and nonprofits (not-for-profit organizations). The Nonprofit Sector is so diverse that general perceptions of it are much like responses to Rorschach tests: they reveal more about the perceiver than what is perceived. Virtue and vice, as well as altruistic service and corruption, are manifested in all economic areas—government, business, the professions, family, and philanthropy. Still, much that I say implies the vital significance of a vigorous Nonprofit Sector.

Third, and most important, I am not endorsing a political ideology that favors private philanthropy as a replacement for government welfare programs. Government bears the primary responsibility for meeting the basic needs of disadvantaged citizens by fairly distributing welfare costs through taxation.[10] There are four reasons for this.

(1) Scale. Homelessness, violence, and poverty (especially of children) have increased dramatically during the past decade. During the same time welfare services have been cut back. Support for disadvantaged people is best delivered through a partnership among government, nonprofit organizations,

and the marketplace, but primary responsibility for funding for the desperately poor belongs to government with its authority to tax and regulate. As Martin Luther King, Jr., remarked with prescience, "philanthropy is [often] commendable, but it must not cause the philanthropist to overlook the circumstances of economic injustice which make philanthropy necessary."[11]

(2) Security. Human capacities for altruism are limited, and hence voluntary philanthropy cannot be relied upon as the mainstay in meeting fundamental needs. Government welfare programs provide assurances to the elderly and jobless that their minimal needs will be met. In an increasingly uncertain world, each of us needs that security.

(3) Fairness. Government provides a mechanism for fairly distributing both burdens on taxpayers and benefits for recipients. While that mechanism is not always used properly, nevertheless it tends to be more reliable than the piecemeal efforts of philanthropic organizations, even when those efforts become coordinated (as they usually are not). Concentrating on the weaknesses of government and the moral limitations of a competitive marketplace should not result in the hyperbole of calling philanthropy "the moral sector."[12]

(4) Symbolism. Government programs express the collective caring of an entire society, symbolically as well as in substance. "An official political concern with issues or problems," writes Robert Nozick, is "a way of marking their importance or urgency, and hence of expressing, intensifying, channeling, encouraging, and validating our private actions and concerns toward them."[13] Government programs are essential to establish the "solemn marking of our human solidarity" within caring communities.

Of course, philanthropy also carries symbolic meanings, as I will emphasize. Most often, however, its symbolism does not express the official view of an entire society. That is both a limit and a strength. Philanthropy enables individuals and groups to express their values, substantively and symbolically, without first having to persuade the majority in a democracy. That frees philanthropy to function as a catalyst for change. It makes possible focused and prompt responses to social problems and community aspirations, sometimes by reforming government. Above all, it contributes to caring relationships and communities in more personal ways than by voting and paying taxes.

Scope of Philanthropy

As children, my friends and I gave to the March of Dimes through our scout troup. We saved dimes in cardboard holders and then mailed them in together. We also sponsored fundraisers, staffed carnival booths, and served community dinners. Helping was a simple gesture, at once a natural impulse, a habit, and a group endeavor. It was clear to us there were other avenues for helping. Family and friends supported victims of polio in a more extensive and intimate way, and scientists such as Jonas Salk helped through creative work in their professions.[14] I do not remember, however, using a word to distinguish our activities from these other forms of service; we simply lumped them all together under the heading of helping out or doing one's share. Today the best single term is "philanthropy"; the best two-word expression is "voluntary service." I use them interchangeably, with some preference for the brevity of the former, to refer to all forms of voluntary private giving for public purposes.

Alternative terms are misleading for one reason or another. Thus, the word "humanitarianism" is either too broad in covering all kinds of service, including work in the professions, or too narrow in referring to the alleviation of suffering but not to cultural patronage. "Charity" may be preferred by some people, but its meaning has become diffused into three specialized meanings: Christian love (in its honorific sense), condescending pity (in its pejorative sense), and the tax-deductible status of organizations (in its legal sense). "Voluntarism" and "volunteerism" suggest a particular ideology about how to deal with social problems, namely, through voluntary service rather than by government involvement.

The definition of philanthropy is somewhat vague. Each of its four interconnected elements needs to be clarified: voluntary, private, giving, for public purposes. It would be futile, however, to seek an absolutely precise definition. "Philanthropy" refers to many kinds of giving which are loosely related by overlapping similarities.[15] The following remarks are intended as signposts which roughly indicate the ground to be explored without setting rigid conceptual boundaries. Or rather, the remarks identify the features of paradigm (clear-cut) cases while also indicating areas of vagueness which for my purposes need not be removed.

(1) Philanthropy is *voluntary* in the sense of being intended and uncoerced. "Intended" means the act or activity is done with the purpose of making a gift. "Uncoerced" rules out legal penalties for not giving, as well as threats of harm and other morally objectionable forms of force, manipulation, and deception. Extortion, not philanthropy, occurs when a donation is made because of a threat of penalties, and abusive force is present when a person is constrained to make a political contribution in order to keep a job.

Voluntariness implies both the absence of coercion and the presence of intentional activity. When one of these elements is missing, nonstandard or borderline (doubtful) cases arise. Suppose I am deceived or otherwise coerced into giving money for a purpose I disapprove of. Perhaps a "charity racketeer" cons me into believing I am giving in order to help build a shelter for homeless people and then uses my money to support his lavish lifestyle. Did I engage in philanthropy? Yes and no. Yes: I acted intentionally for what I thought was a public purpose, even though my intention was subverted. No:

My giving was manipulated and coerced, even though I attempted to engage in philanthropy. Whatever we decide to say about such cases, they are not paradigms that would be used in explaining what philanthropy is.

"Voluntary" is not a synonym for "willingly," in the sense of acting as one wants or wishes to. Loyal citizens concerned with the public good might pay their taxes willingly, without feeling pressured to give. Nevertheless, taxes are not a form of voluntary service. The failure to pay them carries a severe penalty, and hence there is force present, even if some individuals do not "feel" forced. Conversely, some philanthropy is done reluctantly, rather than willingly. Individuals might voluntarily contribute to Amnesty International motivated by a stern sense of duty, all the time wishing they could spend their money in more self-indulgent ways. Perhaps the reluctance indicates an absence of perfect virtue, but it does not make the giving involuntary.

Furthermore, "voluntary" does not mean morally optional or nonobligatory. That is important. Our definition allows that some philanthropy might be a moral responsibility, as many people believe it is. I might give voluntarily, intentionally and without coercion, to help people in serious distress, while believing I have a responsibility to give. My belief, in turn, may be true depending on the circumstances and on justifiable principles of obligation. In general, issues concerning obligations should be left open for inquiry rather than closed by definitional fiat.

Voluntariness is a matter of degree and interpretation, as is coercion. Coercion is obvious when criminals are ordered to engage in community service as the penalty for their crime. A lesser degree of coercion occurs when they are given a choice between community service and spending time in jail. What should we say, however, about Lieutenant Colonel Oliver North's 1,200 hours of community service in working with inner-city youths? The service was not entirely voluntary, since it was court-ordered as part of the sentence for his conviction in the Iran-Contra scandal (a conviction that was later overturned). Nevertheless, he approached his service with an enthusiastic spirit, "attacking this public service with the energy and tenacity of a born Marine."[16] He developed innovative ideas, initiating a "Pied Piper Program" to scare children away from drugs by taking them to observe cocaine addicts. Rather than punching a clock, he put in longer hours and far more effort than was required. While his service is not a paradigm of philanthropy, surely it had a philanthropic dimension.

Sometimes we make donations because we are pressured by fundraisers, employers, friends, religious leaders, or a climate of social expectation. Are these pressures coercive, making giving more like extortion than voluntary service? Occasionally, peer pressure can become extreme so as to generate elements of coercion, and pressures within authority relationships easily become coercive, as with pressures to contribute to an employer's favorite cause. However, most social pressures to give are moderate, of the kind ubiquitous in human affairs. We are free to resist them without penalty, other than the negative attitudes of others—which we must confront in all areas of life.

(2) *Private* giving contrasts with government spending. Philanthropists give their own money and time, unlike government officials who disperse public money. Most philanthropic giving, about 80 percent of it, consists of gifts by individuals. The rest comes from nongovernment organizations, especially private foundations, not-for-profit corporations, and for-profit businesses.

In practice, philanthropy and government spending are interwoven. Many nonprofit philanthropic organizations are funded as much by government funds as by private support. America's welfare programs depend as much on nonprofit organizations as on government agencies to deliver services. The extent of this dependence became clear during Ronald Reagan's administration. Reagan praised nonprofit welfare organizations while severely cutting government funding for them. He also reduced tax incentives for individual gifts to charities.[17] The result was a sharp curtailment of social services.

It is tempting to refer to federal humanitarian aid to other countries as "government philanthropy." I will resist the temptation. It is true that much foreign aid amounts to indirect giving from the citizens of democracies to the citizens of other countries. The government serves as a vehicle for carrying out the humanitarian aims of its citizens, as well as the aims of political expediency, presumably based on their collective consent to be taxed for these purposes. Yet much the same can be said of government spending on welfare programs for its citizens. Even when voluntary giving and taxation promote the same ends, then, it is worthwhile to distinguish them by reserving the term "philanthropy" for nongovernment giving.

(3) *Giving* means donating one's resources without contracting to achieve comparable economic compensation. The resources may take the form of volunteered labor, expertise, money, or items having economic value. Giving differs from economic exchanges, such as selling a car, where there is an explicit contract between two parties who exchange goods or services. Nevertheless, sometimes philanthropy is engaged in to acquire economic benefits, as with most corporate philanthropy, which is tied to marketing and public relations.

Philanthropists often do seek economic benefits. Volunteers might want and need advertised benefits, such as the modest living stipend given to Peace Corps volunteers. Occasionally they even receive indirect economic rewards greater than their contributions, for example, lucrative employment opportunities based on their credentials as volunteers, or business advantages gained from a reputation for community involvement. Since I want to leave open questions about motives, I will allow that self-interest is sometimes the primary or even exclusive motive for philanthropy.

Was Robin Hood a philanthropist? According to legend, he liberally distributed money to needy people without seeking compensation, motivated by compassion and a sense of justice.[18] Yet the money was stolen, hence not his to give. For clarity, let us agree that giving means transferring ownership of one's personal property, as well as volunteering one's time and talent.[19] Assuming Robin Hood was returning money to its rightful owners because the king's taxes were so excessive as to be immoral, Robin Hood qualifies as a philanthropist for his voluntary service on behalf of a public cause. Philanthropy does not occur, however, when one donates to a charity money gained fraudulently. Presumably that was involved in the charitable gifts of millions of dollars by Michael Milken, the junk-bond financier of corporate takeovers during the 1980s who was sent to jail on numerous counts of fraud.

Are foundation officers who distribute grants philanthropists? Probably not, assuming they are paid professionals and assuming they do not own the grant money. Yet suppose a particular officer chooses the job over far more lucrative offers, pursues the work from a desire to help others, and puts in far more time and effort than is normally expected? Our definition is sufficiently flexible to acknowledge a philanthropic dimension to this work.

There is also a philanthropic dimension to workers who serve the public beyond the compensation of a paycheck. For most jobs we can distinguish between (a) the required level of performance and (b) an exceptional (optimal, maximal) level of performance.[20] When workers perform at exceptional levels in order to help others well beyond what they are paid for, their work acquires a philanthropic dimension. For example, consider Wally Olson, the Los Angeles singing bus driver who leads his passengers in songs, each day accepting requests for favorite numbers.[21] He gets to know his regular customers and becomes involved with their problems. And he makes it his job to convey a cheerful, caring attitude that has helped to personalize an otherwise impersonal and occasionally violent work situation.

(4) *Public purposes* comprise virtually all social aims beyond helping one's family and friends. The aims might be civic: citizens' support for cities, counties, states, nations, political candidates and groups, and social movements. They might be religious: support for a church, synagogue, mosque, or religious movement. Some are cultural: gifts for the arts, humanities, science, museums, libraries, or historical monuments. Others are humanitarian: giving to emergency relief efforts, donating blood, contributing to medical research, volunteering in a center for the disabled, or finding shelter for the homeless. Still others are environmental: protecting animals, forests, ecosystems, and clean air and water.

Philanthropy and friendship overlap in many instances. Is philanthropy involved when individuals donate to a literary club or church whose members are their friends? Yes, because the group is open to future members and because there is a public purpose beyond friendship, namely, literary inquiry or religious worship. Even if donors' motives are largely self-interested, the organization may benefit other people and in that sense qualify as a public purpose.

The expression "public purpose" is ambiguous in a helpful way. It refers to either (i) the purposes of givers, that is, their intentions and aims, or (ii) the ends actually promoted by gifts. Thus, philanthropy may occur when donors try to promote what they believe to be a public good, even if they fail to produce the intended results. Philanthropy also occurs when donors successfully promote a public purpose, even though their primary intentions were for other things, such as gaining personal recognition.

To sum up, the definition of philanthropy as voluntary private giving for public purposes contains several areas of vagueness. Nevertheless, it has several clear benefits for exploring the ethics of philanthropy. It avoids building in preconceptions about good motives, admirable aims, desirable consequences, and whether philanthropy can be a moral responsibility. All these matters are left for moral inquiry. Hence the definition is value-neutral, unlike "persuasive definitions" which build in controversial attitudes or assumptions about philanthropy.[22]

Persuasive definitions of philanthropy abound, sometimes pointing in opposing directions. Here are eight persuasive definitions, each of which has some basis in ordinary language and may be useful in other contexts. Since they bias rather than facilitate moral inquiry, I note them in order to set them aside.

(1) Lavish, large-scale giving, whether by very rich individuals or by foundations.[23] (Philanthropy versus small gifts.) —This definition aids and abets the stereotype of philanthropy as the proper domain of the wealthy. Yet, about half the total dollar amounts of voluntary private giving for public purposes comes from lower- and middle-income people.[24] Refusing to regard philanthropy as the province of the upper class is a first move toward appreciating how it permeates all social classes.

(2) Giving motivated by humanitarian love. (Philanthropy versus giving from nonhumanitarian motives.) —This definition has its roots in etymology: *philanthropia* is the Greek word for "love of humanity," although for the Greeks "humanity" meant free citizens and ruled out women, slaves, and barbarians. Nevertheless, the definition is misleading in several respects. It builds in one motive for philanthropy rather than leave the question of motives open for moral inquiry. Moreover, the motive suggests universal concern for humans, whereas much voluntary giving has more focused

intentions, such as to help artists or scientists, Mormons or Baptists, local communities or nations, or to honor a family name or a deceased relative. The definition also disregards philanthropy aimed at preventing cruelty to nonhuman animals.

(3) Morally optional giving.[25] (Philanthropy versus obligatory giving.) —Philanthropy, it might be said in defense of this definition, ought to be a matter of joy and generosity, not onerous duty. Yet many people engage in voluntary service motivated by a sense of responsibility, and that seems quite compatible with joyous giving. Surely these individuals are not confused, much less morally flawed. In any case, rather than separate obligation and philanthropy at the outset, we should leave open for inquiry whether philanthropy is sometimes morally required.

(4) Giving for cultural purposes, such as the arts and sciences, rather than charitable giving to alleviate suffering.[26] (Philanthropy as cultural patronage versus compassionate charity.) —This usage creates another misleading dichotomy. Giving to science and education is sometimes motivated by a desire to alleviate suffering by discovering long-term solutions to disease and suffering. Most important, for the purposes of moral inquiry we need a definition that brings together cultural patronage and relief of suffering in order to invite questions about their relative priority.

(5) Giving to prevent suffering by discovering long-term solutions, rather than short-term alleviation of suffering.[27] (Philanthropy as prevention versus palliation.) —This definition seems to embody an attitude about the desirable emphasis in giving. Yet surely both short-term and long-term solutions to suffering are important. Questions about relative priorities in allocating our resources should be left for investigation into particular situations rather than biased at the outset by a definition.

(6) Giving money, rather than volunteering time and talent. (Philanthropy versus volunteering.) —In fact, volunteered time and talent usually do have economic value, and offering money is one way to volunteer help. That is why I will use "philanthropy" and "voluntary service" as rough synonyms, while using "volunteering" with its normal connotation of service through hands-on participation.[28]

(7) Good giving; giving which is wisely conceived, admirably motivated, and beneficial in its consequences. ("True philanthropy" versus flawed giving.) —This honorific usage has a place in inspirational writings and at ceremonies praising benefactors, but it is not useful in identifying an area of moral inquiry.

(8) The nonprofit (independent, third) sector.[29] (Philanthropy versus government and business.) —It is true that much voluntary giving for public purposes is directed toward such nonprofit organizations as museums, private schools, churches, and shelters for battered women. Nevertheless, it is mis-

leading to use the word "philanthropy" to refer to the not-for-profit sector. Some nonprofit organizations have no connection with voluntary giving, and some are established for tax purposes or other economic purposes, rather than for serving public purposes. Conversely, many profit-making corporations (such as for-profit hospitals) and government organizations (such as public schools and libraries) depend heavily on volunteers and private donations. Philanthropy functions in all economic sectors.

Practices and Virtues

I defined philanthropy as *acts* of voluntary private giving for public purposes.[30] These acts, however, are rarely eccentric gestures; usually they occur in the course of participating in social practices. Here are just a few examples of philanthropic practices: giving by alumni to their alma maters, donating blood, sheltering the homeless, contributing to public radio and television, patronage of the arts, volunteering in community organizations (schools, hospitals, museums, police programs), participating in service groups (Kiwanis Club, Rotary Club, some sororities and fraternities), serving in community safety programs, taking part in social protest movements, joining a watchdog group to improve government, paying tithing, going on a mission, assisting in wildlife preservation, whistle-blowing to warn the public of dangers.

These are social practices in the colloquial sense: patterns of conduct engaged in by many people and continuing over time. They are also practices in Alasdair MacIntyre's technical sense: activities that contribute to human good when participants meet appropriate standards of excellence.[31] Philanthropy encompasses a large cluster of related practices, in the same way as the professions (medicine, teaching, engineering), sports (basketball, soccer, tennis), sciences (biology, physics, sociology), and the fine arts (portrait painting, sculpture, music), to cite some of MacIntyre's examples of practices.

More fully, a practice is

> [1] any coherent and complex form of socially established cooperative human activity [2] through which goods internal to that form of activity are realized [3] in the course of trying to achieve those standards of excellence which are appropriate to, and partially definitive of, that form of activity, [4] with the result that human powers to achieve excellence, and human conceptions of the ends and goods involved, are systematically extended.[32]

I will clarify this definition as I apply each of its four parts to philanthropy.

(1) Practices, including philanthropic practices, are "socially established" in that they are made possible by structured societies and sustained by social traditions. Practices remain coherent and identifiable even when they take

remarkably different forms over time and across cultures. Think of the variations in sports from classical Athens to today's professional athletics, or the changes in science during the same time span. There have been astonishing variations in the goals and functions of these activities, in the techniques and equipment employed, in the organizations promoting them, and in the social functions they serve. Philanthropy has an equally rich history of varied forms, functions, purposes, styles, tactics, and institutional structuring.

For example, foundations have become essential to contemporary philanthropy, but they did not exist a few centuries ago. By contrast, settlement houses were once vitally important urban community centers prior to the development of government programs, but they have all but disappeared. Again, the practice of donating blood became possible with the emergence of suitable medical technology, and someday it may disappear as artificial blood sources are developed. And there are both striking similarities and differences in medieval church-controlled charity (in the religious sense) and today's government-regulated charity (in the legal sense). Increasingly, contemporary philanthropic practices are framed by a complex and ever-changing structure of laws concerning tax deductions, rules for political donations, accountability requirements for nonprofit corporations, and professional credentialing of development officers.

Philanthropy is a "cooperative human activity" in several respects. To begin with, it requires the active involvement of both givers and receivers. Obviously, philanthropy is impossible if no one is willing to offer help or respond to calls for aid; it is equally impossible if no one is willing to accept help. But there is more to be said. It is a misleading stereotype to regard recipients as passive. Often they assert their needs and invite the participation of volunteers and donors. Think, for example, of a person seeking funding from a foundation by writing a grant proposal. Think, too, of a group vigorously trying to get a member of a minority elected as a volunteer member of a community board.

Furthermore, givers and receivers are usually members of groups whose effectiveness depends on cooperation. Donors might belong to organizations such as service clubs, companies, or schools. Alternatively, they may be identifiable as a group only by reference to their philanthropic goal: for example, contributors to relief services for victims of the 1988 Armenia earthquake. Either way, large numbers of benefactors may be required in order to marshal adequate resources for tackling social problems. Beneficiaries, too, are typically members of groups: residents of a country served by a privately funded museum, Americans in need of a kidney transplant, starving people in Bangladesh or Somalia.

In addition, intermediary groups and institutions play important roles in connecting givers and receivers. Many of these organizations have complex

internal structures which enable them to exert social influence. Some organizations facilitate the activity of donors by collecting gifts and distributing
them to beneficiaries. Others aid recipients, such as universities and community advisory groups which help grant writers to solicit foundation funds.
Still others serve both constituencies, gathering and then disbursing funds;
for example, the United Way, CARE, Amnesty International, Alliance for
the Arts, Black United Fund, and various churches and synagogues.

Finally, shifting to a value judgment, philanthropy tends to work best
when it is a two-way interaction between donors and recipients who regard
each other as moral equals, rather than a one-way abandoning of resources
from the rich to the poor.[33] The more both parties actively participate in
what is viewed as a shared enterprise, the more both benefit from meaningful
exchanges and relationships.

(2) The "internal goods" of a practice are those desirable things promoted by the practice in some singular (if not unique) manner that partly
defines the practice itself.[34] They include worthwhile experiences and relationships, the exercise of valuable skills, and useful products and services created by practices. For example, each profession promotes particular social
services: medicine promotes health, law protects rights and serves justice,
education promotes learning, and engineering creates useful technological
products. The fine arts promote several internal goods: artistic expression,
aesthetic enjoyment, and the creation of cultural artifacts and symbols.

Given their enormous diversity, philanthropic practices promote a great
variety of internal goods. They range from alleviating poverty to helping
injured animals, from serving religious needs to improving government, from
increasing literacy to promoting the arts. In general, philanthropic practices
promote internal goods in numerous ways.

Many philanthropic practices directly serve basic needs. Offering shelter
to the homeless, a practice important in nearly all societies, contributes to
survival needs, whether the shelter is temporary or permanent as in Habitat
for Humanity's program of building homes. Working in a soup kitchen sustains people who would otherwise be without food. Serving in a community
security program promotes public safety. And animal rescue and rehabilita-
tion programs respond to the needs of nonhuman animals.

Philanthropic practices may function as indirect or second-order ways to
promote the internal goods of another, primary practice. For example,
alumni giving promotes learning, which is also the internal good of education. Again, patronage of the arts furthers the same internal goods as the
arts themselves. And philanthropic contributions to improve government,
promote justice, and serve the public welfare share these internal goods with
professionals working in government.

Sometimes philanthropic practices are embedded in other, primary practices, and hence directly promote their internal goods. Tithing, for example, is an important part of some religions; it is both a religious and a philanthropic activity. When lawyers engage in *pro bono publico* work, volunteering their services without fee or at reduced fees, they are simultaneously engaged in two practices, law and philanthropy. And unpaid sheriff's deputies in police reserve programs are engaged in both voluntary service and law enforcement.

Finally, and most important for my purposes, philanthropy promotes generic internal goods of its own, distinct from those of a primary practice to which it may be attached—generic in that they can be achieved through virtually all forms of philanthropy. In particular, successful philanthropy creates or sustains caring relationships between benefactors and beneficiaries. These relationships morally benefit giver and receiver alike, in ways I will explore throughout this book. Philanthropy also fosters caring relationships among givers who work together as donors or volunteers. And it can promote caring relationships among recipients who share resources used for public endeavors, for example, among members of a literacy education group which is supported by a foundation grant.

MacIntyre contrasts internal goods with "external goods"—such as income, influence, and fame—which do not define the practice and which can be acquired by engaging in many different social practices. Individuals participating in professions typically have some interest in both external and internal goods. They seek money and professional recognition (external goods), as well as the specific form of excellence or craftsmanship involved in the profession (an internal good). The same is true of organizations connected with practices, such as those serving the professions (for example, the American Association of University Professors), the sciences (the American Academy of Science), or the arts (the Actors Guild). Institutions also have significant interests in external, as well as internal, goods: "They are involved in acquiring money and other material goods; they are structured in terms of power and status, and they distribute money, power and status as rewards. Nor could they do otherwise if they are to sustain not only themselves, but also the practices of which they are the bearers. For no practices can survive for any length of time unsustained by institutions."[35]

Much the same is true in philanthropy. Philanthropic organizations are legitimately interested in their own survival, growth, resources, and reputation, in order to meet their philanthropic aims. Individuals, too, are typically interested in self-esteem, recognition and appreciation, and personal development, in addition to their commitment to some public good. Within limits, the resulting mixture of purposes is morally acceptable, even desirable, insofar as it strengthens the overall pursuit of good ends (as is argued in Chapter 5). Beyond those limits, excessive concern for external goods, such as power and prestige, distorts commitments to the internal goods of philanthropy in ways that cause harm (of the kind discussed in Chapter 4).

(3) "Standards of excellence" define better and worse ways of engaging in a practice and thereby partly define the practice itself. The standards of achievement in baseball, for example, define excellence in batting, fielding, and stealing bases, and partly define the nature and goals of the game. Similarly, philanthropic standards of excellence specify what it means to give well, and thereby partly define philanthropic practices. They specify how to help effectively, without waste and without making recipients feel degraded. They comprise all the norms, guidelines, virtues, and ideals that promote helping and caring relationships in philanthropy.

(4) As numerous individuals and groups pursue excellence in practices, "human powers to achieve excellence, and human conceptions of the ends and goods involved, are systematically extended." Talented engineers, for example, have extended conceptions of technological possibilities as they developed automobiles, computers, space shuttles. Similarly, creative philanthropists have widened the possibilities for caring within communities, as well as for achieving an array of other public goods. To a remarkable extent, the history of philanthropy is the history of social innovation.[36] Many components of modern contemporary society began as philanthropic experiments: public education, community hospitals and libraries, welfare services, and civil rights legislation, to name only a few.

Now that MacIntyre's definition of practices has been applied to philanthropy, consider an objection. I have suggested that philanthropy is largely a set of social practices in a normative or value-laden sense which introduces the ideas of internal goods and standards of excellence. Yet I began with a value-neutral definition of philanthropy as voluntary private giving for public purposes. Is this a contradiction, such that philanthropy is regarded in both neutral and normative terms?

In reply, we need to mark two distinctions. One is the difference between defining a *concept* and developing a normative *conception* of the things to which the concept applies. Defining how to operate a car is one thing; presenting a conception of safe driving is another. Similarly, defining philanthropic acts is one thing; conceiving of them as parts of good-promoting practices is another. The definition of philanthropy remains value-neutral in that it makes no assumptions about when philanthropy is good or bad. By contrast, the conception of philanthropic practices is normative in that it portrays much philanthropy as aimed at internal goods.

I am not claiming that all philanthropic activities are practices in MacIntyre's sense. Racist and violent activities which assault the public good are not social practices, with internal goods. If racists and terrorists disagree, we can set forth reasons to show they are mistaken. Moreover, defining practices as value-laden does not imply that all practices are good on balance. A philanthropic practice might serve an internal good and yet also promote undesirable ends. Serving on a religious mission is a value-laden practice in that it is directed toward some aspect of the public good, but we might see more harm than good in particular forms of proselytizing.

The other distinction is between individual acts and the general practices they fall under. The definition of philanthropy focused on acts, whereas the normative conception applies to philanthropic practices as a whole. We can identify an act as falling under a practice without evaluating the act. To use an illustration from medicine, we can identify a heart operation as a physician's act which occurs within a practice whose internal good is health, and yet judge the act immoral because its ineptness killed the patient. Similarly, we can identify acts as falling under philanthropic practices without implying the acts are good. We can say, for example, that giving cash to a mendicant falls under the practice of alms giving, whose internal good is to meet basic needs of disadvantaged individuals. At the same time, we can criticize the gift as inappropriate if it is likely to be used for drugs and where a more effective gift would have been a donation to a hunger organization which would assure the money's proper use.

Our definition of philanthropy, then, remains value-neutral even though we are now beginning to develop a normative conception of desirable forms of philanthropy. The next step is to extend that conception by relating philanthropic practices to the virtues.

Virtues imply desirable patterns of action, but also much more. Most of them imply valuable patterns of emotions, attitudes, desires, utterances, reasoning, and relationships. For example, kindness is sensitive concern for the well-being of others as manifested in actions, words, reasoning, and feelings. Again, honesty is shown by avoiding cheating and stealing, motivated by respect for others; it is also shown by having respect for truth and evidence, contempt for shoddy thinking, and pride in communicating clearly. Virtues are not private merit badges. They are valuable ways of relating to people, practices, and communities. As such, they promote the good of both ourselves and others.

MacIntyre identifies three ways in which the virtues promote internal goods. First, they enable participants in practices to meet appropriate standards of excellence so as to achieve internal goods. MacIntyre makes this feature part of the definition of virtues: "a virtue is an acquired human quality the possession and exercise of which tends to enable us to achieve those goods which are internal to practices and the lack of which effectively prevents us from achieving any such goods."[37] Standards of excellence differ

greatly among practices, which is not surprising since they partly define individual practices, but the virtues are important in all practices, albeit in
somewhat different ways depending on the context. Such virtues as honesty
and respect for people, for example, promote excellence in professions, parenting, playing sports—and philanthropy.

Some virtues motivate people to participate in philanthropy; for example,
compassionateness, generosity, loyalty, and a sense of justice. Other virtues
enable us to give effectively. Prudence and practical wisdom help us avoid
wasting resources by inquiring carefully into which organizations are worthy
of support. Kindness and humility enable us to avoid snobbery and condescending pity toward recipients. Courage and persistence are vital resources
for volunteers seeking social reform. Honesty and integrity enable fundraisers
to preserve public trust in organizations. And justice and fairness prevent
corruption in organizations. As these examples suggest, the multiplicity of
the virtues in philanthropy reflects the complexity of moral life.

Second, the virtues foster unity of character. Conflict and fragmentation
permeate our lives. Some conflicts derive from threats to those long-term
commitments which provide personal continuity and integrity. The virtues
of self-discipline and self-knowledge enable us to confront temptation and
weakness; courage enables us to meet danger; perseverence helps us to deal
with discouragement. Other conflicts derive from tensions within our set of
commitments. The virtues promote balance and integration among the various practices and relationships we commit ourselves to at any given time.
For example, prudence and conscientiousness help us manage the competing
demands of family, friends, education, work, political involvement, and philanthropic commitments. In general, the virtues provide guidance and coherence in the ongoing "narrative quest" (endeavor over time) to discover how
to live well.[38]

Third, the virtues sustain moral traditions and communities.[39] A moral
tradition is a valuable way of living which maintains an identifiable structure
through time. Traditions are embedded in communities, including communities unified by geography, history, economics, religion, and involvement in
common practices. By permeating communities, virtues sustain traditions
through many generations.

Each of these roles for the virtues is important in understanding the
moral status of philanthropy. Chapter 3 explores how virtues promote excellence in philanthropic practices. Chapter 6 explores how the virtues foster
personal unity during the ongoing search for a fulfilling life. Chapter 4 discusses the harms done to individuals and communities in the absence of
important virtues. And the following section in this chapter says more about
the role of the virtues in sustaining communities. Before proceeding, how-

ever, we should note some additional ways in which the virtues enter into our lives, beyond the three MacIntyre discusses.

A fourth role of the virtues is to function as ideals for the kind of individuals we should aspire to become. Each virtue represents a partial ideal for character, and clusters of virtues define composite ideals. A composite ideal, for example, might be honesty and commitment to excellence combined with generosity toward others. In this way, ideals of virtue function as guides for our actions, commitments, and habit formation, even when they are not explicitly formulated.

Fifth, the virtues guide moral education. Of course, we also use simple rules of conduct in teaching morality: Be honest, Don't steal, Return favors with favors. But the point of citing these rules is largely to convey virtuous ideals of character and ways of relating to other people.

Sixth, as Edmund L. Pincoffs points out, the virtues "provide grounds for preference or for avoidance of persons," and shape the nuances of relationships.[40] Thus, we tend to seek out friendly and kind people and to avoid cruel and selfish people, and our relationships with trustworthy individuals are different from those with unreliable and dishonest individuals.

Seventh, as ideals, virtues guide organizations, as well as individuals.[41] Organizations, including philanthropic ones, can be said to act, assuming they have rules which authorize individuals to act for the organization as a whole. Those acts may or may not reflect patterns of social responsibility, justice, fairness, compassion, prudence, efficiency, collegiality, and fidelity to the group's mission.

One final distinction: If the virtues include all desirable traits of individuals and institutions, then we should differentiate between moral and nonmoral virtues.[42] Moral virtues such as honesty, compassionateness, and courage, involve direct concern for the interests of others (in addition to one's own). Other categories of virtue include aesthetic excellence (gracefulness, charm), intellectual excellence (intelligence, creativity, commitment to excellence), physical excellence (vigor, athletic skill), and religious sensitivity (a sense of the sacred). In what follows, "virtue" will refer to moral virtues, except when the context indicates otherwise.

Having drawn this distinction, we should appreciate that nonmoral virtues may take on moral significance in certain circumstances. As will become clear in the next chapter, the nonmoral virtues of reverence for the sacred, appreciation of beauty, and commitment to excellence in the professions all have moral significance when they motivate morally desirable forms of philanthropy. Moreover, just as moral and nonmoral virtues interact in philanthropy, so do moral and nonmoral purposes. Even when a philanthropic purpose is not moral per se, giving may have moral significance. Giving to the arts, humanities, and sciences has clear moral implications, both in bene-fiting artists, humanists, and scientists and in promoting the well-being of everyone affected by their achievements.

Caring within Communities

Between 1940 and 1944, the 3,500 French villagers at Le Chambon res-cued 6,000 Jews, most of them children, by sheltering them from the Nazis and smuggling many to Switzerland. They took enormous risks. Even though they gained the indulgence of a sympathetic Nazi officer, the entire village could have been massacred if even one citizen betrayed their efforts. No one did.

The community at Le Chambon was unified by ties of religion, geogra-phy, history, and local traditions. Most villagers were descendants of the Hu-guenots, a Protestant minority persecuted in Catholic France from the sixteenth to the eighteenth century. The community was also united by ideals of benevolence, courage, perseverence, and integrity. As Philip Hallie writes, their "caring had to do in part with Saint John's commandment to love one another, but it also had to do with stubbornness, if you will, fortitude, a refusal to abjure . . . [their] commitment" to sheltering people whose pain they shared through empathy and with compassion.[43]

Many of the villagers did not regard their actions as heroic or even ex-ceptionally virtuous. In their eyes they were simply responding to the plight of others: "How can you call us 'good'? We were doing what had to be done. Who else could help them? And what has all this to do with goodness? Things had to be done, that's all, and we happened to be there to do them. You must understand that it was the most natural thing in the world to help these people."[44] Whether or not they were religious, members of the com-munity acknowledged a sense of responsibility to help strangers fleeing for their lives. But the felt responsibility was not experienced as an onerous bur-den. It was a spontaneous and natural response to need, and as such a par-adigm of virtue.

André Trocmé was the local pastor who led the villagers' nonviolent re-sistance to the Nazis. During the years before the war, Trocmé had articu-lated an ethic of service centered on a distinction between giving oneself and merely giving things. Hallie explains:

> [W]hen you give somebody a thing without giving yourself, you degrade both parties by making the receiver utterly passive and by making yourself a benefactor standing there to receive thanks—and even sometimes obedi-ence—as repayment. But when you give yourself, nobody is degraded—in

fact, both parties are elevated by a shared joy. What you give creates new, vigorous life, instead of arrogance on the one hand and passivity on the other.[45]

The distinction between giving oneself and merely giving things is not the distinction between volunteering time and donating money; the villagers gave themselves in both ways. Instead, it is the distinction between giving with care and giving impersonally. However good its consequences, impersonal giving threatens relationships based on moral equality. By contrast, giving with care—with good will and good judgment—enables us to bring our lives into creative relationships based on a sense of shared humanity.

Philanthropy at Chambon expressed existing ties of community and also widened community by creating new caring relationships. A pre-existing sense of community became focused in doing something of moral consequence together. Existing community organizations were transformed in order to help people fleeing for their lives, as well as to protect the villagers. The Boy Scouts, for example, together with some thirteen Bible study groups, were transformed into a communications network which enabled the community to respond quickly to Nazi raids.

As Le Chambon illustrates, philanthropic caring within communities unites people in relationships that strengthen, enlarge, and partly define community.[46] Precisely what is meant by "caring" and "community"?

"Caring" can refer to several things: an attitude, the specific virtue of benevolence, a more generic virtue of moral concern manifested in all the virtues, or relationships based on mutual moral concern. After briefly distinguishing these, I will rely on context to indicate which is meant.

As an attitude, caring is positive regard for the good of someone or something. To care "about" persons (or animals) is to desire their well-being for their sake, rather than solely for benefits to us. To care "for" individuals is actively to promote their well-being or to be prepared to. Their well-being is by itself a reason to act on their behalf, without having to look further for some gain to us.

As the Chambonnais remind us, caring is a sympathetic response to the needs of others. It implies understanding their situation, desires, and beliefs. It also implies a readiness to help if needed. It is shown in a variety of emotions: sympathy, compassion, solicitude, fear for people who are in danger, worry when they are in trouble, hope for success in their endeavors, delight when they succeed, joy when they return our love, and remorse when we fail to offer needed help. And it is shown in beneficent acts, that is, acts motivated by the desire to help and which actually succeed in helping others.[47]

Caring, then, is more than conduct, even though conduct is often its decisive indicator. Caring involves sensitivity, understanding, emotions, and good judgment—aspects of character that are not reducible to obeying simple rules of Do and Do Not. All aspects of the personality are evoked in connecting our lives with others. That is why giving with care is giving oneself.

As the specific virtue of benevolence, caring is the virtue of manifesting the attitude of caring in morally desirable ways. It implies attending to the needs and desires of others, showing compassion for their misfortune, delighting in their good fortune, being kind and generous. In a wide-scoped form, it is a general attitude of active good will toward humanity; in its focused form, it is directed toward particular individuals or groups.

As a generic virtue, caring is moral concern for persons and animals. This is the thematic sense used in the title of this book and that of the present chapter. Beyond just wishing others well, it is a disposition to help when one can, together with a tendency to help effectively. Giving with care means giving in a concerned and careful manner, with good will and intelligence. As such, it is an umbrella virtue which alludes to the full spectrum of philanthropic virtues explored in Chapter 2.

Caring relationships are between two or more people who care (in the generic sense) for each other. Caring is not always reciprocated with complete parity. Parents caring for their newborn baby constitute one paradigm of a caring relationship, even though of necessity it is an unequal relationship. Normally, however, the caring person hopes that the caring will eventually be reciprocated, even when the hope is not fulfilled: regrettably, a beneficiary turns a cold eye toward a benefactor; tragically, an infant dies before it can return its parents' love.

Can philanthropy involve caring relationships? Isn't it more a matter of helping strangers based on one-way positive attitudes, by contrast with family and friendships where talk of relationships is straightforward?

To begin with, much philanthropy is connected with family, friends, and other face-to-face interactions. Much philanthropy is engaged in to honor a family member, living or dead, or offered on behalf of an entire family. Moreover, many philanthropic interactions in local communities are a direct extension of family relationships; for example, participating in the Parent Teachers Association, church groups, and amateur sports. In these and other ways, philanthropy provides ways to express in a public forum the caring relationships rooted in private life.

In addition, philanthropy creates new personal relationships. On the one hand, there are new friendships to be made with people we help. Mary Mac-Anena, who for years has served meals to homeless people at a community park near my college, makes a point of seeking friendship with the people she helps. Again, in serving in a Big Brother or Big Sister program, volunteers become surrogate parents and siblings. On the other hand, volunteers working on behalf of common causes tend to develop ties of friendship. Mary is a friend (and inspiration) to hundreds of students who over the years have volunteered to help with her work.

Admittedly, when direct interactions are not possible, prospects for intimate caring relationships diminish. That may create problems. The increasingly impersonal nature of large organizations and mass movements in philanthropy, as elsewhere, is a cause for genuine concern. United Way, for example, has responded by allowing donors to specify which programs their money is used for, thereby strengthening personal identification with causes. Nevertheless, even when we do not know beneficiaries or other contributors, giving can connect our lives in caring ways with others. Why do we contribute to a particular political party or social cause? Because we share its goals with many other individuals, givers and receivers alike, with whom we identify. In contributing to *our* country, state, or city, we sustain ties to people we care about, even though we do not know them personally.

What about giving to strangers with whom we have no particular affiliation? Is there a caring relationship when we mail a check to help victims of an earthquake or tornado? There is a relationship of shared humanity grounded in faith that our efforts will be appreciated, and in that sense our caring is reciprocated. In giving, we connect our lives with theirs in ways that express and affirm human kinship. A gift shows they matter to us. Our capacity to care for strangers is limited, but it exists and it is important. It can also be cultivated, and one way is through philanthropy.

Some gifts to strangers have an intimacy all their own. Donations of blood resonate with symbolic meaning.[48] So do gifts of body organs. At the same time, the scope of these gifts—their range of possible recipients—is enormous. The donor does not know who will receive the blood, or even whether it will be sold or discarded before it can be used. Even when the gift is not used, however, there is a symbolic relationship: donors hope their gift will help, and they naturally hope the gift will be appreciated; they also express a kinship with people in need of life-saving resources.

Gifts of blood, organs, and emergency funds have strong symbolic meaning precisely because they are offered to strangers. They express our desire to help people because they are people, rather than because they stand in any particular relationship to us. This meaning is not sentimental fluff; it is as palpable as the gifts in which it is embedded.

Philanthropic caring is not always aimed directly at persons. The immediate target may be an ideal, cause, practice, organization, animals, or the environment. There is still concern for the well-being of what we care about, though the type of well-being differs according to the object. The well-being of persons is self-fulfillment. The well-being of animals is their flourishing in the life appropriate to them. The well-being of a community, cause, institution, or practice is its continuance and improvement. And the well-being of ideals means their widespread acceptance and implementation.

Even in these cases, caring relationships with persons are often indirectly involved. To care for a cause or an organization typically implies caring about people affected by them. A gift to a hospital or a medical research foundation is more than impersonal support to promote scientific knowledge. It is an expression of concern for people who will benefit from those organizations. In addition, there are the relationships among individuals who share a commitment to practices and institutions. Commitments to music or historical preservation, for example, link people together in shared endeavors and mutual care. There are also relationships, however formal, with people who represent organizations and groups. Even an acknowledgment letter from a representative of an organization to which we mailed a donation is a minimum form of reciprocity, which explains why its absence prompts resentment.

Turn now to the idea of community, which is a value-laden concept. A community is any group of people joined by shared caring, both reciprocal caring in which they care about the well-being of members of the group and confluent caring in which they participate together in practices on the basis of caring for the same activities, goals, or ideals.[49] For example, religious communities are identified by confluent commitments to religious ideals as well as by reciprocal caring among church members. Professional communities unite people with shared goals and also evoke reciprocal caring among colleagues. Neighborhood communities combine shared interests (such as interest in neighborhood safety and beauty) with mutual concern for the well-being of the members. Many philanthropic organizations are themselves communities which serve wider communities. Widest of all is the "moral community" that includes all morally concerned humans, past, present, and future. Next in scope is the "global community" comprising all people presently alive. Then come societies and the smaller communities they integrate: intimate small groups (families, a circle of friends), more impersonal large-scale structures (such as governments), and a variety of intermediate groups serving special needs. Philanthropic organizations generally function as intermediate or "mediating groups" which link individuals and families with larger social structures.[50]

Communities, including philanthropic ones, provide a variety of contexts for fostering virtues. Churches, scouts, amateur athletics, educational facilities, and service organizations are examples of groups that help in developing virtues and promoting caring relationships which sustain communities. Obviously not all communities are equally effective in this regard, just as not all are good overall.[51] Fully desirable communities—the ones in which the virtues are most successfully developed in individuals and organizations—have six features.[52]

First, fully desirable communities generate extensive networks of reciprocal caring relationships. Typically, individuals have some awareness that others return their caring. This makes it rational to give to strangers with the hope that our caring will be reciprocated even when we are unable to determine whether it is.

Second, fully desirable communities are just, in that they do not unfairly discriminate. They may set eligibility requirements that restrict membership, but those requirements cannot be based on prejudice. They recognize all people as having equal rights to participate in and benefit from the wider society in which the community is embedded. With respect to political societies, justice forbids gross economic inequalities unless the minimal needs of all members are met.

Third, a desirable community is characterized by widespread appreciation of the community. That means valuing its practices, institutions, traditions, ideals, and norms. It implies cherishing the community's heritage, hoping for its future, and desiring to promote its present possibilities. These attitudes need not be universal, but they must be widespread.

Fourth, in desirable communities there are numerous valuable activities and few undesirable ones. The activities may be political, economic, professional, vocational—or philanthropic, as in giving together. Cooperation, together with awareness of the importance of that cooperation, is essential.

Fifth, there is widespread faith and trust in the prospects for the community which evoke full participation of community members. Without these, all forms of social cooperation are at risk.[53] In particular, without trust in communities philanthropic giving loses its hope and its point. At the same time, when philanthropic giving is value-centered and virtue-guided, it is a major forum for strengthening social trust.[54]

Sixth, there is extensive rational public discourse and shared reflection about the goals and activities of a group. Moral discourse and reasoning are especially important. Philanthropic organizations improve their chances of contributing to the public good insofar as they maintain open dialogue with their constituencies and the public. Insofar as they contribute to public discourse about moral issues, they strengthen the conceptual framework essential for maintaining caring within communities. A vocabulary of the virtues is a large part of that framework.

Moral discourse has eroded in American society, in the view of Robert Bellah and his co-authors of the sociology-based study *Habits of the Heart*. The book's title was borrowed from a phrase used by Alexis de Tocqueville to refer to the mental and moral dispositions which unify a society. One such habit of the heart, observed by Tocqueville during his famous visit to the United States in 1831, is the tendency to form and participate in voluntary organizations. According to Tocqueville, this tendency counterbalances the danger of excessive individualism in isolating people from the wider community. According to Bellah, this danger threatens the very community which makes individual freedom possible.

Bellah occasionally portrays Americans as behaving selfishly: "We have put our own good, as individuals, as groups, as a nation, ahead of the common good."[55] His main thesis, however, is that Americans suffer from a kind of conceptual selfishness: "If there are vast numbers of a selfish, narcissistic 'me generation' in America, we did not find them, but we certainly did find that the language of individualism, the primary American language of self-understanding, limits the ways in which people think."[56] During their study of some two hundred individuals, Bellah and his colleagues repeatedly heard descriptions of family, work, and community involvement cast in self-centered terms. Americans' primary language in thinking about values is the language of personal success through material rewards ("utilitarian individualism"), together with personal pleasures through satisfying preferences ("expressive individualism"). Even in portraying their moral commitments, they emphasized individual choices rather than responsibility. Their conceptual world centers in "lifestyle enclaves" of private consumption rather than in public community.

Bellah urges us to rethink individualism. Its valuable aspects, especially personal initiative, self-reliance, and respect for individual dignity and freedom, should be retained. Personal initiative, however, needs to be understood as exercised in and through community. That understanding can be fostered by returning to two traditions deeply embedded in American culture. One is the republican tradition of active democratic citizenship. The other is the biblical tradition which has kept alive the ideal of a compassionate and just society. Reclaiming the moral languages of these two traditions will enable us to reconceive individualism as a product of communities and in turn be fulfilled by giving back to communities.

I have some sympathy for Bellah's recommendations (even though the moral language he proposes is not altogether clear). At the same time, given our increasingly pluralistic culture, it would be parochial to recommend a biblical emphasis to the neglect of Muslim, Hindu, and Buddhist scriptures and the rich literature of nonsectarian humanism. If we are to communicate across religious boundaries, as well as reconcile individualism and community, we need to emphasize what is common or at least overlapping among our moral languages, and do so within a pluralistic world view which is tolerant of alternative religious and moral perspectives. A first step in that direction is to become more fully acquainted with the language of the virtues.

2

Virtues in Giving

Actions expressing virtue are noble, and aim at what is noble. Hence the generous person . . . will aim at what is noble in his giving and will give correctly; for he will give to the right people, the right amounts, at the right time, and all the other things that are implied by correct giving. He will do this, moreover, with pleasure or [at any rate] without pain. . . .

—Aristotle

[V]irtue is the attempt to pierce the veil of selfish consciousness and join the world as it really is.

—Iris Murdoch

ARISTOTLE CONCEIVED OF the virtues as tendencies to hit the mean, that is, the reasonable middle ground between the vices of too much (excess) and too little (deficiency). He classified the virtues according to the kinds of emotions, desires, and actions they govern. Thus, courage is the mean between cowardice and foolhardiness when confronting danger and experiencing fear; temperance is the mean between overindulgence and apathy in satisfying the appetites; pride is the mean between vanity and a sense of inferiority when making self-appraisals or feeling self-esteem. According to Aristotle, there are two virtues in giving wealth, depending on one's economic resources. *Eleutheriotes*, sometimes translated as "liberality," is the virtue of openhanded givers who have modest resources. *Megaloprepeia*, translated as "magnificence," is the corresponding virtue of wealthy individuals who are able to make lavish gifts. For liberality the extremes are wastefulness and stinginess, whereas for magnificence the extremes are vainglory and pettiness.

Liberality and magnificence are usually understood as two dimensions of the virtue of generosity. Yet the word "generosity" is not a perfect translation of Aristotle's terms. In its ordinary sense, "generosity" means benevolent giving beyond what is required or customary. By contrast, Aristotle had in mind the far more robust idea of *correct giving*, whether on modest or on lavish scales. He meant voluntary giving to worthy recipients, in fitting amounts, on suitable occasions, for apt reasons, with appropriate attitudes and emotions, and "all the other things that are implied by correct giving."[1] Plainly, correct giving is an umbrella virtue that covers the full spectrum of philanthropic virtues, that is, the admirable character traits manifested in voluntary giving for public purposes. In this respect it is akin to giving with care—with caring and carefulness, with good will and wisdom.[2]

All the major virtues are important in philanthropy. I will discuss about thirty virtues, illustrating them with examples from literature and the history of philanthropy. My list is not a complete taxonomy, but I hope it overthrows a narrow preoccupation with any one or two virtues.

We can sort the philanthropic virtues into two broad and overlapping categories. *Participation virtues* are especially important in motivating giving. Most of them cluster around benevolence, justice, reciprocity, enlightened cherishing, and self-affirmation. *Enabling virtues* provide the moral resources for effectively pursuing philanthropic endeavors. They include the virtues of self-direction, moral leadership, and respect for others. Here is a catalogue of the virtues to be discussed:[3]

PARTICIPATION VIRTUES
    Benevolence
        1. Compassionate   2. Kind
        3. Generous   4. Loving

    Justice
        5. Sense of Justice

    Reciprocity
        6. Gratitude   7. Fairness

    Enlightened Cherishing: Sense of Community
        8. Public-Spirited   9. Convivial
        10. Loyalty   11. Faith and Hope in Community

    Enlightened Cherishing: Sacredness, Beauty, and Practices
        12. Sense of Reverence
        13. Sense of Aesthetic Appreciation
        14. Committed to Excellence

    Self-Respect
        15. Integrity   16. Dignity   17. Pride

ENABLING VIRTUES
    Respect for Others
        18. Honesty   19. Respect for Autonomy

Self-Direction: Understanding
  20. Wisdom   21. Good Judgment
  22. Self-Knowledge   23. Humility

Self-Direction: Commitment
  24. Perseverance   25. Courage   26. Sincerity

Moral Leadership
  27. Morally Creative   28. Responsible Authority
  29. Peaceloving   30. Inspirational

Benevolence

The relative importance of specific participation virtues, as well as their precise manifestations, varies greatly among cultures, communities, and individuals. Yet the virtues I discuss have wide cross-cultural significance. Benevolence is a good place to start because of its central role in our Judeo-Christian heritage, as well as in Buddhist, Hindu, and Islamic cultures. I will be concerned with both focused benevolence, which is directed toward specific individuals or groups, and general benevolence or humanitarian love, which is aimed at persons in general.

In either form, benevolence is active direct concern for other sentient creatures, including human and nonhuman animals. Its core is the desire for others' well-being for their sake, rather than solely for some advantage to us. That desire generates intentions to help, reasoning about how best to help, and beneficent conduct which succeeds in helping others. The desire is also embedded in feelings of affection, sympathy, and compassion. And it fosters relationships based on caring and commitment to others. Thus, benevolence affects all dimensions of character: desires, reasoning, intentions, conduct, emotions, commitments, and relationships.

Benevolence is an intrinsic good. It embodies desires, attitudes, and intentions which are inherently valuable because they manifest appreciation of the value of other lives. Benevolence is also an instrumental good because it tends to produce good consequences. In addition to motivating helping behavior, it makes other people feel valued so as to strengthen their self-esteem and self-respect.

Benevolence is a generic virtue which encompasses many more specific virtues, among them compassionateness, kindness, generosity, and love.

1. *Compassionate.* The virtue of compassionateness is the tendency to feel and act on the emotion of compassion in appropriate contexts and in desirable ways.[4] Compassion is sorrow combined with an active desire to help in

response to suffering or distress. The active desire distinguishes it from momentary sorrow and sentimental moods. Compassion motivates acts of helping perfect strangers, as well as people we know. It stirs people to mail money to starving people in foreign countries, volunteer time in centers for battered women, support political groups seeking government aid for the homeless and for victims of AIDS, and participate in groups that raise public awareness about the plight of animals.

Mother Teresa is a paradigm. As a young nun she visited the slums of Calcutta and experienced an overwhelming desire to help and also a sense of belonging there. Later, after acquiring her convent's permission, she devoted her life to feeding, clothing, healing, and ministering to Calcutta's desperately poor. She lovingly identified with them: "My community are the poor. Their security is mine. Their health is my health. My home is the home of the poor . . . the poorest of the poor."[5] She adopted an austere life close to the level of the people she served. Gradually she attracted hundreds of other nuns to similar service in the religious order she founded, the Missionaries of Charity.

As this example suggests, compassion is grounded in a sense of moral equality and shared humanity. In this respect it differs from pity. Compassion and pity are both sympathetic responses to the plight of others, and as such contraries of callous indifference and malicious glee. However, pity, in the pejorative sense, suggests an attitude of condescension, of looking down on others as inferior to us in some way.[6] The condescension may be mild, even tinged with affection, or it may be harsh, mixed with contempt and an impulse to degrade. Occasionally it is even a reasonable response to the stupidity of self-destructive people who are responsible for their own suffering and degradation. Nevertheless, pity puts people at a moral distance, whereas compassion promotes caring relationships.

Not surprisingly, we appreciate compassion toward us and dislike feeling pitied (unless we are masochists). Compassion reveals that people value us and regard us as moral equals whose suffering "is seen as the kind of thing that could happen to anyone."[7] Accordingly, philanthropic relationships are strengthened when recipients perceive benefactors as compassionate; they are undermined when recipients feel pitied. Misfortune is bad enough; pity adds the torment of being regarded as pathetically inferior.

2. *Kind.* Whereas compassion is directed toward distress and suffering, kindness ranges more widely. Kind people take pleasure in furthering the well-being of other people, whether or not they are suffering. For example, a kind philanthropist might fund a neighborhood carnival because she delights in making children happy.

Kindness blends benevolence with sensitivity. It is the tendency to help people (and other animals), motivated by a desire to promote their good and guided by a sensitivity to their needs, desires, and situation.[8] Kind people tend to offer the right kind of support at the right time, and they avoid insulting and hurting feelings. As a result, they tend to be effective in helping, rather than just "kindly" in their intentions. If they fail it is usually because of bad luck or unusual complications.

Daniel Ponder, Eudora Welty's character in *The Ponder Heart*, is an exceptionally kind man.[9] He is finely attuned to the needs of people, and his sweet disposition makes him eager to help by giving. As a result his gifts are tailored to the specific needs of his rural neighbors: a string of hams, a suit of clothes, two iron wheels, a fine Shetland pony (for a child), a pick-up truck, and in one case a hotel! His father viewed the last gift as excessive and consigned him to an asylum. But Daniel Ponder is not crazy. He is simply kind—and generous.

3. *Generous.* To give generously is to give more than is required, customary, or expected in light of one's resources and circumstances, and to do so motivated by benevolence. The virtue of generosity may be shown in a pattern of small gifts or with one or a few very large gifts.

Degrees of generosity are measured on three scales: (i) the depth of caring expressed, (ii) the amount given, relative to required or customary gifts, and (iii) the amount given, relative to the resources of the giver; roughly, the degree of sacrifice involved. For example, people with large resources must give more in order to be as generous as givers with more modest resources. A familiar parable illustrates how generosity can be shown in giving small amounts:

> Then Jesus sat down opposite the Temple almsbox and watched the people putting their money into it. A great many rich people put in large sums. Then a poor widow came up and dropped in two little coins, worth together about a halfpenny. Jesus called his disciples to his side and said to them,
> "Believe me, this poor widow has put in more than all the others. For they have all put in what they can easily afford, but she in her poverty who needs so much, has given away everything, her whole living!"[10]

The widow gave more generously because she gave a greater percentage of her resources, so that her gift represented a greater sacrifice, and perhaps also because her sacrifice revealed a higher degree of benevolence. The rich people who gave modestly relative to their wealth were dutiful in meeting the requirements of their religion, but not generous. In praising the widow,

Jesus was prescribing an ethics of high ideals which transcends an ethics of minimum duties.

Actions can be divided into four moral categories: (i) required by obligations (morally right), (ii) forbidden by obligations (immoral), (iii) neither right or wrong, nor good or bad (morally indifferent), and (iv) good or admirable beyond the requirements of obligation incumbent on everyone in similar circumstances (supererogatory).[11] Generous acts, like those of Mother Teresa and the poor widow, fall into the fourth category: they are good beyond what is obligatory for everyone.

Does this mean that generosity is an entirely optional virtue? Perhaps it can be argued that we should aspire to become generous people. It would follow that we ought to engage in some generous acts, even though such acts are still defined as not obligatory for everyone in a given situation. That is because the generous person has discretion about where to perform generous acts, and because no one has the resources to be generous all the time.

We admire generous people for two reasons. On the one hand, their deeds tend to produce good results in a degree beyond what is morally required. On the other hand, their willingness to help suggests exceptional benevolence. To be sure, generous giving can be harmful when unaccompanied by prudence and practical wisdom. People can be "generous to a fault" when they give beyond their means or in ways that unintentionally harm others. Yet even misguided generosity can reveal admirable benevolence when there is a desire and sincere intention to help.

I have been discussing economic generosity: giving money or things with monetary value (such as clothing, blood, services). Two additional forms of generosity are relevant to philanthropy: generous-mindedness and emotional generosity.[12]

Generous-mindedness concerns judgments about people. It implies readiness to give them the benefit of the doubt, to discern extenuating circumstances for their failures, to appreciate their virtues, and to find encouraging words to counterbalance criticisms of them. It also implies a willingness to forgive them, at least when they feel remorse for wrongdoing. Generous-minded philanthropists are prepared to trust in the good will of both recipients and other donors. Being slow to blame people for their misfortune, generous individuals are quick to help when they can. Conversely, the absence of generous-mindedness discourages giving. Petty and spiteful persons are eager to blame others for their plight. Nevertheless, overgenerous judgments can lead to naive and even hurtful giving that encourages dependency. Finding the golden mean in philanthropic generosity is notoriously difficult.

Emotional generosity is freely giving emotional support, including the time and energy required, whether or not those gifts have an economic value.

Even when busy and hurried, emotionally generous people are willing to listen, provide reassurance, offer suggestions, and convey supportive faith and good will. Many of them volunteer for jobs requiring this kind of support, such as Candy Stripers who bring comfort and support to hospital patients, hospice volunteers who help victims of AIDS, and counselors of rape victims.

4. *Loving.* "Love" can refer to a variety of emotions, attitudes, and relationships. Here I have in mind a combination of benevolence and pleasure. Loving persons care deeply about and seek to promote the good of others for their sake. They also take special delight and joy in the happiness of others. A loving person not only promotes the good of others, but takes delight in doing so.

The disposition to delight lovingly in helping others is a virtue that evokes the energies of many philanthropists. Certainly that is true where focused giving is involved, as in adopting a child—perhaps a child whom others have ignored because of its illness or disabilities. Again, scout leaders become lovingly involved in helping children in their troups, and caregivers in hospitals and hospices find joy in bringing happiness to patients.

What about attachments to larger groups, including international groups? Often it is said that love by its nature is restricted to face-to-face interactions and that trying to love everyone leads to disingenuous sentimentalism. If so, what are we to make of the injunction to love all people?

Immanuel Kant insisted that the commandment to love one's neighbor is sensible only when understood as the dictum to act beneficently.[13] Since emotions and inclinations are not under our direct control, he argued, they cannot reasonably be commanded. Yet, contrary to Kant, we can indirectly shape our emotional life. Through self-discipline and reflection on our attitudes we can at least lessen hatred, spite, and envy, and to some extent reorient our lives toward finding pleasure in the well-being of others. The ideal of loving everyone can only be approximated, and perhaps it is unrealistic for most of us, but it is intelligible, and it is an ideal that inspires much philanthropic giving.

Justice and Reciprocity

Justice entails giving what is deserved, whereas reciprocity is giving back in appropriate ways. The ideas are overlapping in that each implies obligations of fairness. In fact, given a sufficiently rich conception of fairness, justice and reciprocity tend to coalesce, as justice expands to include making fair returns and reciprocity expands to include fair treatment. I will keep the two ideas distinct, however, by understanding justice as respect for rights, including making amends for past violations of rights, and reciprocity as returning good for good.

5. *Sense of Justice.* Justice is treating people as moral equals, especially in situations involving competing interests or inequalities in power and opportunity.[14] The most straightforward way to understand moral equality is in terms of human rights, that is, the moral rights everyone has simply because they are persons, and whether or not the laws of a given society recognize the rights. A sense of justice, then, implies a readiness to respect and support people in their exercise of rights. It also implies a willingness to support those institutions and laws which protect human rights.[15]

Justice and benevolence are often contrasted, but they are connected in an important way.[16] We could not appreciate the rights of others to pursue their well-being unless we cared about their well-being, at least to some extent. Of course, our self-interest might motivate us to avoid violating their rights so as to avoid social and legal penalties, but appreciating rights means more than that. It means appreciating the inherent worth of persons.

Setting aside utopian dreams of ideal societies, a sense of justice is largely a sense of injustice. That explains why it can evoke vehement resentment and outrage.[17] Its most distinctive manifestation is indignation in response to specific violations of our rights or the rights of people we especially care about. Indignation functions as a potent philanthropic motive. Historically it was central to the causes of abolition, women's suffrage, and the 1960s civil rights movement. Today it motivates many people to join Amnesty International in order to voice the concerns of political prisoners throughout the world.

Not everyone shares the same sense of justice, as is clear from debates about rights.[18] Libertarians recognize only liberty or negative human rights: rights not to be interfered with while pursuing one's legitimate interests. Yet liberty rights mean little without the minimal resources necessary for pursuing them. Because of this, most human rights ethicists also recognize welfare or positive human rights: entitlements to the minimum necessities for decent life, when circumstances make it impossible to obtain those necessities through one's own efforts and when society has ample resources to provide help.

Sometimes philanthropists are motivated by respect for both liberty and positive rights. They may (correctly) believe that their government has a grossly inadequate tax system that fails to transfer from the wealthy what is essential for economically disadvantaged individuals to pursue decent lives. As a result, they feel that impoverished citizens have some legitimate claim on their resources, hence that philanthropy is a responsibility rather than a supererogatory act of generosity. Also, they might be motivated by indignation, as well as compassion, in doing volunteer work on behalf of the homeless whose rights to basic resources have been denied.[19]

Positive rights also enter into philanthropy through promises.[20] If I pledge to contribute a certain amount of money or time to an organization, I bestow a moral right on others to the pledged amount (even when no legal right is created). This is a "special" right, possessed by those to whom the promise is made, unlike human rights, which all people have.

Justice looks to the past as well as to the future. It concerns making amends for previous wrongs. A person whose wealth was unjustly acquired, whether by fraud or by exploiting workers, appropriately feels contrition. Direct compensation may be impossible, perhaps because the wronged individuals are dead or cannot be identified. Yet some gesture of good faith is possible by giving to philanthropic causes, thereby compensating for past harms in ways that are indirect or symbolic.

The past wrong may have been unintended. Consider Eliot Rosewater in Kurt Vonnegut's novel *God Bless You, Mr. Rosewater*.[21] As a platoon commander during World War II, Rosewater led his soldiers in an assault on a building partly engulfed by fire. Largely blinded by smoke, he killed two Germans with a grenade and bayoneted another German who was wearing a gas mask. He quickly discovered that the Germans were two old men and a fourteen-year-old boy who were unarmed civilian fire fighters. Rosewater cracked, attempted suicide, and later traveled aimlessly for years. Gradually he began to feel called to a philanthropic mission. To his father's chagrin, he distributed his inherited fortune to public causes. He also became a volunteer fire fighter. We do not blame Rosewater, as he blamed himself, since killing the civilians was an excusable error in the midst of a tragic but justified war of self-defense. Yet we understand his remorse. We understand how it fostered an authentic sense of personal responsibility to help others as a way to make amends and find some peace in living with himself.

Whereas making amends for past injustice implies returning good for harm we have done, reciprocity is the virtuous disposition to return good for good we have received, motivated in part by caring.[22] Gratitude and fairness are especially important participation virtues which motivate giving something back to groups and communities from which we benefit.

6. *Gratitude.* At first glance, gratitude seems to be a virtue of receivers rather than of givers, but it is both. When we feel grateful, we desire to show appreciation with a reciprocal expression of caring, often through giving.

We feel grateful for gifts to ourselves and to people we care about, but even more for the benevolence expressed in those gifts.[23] In fact, sometimes we cannot be expected to appreciate a gift ("Another tie and I will go crazy"), even though we appreciate the benefactor's good motives ("It's the thought that counts"). To appreciate benevolence is to value the benefactor as a person, not merely as a supplier of goods. In turn, we want to show appreciation with a reciprocal expression of caring. Appropriate reciprocation takes many forms. A thank-you note or phone call may suffice, or perhaps a gift to the benefactor is appropriate. Sometimes, however, the most fitting way to reciprocate is to make a philanthropic gift. Perhaps the benefactors are dead; yet we know they would have appreciated a gift on their behalf to their favorite cause.

Most of us have received help from groups whose members we do not personally know and whose gifts were not aimed specifically at us. I am grateful, for example, to the donors who established the foundation which awarded me a scholarship, even if they were not directly involved in giving me the scholarship. The gratitude might motivate me to contribute to the foundation when, later in life, I have the means to do so. Or, if I know the foundation has sufficient funds, I might instead contribute to a related foundation or even establish a new one. Similarly, many people contribute to civic causes out of gratitude toward their community, city, state, or country. They "give something back" in appreciation of the cumulative acts of good will by many individuals who helped make their achievements possible.

In addition to appreciating specific donors and communities, gratitude can be a more comprehensive appreciation of one's good fortune in life. One form is religious appreciation for the gifts of a benevolent creator in whom one has faith. Another form is a broad-scoped moral appreciation for the web of supportive influences in one's life. Whether religious or secular, comprehensive gratitude becomes woven deeply into the lives of many philanthropists. It becomes what Paul F. Camenisch calls "the salient characteristic, the dominant mood or theme of a total way of life":

> The person or group living out of such a comprehensive sense of gratitude will live with a joyful sense of the interrelatedness of things whereby life is enriched by the generosity of persons or powers outside themselves. Their lives will reflect the conviction that the goodness of life is not grounded primarily in themselves, in their own efforts and accomplishments—what they have earned, nor in their rights. . . . Rather they will see much of life's goodness grounded outside themselves in the uncoerced, undeserved bounty of other agencies well-disposed toward them.[24]

7. *Fairness.* Fairness is a primary virtue in sustaining cooperative practices. If I benefit from the efforts of others, I should do my fair share in return. That implies, for example, contributing to the publicly supported tele-

vision channel I watch daily, volunteering time in a neighborhood cleanup campaign, or donating money to expand the library at my child's school.

Being fair implies reasoning fairly. It is incompatible with the intellectual and moral cheating involved in rationalizing away responsibility. That cheating is shown in the biased and self-deceptive reasoning used by "free-riders" who profit from group endeavors without contributing their fair share in return: "My donation would be too insignificant to be worth sending"; "Programs should be better before I contribute to public television"; "I just made a [small] donation a few years ago."

Like gratitude, fairness has a more global form, beyond its role within particular cooperative practices. This widened sense of fairness inclines us to do our fair share in solving social problems. It is based on understanding how we depend on others, economically, socially, and morally. And it is based on appreciating how privilege and wealth make it appropriate for us to help people who suffer from great disadvantages.

Enlightened Cherishing

As Harry S. Broudy explains, "Cherishing is a special kind of love and desire. It is not merely a desire for possession of the object but, rather, a desire to preserve and care for the object because it has properties that delight us, i.e., properties intrinsically valuable. *Enlightened cherishing* can be thought of as a love of objects and actions that by certain norms and standards are worthy of our love."[25] Enlightened cherishing can also be understood as a cluster of virtues which have enormous significance in motivating and guiding philanthropy.

I begin with enlightened cherishing of communities, that is, of groups of people joined together by valuable forms of cooperation and caring. All philanthropic virtues tend to support communities, but some are directly aimed at promoting them. These community-centered virtues include public spiritedness, conviviality, loyalty, and faith and hope in the prospects for communities. Together they largely define what it means to have a (desirable) sense of community.

8. *Public-Spirited.* Public-spirited individuals have a deep and abiding commitment to sustain and advance their communities. Construed as a virtue, public-spiritedness refers to desirable forms of identification with and involvement in communities.

Benjamin Franklin is a paradigm. Industriousness, frugality, moderation, and the other prudential virtues he espoused helped to make him financially secure early in life. After turning forty-two he devoted most of his energies to public service, including service as a civic leader, ambassador, and peacemaker.[26] He spearheaded the development of Philadelphia's first public library, volunteer fire company, and hospital, as well as founded the academy which became the University of Pennsylvania and started a program for clean and well-lit streets. He offered his scientific and technological inventions free to posterity, rather than patent them for personal profit. Taken together, his community involvement brought a new direction to American philanthropy, moving it away from the personal piety of colonial days toward the more secular spirit of advancing public welfare. In doing so he shifted attention from short-term alleviation of poverty toward long-term solutions.

9. *Convivial.* Understood as a virtue, conviviality refers to temperaments which contribute to constructive forms of social involvement and cooperation.[27] It means the willingness to participate in desirable shared activities, the tendency to take delight in them, and the ability to get along with other participants. It is a virtue because most human goods are made possible by cooperative endeavors.

Convivial people are fond of good company, and they are themselves good company. They give pleasure to other participants in cooperative activities, whether through congeniality, friendliness, pleasant conversation, warmth, kindness, cheerfulness, infectious enthusiasm, humor, or lively wit. Whatever their personality style, convivial individuals spread delight in ways that make other people feel valued. So understood, conviviality is a key virtue in motivating and sustaining effective voluntary service.

Again, Franklin is a paradigm. He enjoyed working with people on behalf of the community, and people liked to work with him. His good will and wit won him friends throughout the colonies and in France and England. Interestingly, while Franklin did not place conviviality on his famous list of thirteen virtues, he alluded to something like it as the culminating effect of all the virtues. "The joint influence of the whole Mass of the Virtues," he wrote, produced in him "that Evenness of Temper, and that Cheerfulness in Conversation which makes his Company still sought for, and agreeable."[28]

10. *Loyalty.* According to Josiah Royce, loyalty is "the willing and practical and thoroughgoing devotion of a person to a cause."[29] More than any other philosopher, Royce explored how loyalty tends "to unify life, to give it centre, fixity, stability."[30] Loyal service widens our sense of what is good for us, revealing and expressing the connections between our interests and those of others. It enriches our identity by making us part of groups and shared endeavors.

Royce thought that loyalty is intrinsically good. He recognized, of course, that some causes are bad and damage communities, hence that loyalty is best when "enlightened" by being tolerant of other people's loyalties. But he thought that even loyalty to bad causes was somewhat good in that it served to focus and unify one's life. In my view, by contrast, loyalty is a virtue, having intrinsic value, only when it is directed to good causes—those which can unify a personality in desirable ways.[31] Nothing is good about centering one's life by becoming a Nazi or committing oneself to terrorist groups.[32]

Loyalty is a virtue, then, whenever it joins individuals to desirable causes (an intrinsic good), and it is most desirable when it advances those causes (an instrumental good). As such it provides a valuable motive for philanthropy. Royce's favorite example was loyalty to humane religions, which he defined as "the interpretation both of the eternal and of the spirit of loyalty through emotion, and through a fitting activity of the imagination."[33] In an ecumenical spirit, we might agree that a variety of religions promote good ends, whether or not we agree with their particular articles of faith.

Many philanthropic organizations depend for their effectiveness on the long-term loyalty of their donors. A cure for polio was found because millions of people developed ties of loyalty with the National Foundation, a private organization created to support medical research into and care for victims of polio. The ties developed during two decades of contributing (usually small amounts) to the March of Dimes:

> By enlisting so many people as active contributors to their cause, the National Foundation secured more than money. The principal weapon the foundation used in its war against polio was the tremendous loyalty people felt to the organization itself, loyalty that began with the first dime they gave and grew every time they read a progress report that told about what 'we' have accomplished and what remains for 'us' to do.[34]

11. *Faith and Hope in Community.* As moral virtues, faith and hope both imply anticipation of moral possibilities and active pursuit of a moral good. Faith is belief and trust in the anticipated good despite the absence of proof it will be secured. Hope is the fervent desire for a good believed to be possible but not certain. Both rule out mere complacency and sentimental wishing. And both imply risk-taking: venturing forth to achieve a strongly desired good whose achievement is uncertain. Specifically, the good might be the continuation and improvement of valuable communities and organizations. Faith and hope in community imply dispositions to act, desire, feel, and reason with optimism about the prospects for the valuable network of caring relationships that define communities.

Faith and hope in community can have either religious or secular roots.[35] Often both are involved, as in Communities Organized for Public Service (COPS).[36] Initiated largely through the efforts of Ernesto Cortes, COPS is

San Antonio's umbrella organization for local community groups, including religious, civic, and self-help groups. While COPS is not a Catholic organization, Catholicism clearly played a unifying role among its constituency—some 150,000 Mexican-American families. During the 1970s it was born of desperation and hope: desperation, because many Mexican-Americans were disenfranchised and impoverished; hope, because COPS became a catalyst for positive change.

COPS raised hundreds of millions of dollars and was able to exert political pressure, improve basic facilities and cleanup, and build public parks and libraries in the poorest neighborhoods in San Antonio. For example, it generated a $46 million drainage bond that ended the devastating flooding caused annually by heavy rainfall. By supporting a variety of volunteer groups, it empowered individuals to deal with governments and large corporations.

Faith and hope tend to be self-fulfilling. They generate commitment and energy, and they inspire others to join with us in cooperative endeavors whose success is uncertain. By providing reasons for the prospects of success, they function metaphorically as "evidence of things not [yet] seen."[37] To the degree they are present, they provide evidence for a community's favorable prospects.

Some virtues of enlightened cherishing concern nonmoral (other-than-moral, not immoral) forms of goodness which have moral implications in philanthropy. I will discuss three primary excellences: reverence for the sacred, aesthetic appreciation, and commitment to excellence. A fourth category will be left tacit, both here and throughout this book: enlightened appreciation of the efforts of other philanthropists.

12. *Sense of Reverence.* Reverence is enlightened cherishing of sacredness. It is an appreciation of things that embody or symbolize pure goodness. In this case, appreciation takes the form of awe, veneration, and voluntary submission toward goodness as a unifying focus for our lives.

Having a sense of reverence is a religious virtue, and religious matters are notoriously contestable. How, then, can reverence be understood as a virtue of enlightened cherishing, as love for what ought to be revered, without immersing us in religious disagreements? Indeed, given that some religions are intolerant or in other ways immoral, how is reverence a virtue?

Let us distinguish between religions and the religious.[38] Religions are systems of belief, ritual, and social organization. Most are theistic, grounded in beliefs about a supernatural deity. A few are nontheistic, such as Zen Buddhism, Confucianism, and some forms of Unitarianism. The religious, by contrast, refers to attitudes and modes of experience involving a sense of the sacred. Each religion interprets sacredness in terms of its own system of beliefs, and sacredness can also be interpreted in purely secular terms.[39] This allows us to understand reverence for the sacred dimension of life independently of the dogmas of any particular religion.[40]

Having said that, I will use theistic faiths to illustrate reverence. After all, half of all individual philanthropic gifts in the United States go to religious organizations. In addition, religious faith motivates a variety of additional philanthropic commitments and supports other philanthropic virtues such as gratitude, loyalty, faith and hope. Religions also foster their own distinctive virtues important to philanthropy, including Christianity's charity (*agape*), Judaism's righteousness (*tsedakah*), and Islam's almsgiving (*zakah*).[41] Within most Western religions, reverence is understood in terms of faith in God. That faith is not merely intellectual assent to propositions about God's existence and commandments, but also a loving trust in God's goodness, a trust which provides guidance, peace, and hope.[42]

One religious motive for philanthropy is self-interested concern for personal salvation, but that is hardly the only one. Here are some more: obeying (what are believed to be) God's commandments about tithing and helping others; desiring to become less selfish as part of emulating saints; expressing gratitude for God's blessings; honoring God by supporting religious institutions; expressing communion with other worshipers; expressing joy in God's creation.

We need not share someone's religious faith to admire their sense of reverence and how it motivates them to help others. For example, although I do not share her religious beliefs, I greatly respect Dorothy Day for her profound sense of sacredness about human life and the life of service it generated.[43] Beginning in college, and for a decade following, Day had been involved as a journalist and protester in the cause of economic justice for the poor. Her conversion to Catholicism in 1927 intensified and focused that commitment. The conversion came at enormous personal cost, ending a common-law marriage to a man she dearly loved but who would not accept her new faith.

Together with Peter Maurin, Day founded the Catholic Workers Movement as a Christian response to the 1930s depression. They published *The Catholic Worker*, a monthly newsletter which became a forum for religious reflection on economic values and attracted hundreds of thousands of readers. They also initiated dozens of "hospitality houses" to serve the homeless, and several farming communes as experimental Christian communities. During most of her fifty years of Catholic service, Day lived among the inner-city poor she served in a spirit of reverence and joy.

13. *Sense of Aesthetic Appreciation.* Aesthetic appreciation is valuing beauty, whether in the arts, in nature, or elsewhere. Enlightened cherishing of beauty

motivates contributions to orchestras, theatres, museums, preservation of historic architecture, and protection of the environment.

Aesthetic appreciation of the arts is a nonmoral excellence which has considerable moral importance in philanthropy. On the one hand, gifts to the arts promote the self-fulfillment of artists and audience alike. On the other hand, the arts often express moral themes that evoke moral change. For example, the Kentucky Foundation for Women was created with this in mind during the 1980s to support women artists.[44] Sallie Bingham, who created the foundation with a $10 million gift, was a playwright, short story writer, and feminist who believed that advocacy of women artists promotes social improvement.

Appreciation of beauty in nature has moral implications when it motivates efforts to preserve the environment. Indeed, such giving is often blended with moral concerns for the health of present and future generations. John Muir, for example, combined moral and aesthetic motives, as well as reverence for nature, as wellsprings for environmental activism. This combination of motives guided his efforts to preserve wilderness areas, create natural parks, and establish the Sierra Club. The same motives are reflected in his writings:

> Watch the sunbeams over the forest awakening the flowers, feeding them every one, warming, reviving the myriads of the air, setting countless wings in motion—making diamonds of dewdrops, lakes, painting the spray of falls in rainbow colors. Enjoy the great night like a day, hinting the eternal and imperishable in nature amid the transient and material.[45]

14. *Committed to Excellence.* Commitment to excellence is shown in striving to meet high standards and in contributing to others' efforts to meet high standards. Here my interest is in the standards of goodness (partly moral, partly nonmoral) in social practices such as the arts, sciences, humanities, and sports. Achievements in these areas often serve morally desirable purposes, as do philanthropic contributions to them. Commitments to excellence motivate philanthropic contributions to professional organizations in medicine, law, engineering, teaching, and other vocations that serve moral purposes. They also motivate donations to foundations that fund the arts, education, and scientific research.

For example, Arnold Beckman's gifts to science and engineering have included $50 million to the California Institute of Technology, $40 million to the University of Illinois, and $20 million to the National Academy of Sciences and the National Academy of Engineering.[46] Beckman is a humanitarian who has sought long-term solutions to human ills. His benevolence merges with a commitment to scientific excellence that was also present in his earlier careers as a chemistry professor and an entrepreneur who marketed

his inventions for improving scientific measuring. His gifts have been innovative as well as generous. Beckman is a pioneer in allowing universities
rather than private foundations to distribute his money, seeing them as best
able to channel funds to worthy research projects. Many of his gifts created
interdisciplinary research facilities which attracted top researchers, in part because his high standards made his grants highly prestigious.

According to Jose Ortega y Gasset, commitment to excellence relates to
nobility, not in the sense of membership in a favored social class, but as a
mark of good character in being devoted to high standards of excellence:
"Nobility is synonymous with a life of effort, ever set on excelling oneself,
in passing beyond what one is."[47] Nobility has to do with *noblesse oblige* in
the positive sense that links privilege with responsibility (and which does
not imply self-righteousness and condescension). It also has to do with a
strong sense of self-worth, which brings us to the next set of virtues.

Respect for Persons

Some philanthropic virtues are, ironically, self-oriented. I will discuss
several of them under the heading of self-respect: integrity, dignity, and
pride. Self-respect is valuing one's moral worth in a stable and deep way.
Each of us has that worth, and hence self-respect is a justified attitude of
self-affirmation. Self-respect is distinct from self-esteem, that is, a positive
feeling about oneself or a disposition to have that feeling. At the same time,
self-respect is a major source of self-esteem and a more reliable source than
social reputation or achievements.

15. *Integrity. Personal* integrity is a complex notion which implies coherence among one's activities and relationships, as well as coherence between
outer conduct and the inner life of emotions, attitudes, commitments, and
convictions. *Moral* integrity is personal integrity built around a core of moral
concern—concern which affects all areas of one's life. Members of the Ku
Klux Klan may have personal integrity, but they subvert their moral integrity.

Desirable forms of philanthropy enable us to join our lives with others
in ways promoting moral integrity. They provide numerous opportunities to
act voluntarily on our personal vision of the public good, and to put our
money (and time) where our mouth is. As we (literally) become part of philanthropic groups, they (symbolically) become part of our identity in ways
that strengthen integrity.

Moral integrity implies conscientiousness—the virtue of diligently meeting moral obligations. If there are obligations to engage in philanthropy, as
in Chapter 3 I argue there are, then conscientiousness about philanthropic
responsibilities plays a role in maintaining moral integrity. Sometimes we

must help, or else do violence to our integrity. The villagers at Le Chambon who gave shelter to Jewish refugees maintained their integrity; some others who closed their doors betrayed their integrity.

The villagers were motivated primarily by benevolence, and integrity was at most a secondary motive. As this example suggests, maintaining integrity can play a supportive role in philanthropy by setting limits. It precludes involvement in bad causes (such as hate groups like the American Nazi Party). It also limits the extent of our involvement in good causes so as to give due attention to the needs of our family and ourselves. At the same time, it reinforces involvement in good causes with which we strongly identify.

16. *Dignity.* Self-respect is also manifested in appreciating one's dignity and rights as a human being. This is illustrated in the life of the great abolitionist Frederick Douglass. A standard tactic of white abolitionists was to evoke the compassion of the white majority by drawing attention to the suffering of slaves. Douglass argued, however, that black people need to become leaders in the abolition movement by asserting their own human rights:

> [T]he man who has suffered the wrong is the man to demand redress . . . the man STRUCK is the man to CRY OUT—and . . . he who has endured the cruel pangs of Slavery is the man to advocate Liberty. It is evident that we must be our own representatives and advocates, not exclusively, but peculiarly—not distinct from, but in connection with our white friends.[48]

A sense of our moral worth is an impetus to contributing to desirable philanthropic endeavors. Like integrity, self-respect leads to giving that is self-affirming as well as helpful to others, and it guides us away from philanthropic involvements where we are unappreciated and simply used by others for purposes we cannot identify with. In that way, integrity is an enabling virtue, as well as a participation virtue.

17. *Pride.* If self-respect is appreciation of one's worth as a human being, pride is an attitude of self-affirmation specifically because of particular features about oneself. Understood as a virtue, pride in oneself is justified self-love and self-esteem based on one's abilities, accomplishments, and social roles.[49]

"I'm glad I could help," when uttered sincerely, usually implies altruism, but in addition it may convey pride in being able to help by having the requisite resources, talent, and commitment. We also take pride in receiving recognition for service, whether awards or simple expressions of appreciation. Within limits, pride from honors received is a legitimate affirmation of achievements in service. Our sense of self-worth is strengthened when we know we were able to make a difference, and when we are recogniz~~ ~~ our contributions.[50]

We are social beings whose identity consists largely in how we relate to others, including the groups and organizations we identify with. Pride can be pleasure in the excellence of one's community and its institutions— schools, museums, zoos, and other organizations we contribute to. Pride is closely linked to enlightened cherishing. In particular, civic pride is a potent motive for voluntary service within one's local community, as is patriotism at the national level.

Pride in oneself is often directly linked to pride in one's family. Thus, the philanthropy of people with inherited wealth or "old money" is often motivated by piety for the family tradition.[51] This is especially true of giving to schools and other organizations to which one's family has special historical links. To continue traditional family patterns of giving is a way of showing pride in one's family. Similarly, the "new money" of the entrepreneur can be used to establish the family name in a community that extends beyond the lifetimes of immediate relatives.

Pride is underappreciated as a philanthropic virtue, perhaps because it is easily confused with less desirable traits. Justified pride differs from the egotism and hubris condemned as the worst of the Seven Deadly Sins.[52] The egotist's objectionable self-elevation takes several forms. Narcissism is excessively focusing attention on oneself so as to become self-absorbed. Conceit is exaggerating one's talents, accomplishments, or beauty. Vanity is preoccupation with gaining and enjoying praise. Arrogance is putting others down in order to elevate oneself. Snobbery is arrogance shown in making others feel inferior.

Warranted pride and unwarranted egotism are frequent companions in philanthropy, as elsewhere in life. They were inextricably woven in the character of Andrew Carnegie. Carnegie was justifiably proud of the entrepreneurial talent and hard work that enabled him to acquire the wealth he later gave away on an unprecedented scale. At the same time, he arrogantly embraced Social Darwinism, the repugnant view that a privileged few like himself are entitled to dominate.[53] He was also known for his vanity in reveling in the honors bestowed at hundreds of dedication ceremonies for the libraries he endowed: he "dearly loved the pomp and circumstance of . . . riding in an open carriage through the old twisting streets, lined with crowds and flags."[54] A balanced appraisal of Carnegie's motives would acknowledge both his unsavory arrogance and his legitimate pride.

I shift now to respect for others, an umbrella virtue which underlies many participation virtues but which is also the most essential cluster of enabling virtues—those which enable us to carry out our intentions to help others. Honesty and respect for autonomy are especially important in placing limits on how we go about helping others. They are dealt with briefly here because Chapter 4 deals with them more fully.

18. *Honesty*. At first glance honesty seems to be a grab bag of Do Nots: Do not lie, steal, cheat, break promises, violate rights to truth, be hypocritical. These negative prescriptions, however, are unified by the positive theme of trustworthiness. To be honest with people is to be worthy of their trust.[55] Dishonest people violate trust, typically by using deception to advance their selfish interests at the expense of other people.

Trust makes philanthropy possible. We give voluntarily only when we trust that our money and efforts will not be misused. Fundraisers, in particular, have a fiduciary relationship with donors: they have a shared understanding and trust to carry out the intentions of their constituencies. By virtue of that relationship, fundraisers are required to make available that information which is necessary for donors to make informed decisions about giving. They are also obligated not to use donations in ways that sharply conflict with the donors' intentions. We are justifiably outraged when our money is used fraudulently or in other ways that subvert our intentions to help others, and we are easily disillusioned when that occurs. As a result, even a few instances of widely known fraud and negligence can have inordinate influence in discouraging philanthropy.

For example, the downfall of Jim Bakker hurt all television evangelists. Bakker was convicted in 1989 on twenty-four counts of wire and mail fraud and conspiracy.[56] Fifteen years earlier he and his wife, Tammy Faye Bakker, had created the lucrative PTL. (Praise the Lord, or People That Love) ministry. Using deceptive advertising, he oversold lifetime partnerships in his TV ministry's resort, Heritage USA. At least $4 million of the money was used to support a lavish lifestyle of expensive homes, cars, jewelry, and vacations. Also contributing to his downfall was a well-publicized sexual liaison with a church secretary. One of his accusers was Jimmy Swaggart, another prominent televangelist who later confessed to having frequented prostitutes to watch them perform sex acts. The combined debacle of Bakker and Swaggart did great harm to televangelism.

19. *Respect for Autonomy*. In large measure, to respect people is to respect their self-determination. As Kant said, it is to recognize people as "ends in themselves," as free, rational, and self-determining agents who have purposes of their own, rather than as things to be used as mere means to our own ends. This implies having a sense of justice, in respecting others' rights to live without interference and to receive help from others when they cannot by themselves meet their basic needs and when we have ample resources to help. Hence, respect for rights is an enabling virtue just as much as a participation virtue in philanthropy.

Respect for autonomy is crucial if philanthropy is to be a source of caring relationships rather than of exploitation. The following three violations of autonomy are among those discussed in Chapter 4. First, fundraisers sometimes manipulate benefactors. Perhaps the manipulation is unintentional, due to negligence. Or perhaps it constitutes cynical exploitation using coercion, duress, fraud, or deception. Either may occur as fundraisers fall into the habit of viewing people as moneybags, as mere means for promoting their ends (even when those ends are desirable).

Second, philanthropy can harm third parties, nonparticipants. Usually the harm is unintended: giving resources to one nonprofit organization may indirectly harm other organizations that compete with it in a free market economy. Other times the harm is intentional. Contributions to the Ku Klux Klan are deliberate acts of harming minorities. Though it has undergone variations since being founded after the Civil War, the Klan has a terrifying history of cruelty stemming from its central theme of bigotry and white supremacy.[57] It is a tragic reminder that philanthropists sometimes lack even the minimal virtue of nonmaleficence, the tendency not to intentionally inflict harm.

Third, philanthropists sometimes fail to respect the people they are supposed to help. The failure may be intentional, as in making a large donation in order to exert power abusively within a nonprofit organization. But usually the failure is unintentional in ways that cause dependency (pauperizing) or subvert the autonomy of recipients in pursuing their own vision of the good (paternalism). Sometimes the failure is institutionalized in social practices.

In nineteenth-century New England, the custom was to "auction" poor people to residents who offered to take them in for money paid by the town. City officials accepted the lowest bid. In "The Town Poor," Sarah Orne Jewett portrays how degrading this practice was to victims of poverty who lost any chance of regaining their independence. Two sisters were auctioned when their father died, leaving them without a source of support. They are forced to live in conditions of desolation. Two other women discover their plight and visit them in a moment of tenderness and communion. One of those women sadly reflects, "I've always heard the saying, 'What's everybody's business is nobody's business,' an' I've come to believe it."[58] She resolves to take personal responsibility for helping to restore the sisters' ability to exercise self-determination.

Self-Direction

The virtues of self-direction enable us to guide our lives so as to achieve worthwhile lives.[59] The first group of these virtues are aspects of understanding—wisdom, good judgment, self-knowledge, and humility.

20. *Wisdom.* Wisdom is practical understanding and skill in living a good life, rather than abstract theoretical knowledge.[60] It can be general or specific. General wisdom is wide-scoped understanding about life as a whole; specific wisdom is practical understanding about particular aspects of life.

General wisdom serves to unify our endeavors and relationships so as to promote coherence and self-fulfillment. It implies understanding many things: the goals worth seeking in our circumstances and their relative worth, the means to those goals and how to confront dangers which threaten them, our abilities and weaknesses, how to keep things in perspective when dealing with misfortunes, other people's motives, the importance of community, and so on. General wisdom is not esoteric knowledge, but instead a vivid, detailed, and contextual grasp of familiar truths, for example, that life is short, that selfishness hurts us as well as others, and that love is more valuable than power.

Lacking general wisdom, we can still have specific wisdom about our health, family, careers—or philanthropy. Wise philanthropists know how to give effectively (skill knowledge), they master pertinent facts (fact knowledge), and exercise appropriate sensitivity (emotional understanding). Experienced volunteers acquire practical know-how which combines caution and creative imagination in deciding when, where, how, and to whom to give. They understand why giving is valuable, how to balance public service with personal and family commitments, and when to abandon one service commitment in order to pursue another.

Specific wisdom about philanthropy can exist without general wisdom, but there is an open question about whether the reverse is true. Many moral leaders have made (specific) wisdom about philanthropy central to their vision of (general) wisdom about life: for example, Moses (righteousness), Jesus (love), Buddha (compassion), Muhammad (almsgiving), and Confucius (humanity). All these teachers emphasized the simple truth that human life is social. In precept and practice, they emphasized how philanthropic giving contributes to caring relationships within communities.

Certainly the absence of specific wisdom about philanthropy is often accompanied by a lack of general wisdom. The cryonics fad provides a macabre example. Certain wealthy Americans, most of them men, have paid vast sums to have their bodies (or just their heads) placed in permanent frozen storage and invested the remainder of their fortunes in cryonics research, hoping that new discoveries will make it possible to rejuvenate their bodies from frozen cells. Gullible and afraid, they waste resources which could have been used in more beneficial ways.

General wisdom is especially important in achieving moral balance among worthwhile goals, not just in identifying more and less urgent philanthropic opportunities, but in integrating philanthropy with other areas of one's life. In fact, wisdom leads us to withdraw from philanthropy when it threatens overriding obligations, such as to one's family. Consider Mrs. Jellyby who engaged in what Dickens called "telescopic philanthropy": the involvement in misperceived distant causes at the expense of immediate responsibilities.[61] Mrs. Jellyby is devoted to improving the economy and education of Africans in Borrioboola-Gha, on the bank of the Niger River. She finds time to consult with donors, attend and give lectures, and engage in lofty discussions about human solidarity. No time is left for the most basic needs of her family. Her house is filthy and her young children go unattended. Her older daughter, who is forced to serve as her secretary, moans, "The whole house is disgraceful. The children are disgraceful. I'm disgraceful. Pa's miserable."[62] Lacking a sense of moral priorities, as well as lacking self-knowledge about her motives, Mrs. Jellyby's philanthropy is an escape from family responsibilities, a way to gain notoriety, and more a service to the abstraction of humanity rather than to real people.[63]

Or is this portrayal of Mrs. Jellyby unduly harsh? Today we are more sensitive than Dickens to the importance of a wife's social involvements beyond the home, and less sympathetic to a husband who fails to do his share of the housework. Furthermore, if we criticize Mrs. Jellyby we should also acknowledge that many admired male philanthropists have neglected their families by engaging in voluntary service. If we excuse this neglect in Mahatma Gandhi, for example, it is because his service to humanity was extraordinarily effective, unlike that of Mrs. Jellyby.

21. *Good Judgment.* Wisdom implies and overlaps with good judgment. Combining sensitivity and sound reasoning, good judgment enables us to discern the means to the good ends envisioned by wisdom. It calls for objectivity to eliminate distorting biases, imagination to identify fresh approaches, breadth to evaluate alternatives, deep insight, and ability to deal with complexity. Like wisdom, it may be general in scope and concern life as a whole or be exercised in only some areas of life.

Moral judgment is especially important when there is no one perfect solution, but only better and worse solutions, to problems. The best solutions tend to integrate the moral traditions of the communities we live in with our personal needs for self-fulfillment.[64] That integration is accomplished by insight based on a foundation of a good upbringing and wide experience, rather than by applying a simple set of moral rules ranked in order of priority.[65]

Good judgment is required in dealing with problems of vagueness and conflict concerning moral principles. Precisely what, for example, does the

rule "Help people in desperate need" require us to do when confronted with
ongoing massive world hunger? And how should that rule be balanced with
the principle to give something back to communities from which we benefit,
when the two principles conflict because our resources are limited? There is
also the problem of conflicting principles, when two or several moral principles may come into conflict to create moral dilemmas. In coping with moral
vagueness and conflict, moral judgment is at least as subtle as judging a work
of art.[66]

Poor judgment takes many forms, but fanaticism deserves special mention. It occurs when one moral principle is exaggerated to the point where
it undermines equally valuable principles. For example, the National Rifle
Association (NRA) has zealously defended the right to own firearms even at
the expense of public safety. It has consistently opposed all legislation placing
restrictions on gun ownership, including assault rifles whose use is primarily
among gangs and organized crime. It has even blocked legislation requiring
customers to wait two weeks between purchase and delivery of handguns so
that police have a chance to enforce existing laws against ownership of guns
by parolees, mental patients, and drug addicts. In doing so the NRA has
been been influential in lobbying against bills favored by the overwhelming
majority of Americans.

Rashness is another source and sign of poor judgment. Consider Rose
Vassiliou, the protagonist in Margaret Drabble's novel *The Needle's Eye*, who
gave away her inherited wealth when she was twenty-four. She attended a
fundraising talk by a representative of a central African country. Without
making further inquiries she wrote a check giving him nearly all her money
to build a school. The school was built but then destroyed within a few
months during a bloody civil war that killed most of the children and their
parents. The fundraiser spent much of the money on himself, as Vassiliou
later learned from a newspaper article with a picture of him standing in front
of his new Mercedes. Her decision was a benevolent expression of her faith
that it is easier for a camel to get through a needle's eye than a rich person
to enter the kingdom of heaven. But her good intentions were not enough
to justify what she realized in retrospect was a "rash and foolish," "flamboy-
ant, histrionic, disastrous, ruinous gesture."[67]

Rashness implies poor quality of judgment, not mere quickness. Thus,
good judgment can be spontaneous without being rash, as is illustrated by a
gift from Alex Spanos, a multimillionaire who is said to be the largest builder
of apartments in the world. Spanos received a phone call from a woman who
was on the board of directors for a San Francisco museum which was spon-
soring an exhibit on Alexander the Great. She asked Spanos whether he
would be interested in helping to sponsor the exhibit. It took Spanos only
seconds to make his decision:

The moment he heard the idea, he was excited about it and decided to go ahead. "I thought it was a great idea, and expressed a part of my heritage. On top of all of that, I was named for Alexander. Everything just fit into place. I don't believe I found out until much later what the cost was—it was a quarter of a million. But that really wasn't important to me. The idea was right and it was right for me."[68]

Spanos's gift was impulsive in that it immediately evoked his enthusiasm and identification with a cause. But it was not rash or foolhardy, assuming he had better grounds than Rose Vassiliou did for confidence in the people involved in the project, and assuming he made further inquiries before writing out a check.

22. *Self-Knowledge.* Wisdom implies self-knowledge in a value-laden sense which implies valuable forms of self-understanding, in particular those which enable us to pursue self-fulfillment and meet our moral responsibilities. Self-knowledge means knowing *how* to live a meaningful life based on knowing *that* certain things are true, including truths concerning our primary motives and their relative strength, our values and character, our relationships with individuals and communities, and our strengths, weaknesses, potentials, and limitations.

Self-knowledge is often developed through voluntary service. The willingness to experiment by volunteering is a way to learn about our interests, abilities, and sources of happiness. At the same time, blindness to ourselves can cause much harm despite good intentions to help.

In *The Warden* Anthony Trollope presents a comedy of errors about the lack of self-knowledge and good judgment.[69] Inspired by an early nineteenth-century scandal, Trollope's novel focuses on shortsightedness in establishing foundations, in carrying out the aims of donors, and in volunteering for social causes. A fifteenth-century landowner had established a hospital for his workers, leaving each of them a fixed income from rent on his land and giving the remainder to the steward, now the Reverend Septimus Harding. Lacking imaginative vision, the landowner had failed to foresee the effects of fixing the income of his beneficiaries while allowing the steward to profit. As careless as he was compassionate, the Reverend Harding failed to look into the details about the century-old arrangement, thereby profiting from the land appreciation at the expense of the poor.

Along comes John Bold, a zealous crusader against church malfeasance. Bold is Pollyanish about the poor and oblivious to how merely adding to their income would only deepen their dependency. He is also blind to the genuine services provided by the Reverend Hardy. Bold's tunnel vision results in harm to everyone: the Reverend Harding resigns the position in which he did so much good; the church's reputation is sullied; the bene-

ficiaries' money goes to legal and adminstrative fees; and Bold's own professional integrity is compromised as he tries to reverse the legal proceedings
because he fell in love with Harding's daughter.

23. *Humility*. Humility is the proper assessment of one's character, accomplishments, and position in the world. It is "an attitude which measures
the importance of things independently of their relation to oneself or to
some narrow group with which one identifies."[70] It is fully compatible with
self-respect and pride in oneself, and it should not be confused with feeling
inferior.

Here are three types of humility: humility about one's character, social
humility, and intellectual humility. Humility about one's character implies
awareness and realistic assessment of one's moral strengths and weaknesses.
As such, it overlaps with sincerity. The humble person avoids self-righteousness and other attitudes that typify an inflated ego: conceit, snobbery, and
hypocritical pretense. Self-righteousness can cause great damage in philanthropy, inclining givers to be paternalistic in assuming they know better than
recipients what recipients need.

Social humility is tact and sensitivity to others' feelings, even when there
is reason to be confident about one's views. Benjamin Franklin was modest
and clever, not hypocritical, when he stopped asserting his convictions forcibly, replacing words like "certainly" and "undoubtedly" in his speech with
"I conceive" and "I imagine," and foregoing "the Pleasure of contradicting"
others abruptly while learning more indirect ways to refute them. As a result,
"The Conversations I engag'd in went on more pleasantly," and had "much
Weight with my Fellow Citizens, when I proposed new Institutions, or Al-
terations in the old; and so much Influence in public Councils."[71]

Intellectual humility is modesty about the extent of one's understanding
and about how much weight should be given to one's opinions. Much philanthropy is wasteful because it operates on the basis of overcertainty about
how best to help others. In addition, intellectual humility has historical, cultural, and biological dimensions. A humble sense of one's place in history
adds to an enlightened cherishing of historical monuments and museums.

A humble acceptance of oneself as a natural creature reinforces appreciation of the environment on which all creatures depend for their survival.[72]
A sense of oneself as a member of a community, or rather communities,
helps develop the virtues of loyalty, public-spiritedness, and gratitude. And
a sense of realism prevents fanaticism and harmfully grandiose philanthropic
schemes. Such schemes are nearly always accompanied by a failure to show
respect for the legitimate self-determination of other people.

Wisdom, good judgment, self-knowledge, and humility are largely cog-
nitive in nature, even though they are grounded in sensitivity to values. They

are useless without the virtues of commitment, including perseverance, courage, and sincerity.

24. *Perseverance.* Perseverance is steadfastness in pursuing worthy endeavors despite opposition and discouragement. It implies intellectual and physical self-control, but also a toughness of spirit in being patient and persistent.

Dorothea Dix is an exemplar.[73] In 1841 she happened to accept an invitation to conduct a Sunday school class for women prisoners in Cambridge, Massachusetts. There she found psychotic women chained and locked in unheated, filthy cells. Outraged, she began writing letters and giving talks to rouse public awareness. Thus began a forty-year crusade throughout the United States and a half-dozen other countries to reform institutionalized care for the mentally disabled. Confronting widespread ignorance and indifference, she tenaciously persuaded politicians to fund improved hospitals. The same perseverance continued when she later served without pay as the head of the Union's nursing staff during the Civil War.

A more recent example of perseverance in volunteer work was the drive to gain adequate funding for research on AIDS (acquired immune deficiency syndrome) and to provide caring for AIDS patients.[74] Social activists and fundraisers had to confront massive prejudice toward gays. Caring relationships with AIDS patients require compassion and toughness, and, once begun, the willingness to reliably continue involvement. Volunteers must cope with their own fears of death, as well as with burnout, that is, chronic fatigue, depression, and despair.

25. *Courage.* Courageous people cope with danger and fear in admirable ways.[75] They undergo risks with self-control and with the intention to achieve a significant good.[76] Risking one's life by "playing chicken" is foolish rather than courageous because no significant good is pursued. Again, if we are willing to ascribe courage to enemy soldiers, rather than just daring or "guts," it is because we see something good in their pursuit of duty, albeit for a misguided cause.[77] Like most virtues, courage is both intrinsically good and desirable as a means to other valuable ends. We admire courageous individuals for their strength and intentions in pursuing good at the risk of personal harm, as well as because they tend to produce good results.

Types of courage vary according to the kind of dangers involved. Physical courage confronts dangers to one's life or body. Social courage confronts the risk of adverse judgments by other people. Intellectual courage, or the courage of one's convictions, is pursuing one's beliefs in the face of either physical or social dangers. All these forms of courage were shown, for example, by activists in the civil rights movement.

Physical courage requires the intellectual skills of good judgment about when and how much force to use. Consider the Guardian Angels, a civilian patrol founded in New York City by Curtis Sliwa in 1979.[78] Volunteers ride New York subways wearing uniforms that the public has come to recognize. They function as visual deterrents to crime, in addition to making hundreds of citizen arrests of criminals. There is real danger, and several members have been killed. Because they have avoided the use of violence, they have been able to maintain public confidence.

Whistleblowers are perhaps the most unheralded courageous philanthropists. While not all whistleblowing is warranted, justified whistleblowers draw attention to a major harm to the public, whether a safety threat or corruption (in business, government, or nonprofit organizations). After attempting to remedy matters through normal channels, they convey relevant information to the public. The consequences of this public service are usually beneficial to the public but disastrous to the whistleblower, who may suffer harassment by employers, shunning by colleagues, demotion, firing, or blacklisting.[79]

Frank Serpico, for example, was a New York City police officer who tried in vain to get his superiors to end widespread bribe-taking and other corruption in the police force.[80] By revealing what he knew to a reporter, he became the catalyst for sweeping improvements. He also became the object of persecution by colleagues for the remainder of his career. Engineers and scientists have met a similar fate when they warn the public about their companies' illegal dumping of toxic wastes or life-threatening defects in their products.

26. *Sincerity.* Sincerity takes two forms. The first is part of personal integrity: coherence between inner life and outward behavior. People are sincere when their motives, beliefs, attitudes, and commitments are what they are seriously presented as being, where "seriously" rules out contexts such as practical jokes and acting on a stage. Sincere people are honest, whereas insincere people culpably lie, deceive, hypocritically pretend, or fail to have good faith in trying to meet their commitments.

The second form of sincerity is genuineness or purity of inner states. Purity means a lack of corrupting mixtures of hurtful motives. It is compatible with many types of mixed motives, as I argue in Chapter 5, and demands for absolute purity of motives are both unrealistic and a source of fanaticism.[81] At the same time, some motives obviously do distort giving, especially in the absence of self-awareness of them. Self-righteousness, snobbery, and hypocrisy corrode caring relationships. Sincerity enables us to focus on the needs of people we seek to help without the distortions caused by self-preoccupation.

In "A Mistaken Charity," Mary E. Wilkins Freeman presents us with a memorable example of how good intentions distorted by egotism can undermine helping. Mrs. Simonds is "a smart, energetic person, bent on doing good . . . in her own way."[82] With great effort and "with the delight of successful benevolence," she persuades the elderly Shattuck sisters to move into the town's rest home, unfortunately rendering them forlorn and desperately unhappy. The sisters' life had been hard, especially with one of them blind and the other deaf. Yet they managed to live independently in the dilapidated house in which they had been born, taking pride in fending for themselves and "indescribable" delight in growing their own food. The rest home is clean and safe, but also regimented and joyless. Mrs. Simonds is oblivious to all this as she conducts her self-congratulatory "helping" campaign. As Freeman wryly remarks, she serves as "an impressive illustration of the truth of the saying that 'it is more blessed to give than to receive.' "[83]

Moral Leadership

Leaders make things happen within and by groups.[84] Their influence may be undesirable—witness Hitler, Stalin, and Saddam Hussein. *Moral leaders*, however, have good intentions and initiate or guide desirable endeavors. Philanthropic leadership takes many forms: guiding a social movement, organizing a nonprofit organization, directing a group of volunteers, becoming a lead donor whose gift challenges others to contribute, making a courageous gift to a controversial and neglected cause, articulating new and timely directions for philanthropy, developing innovative tactics for social reform or fundraising, and inspiring others to have greater faith and hope in communities.

Depending on circumstances, all the virtues contribute to moral leadership. Good judgment, courage, integrity, trustworthiness, and public-spiritedness tend to be especially important. A few additional virtues which partly define moral leadership are moral creativity, responsible exercise of authority, love of peace, and moral inspiration.

27. *Morally Creative.* To be morally creative is to achieve something new and morally valuable. Newness may be assessed relative to several standards: the status quo, the accomplishments of previous generations, or (in the case of self-transcendence) one's own previous accomplishments or present habits. In philanthropy the achievement may be a discovery, a fresh approach to a problem, or exemplary conduct.

A moral discovery is an insight into a moral issue or challenge. Moral leaders do not invent moral values; instead they envision new possibilities and offer fresh perspectives. Their creative insight uncovers novel approaches while preserving traditional values. Often it consists in forcefully showing which virtues have been neglected or are especially important.[85] Creative leaders are focusers and simplifiers. They thrust to center stage the things that should matter most at a given time and place, and they successfully convey their insights.[86]

Moral achievement sometimes consists in inventing new approaches to helping. Today, for example, a familiar fundraising technique is the matching gift, whereby a donor makes a gift conditional on raising matching funds. Jacob Henry Schiff is credited with inventing the technique, or at least for first applying it on a large scale. Schiff was the leading Jewish American philanthropist for the decades before and after 1900.[87] He pioneered the use of matching gifts with an array of philanthropic projects, including founding New York's Montefiore Hospital and Young Men's Hebrew Association.

Exemplary philanthropic conduct is as varied as the social contexts in which it is shown. Cora Tucker, for example, who in her youth worked as a sharecropper, became a leading community activist in the rural area of Halifax County, Virginia.[88] One of her many philanthropic projects was to organize a letter-writing campaign supporting the Voting Rights Act which improved voting opportunities for black people. In doing so, she used the innovative approach of supplying the local beauty parlors with pens and paper so that women could write letters while having their hair dried.

Volunteering in the radically different setting of Orange County, California, Judie Argyros found a new way to involve her wealthy business friends in the Orangewood Home for Abused and Abandoned Children. She sent a note to them, asking, "When was the last time you had love in the afternoon?" Accompanying the note was an invitation for a limousine to take them to an undisclosed location during a lunch hour the following week. The limousines delivered them to Orangewood, where she provided a tour. Without explicitly asking for money she received a number of large donations.

Entrepreneurship plays an important role in the nonprofit sector as well as in profit-making corporations. In a typical sequence, individuals identify a community need, develop resources for meeting it, and establish a new organization to deliver services.[89] For example, concerned citizens see that their city's services are inadequate to respond to an explosion of teenage runaways. They successfully lobby for state funds and obtain free radio time to invite private donations. Then they rent a building as a temporary shelter and sanctuary, staffing it with both volunteer and professional workers.

Creative philanthropic achievements include most of the recent social movements, including civil rights, feminism, antiwar activism, environmentalism, and animal rights. They also include the nineteenth-century movements which were guided by some of the great leaders in the history of philanthropy: abolition (Frederick Douglass, William Lloyd Garrison), women's suffrage (Sylvia Pankhurst and her family), establishment of public libraries

(Andrew Carnegie), reform of mental health care (Dorothea Dix), and the guarantee of public education for all citizens (Horace Mann). It is plausible to argue that philanthropy's "central value is the extra dimension it provides for seeing and doing things differently."[90]

28. *Responsible Authority.* "Authority" has two relevant meanings which parallel two forms of leadership. Expertise leadership centers in applying special skill and knowledge, whereas role leadership is the effective use of power attached to social roles. Both are important in philanthropy.

Expertise is the authority based in knowledge, both knowing-how and knowing-that. Philanthropic leadership can be shown in using one's expertise to help others, ideally to help others help themselves. Saul Alinsky showed leadership of this kind.[91] He was an expert in helping local community groups solve their own problems, especially in poor areas of the country. From the 1940s until his death in 1972, he became the most effective organizer in American philanthropy, empowering one group after another to assert their interests within the democratic process. Today many of the techniques he pioneered are still used by community organizers.

Role leadership differs from "headship."[92] To head a group is to have a position with rights and responsibilities specified by the rules of an organization. But holding a position is no guarantee of exercising influence, as ineffective managers are painfully aware. Moreover, usually the authority of leaders comes directly from respect earned within a group, rather than from institutional rules per se. Cesar Chavez is an example of respect-based role leadership. In forming and directing the United Farm Workers, Chavez faced an enormous challenge.[93] Powerful agricultural interests dominated all aspects of farm labor, often making working conditions little better than those of slaves. It was common not to respect child labor laws, not to provide basic sanitation facilities, and not to protect workers from pesticide poisoning. In addition to being desperately poor and without permanent homes, farm workers were divided by racial and language barriers. Chavez mobilized their commitment to long-term change. He organized and led nonviolent strikes, pickets, and boycotts that drew public attention to their plight.

29. *Peaceloving.* Because groups are prone to conflict, the ability and disposition to be a peacemaker is an important leadership virtue. Peace is not the mere absence of conflict. In fact, often moral leaders, even in their capacity as peacemakers, must stir things up in order to stimulate healthy tensions and remove unhealthy conflicts. Peace is less an end state than a process of evoking and sustaining shared loyalties: "a process in which people freely and responsibly cultivate shared commitments to common expressions, projects and practices."[94] As a virtue, love of peace is the disposition to enter into and to help guide that process.

The specific techniques of peacemaking vary according to the best way to mediate hostile conflicts, negotiate disputes, develop compromises, and restore troubled relationships. Here are three examples: (1) The Quaker-inspired process of fostering concensus through calm dialogue based on mutual good will is best suited for intimate relationships within groups. (2) Rational negotiation of shared principles works best in competitive situations where opposing sides need to reconcile conflicting interests in order to form contracts.[95] (3) The love-inspired nonviolent resistance used by Mohandas Gandhi is often the best way to pursue peace by empowering oppressed groups.

Gandhi was able to overthrow British control of India by creatively using civil disobedience: disobeying laws in a manner that is nonviolent, public, conscientiously motivated, and accompanied by a willingness to accept legal penalties. Civil disobedience was used to generate test cases for challenging unjust laws in the courts. But its main effectiveness was in attracting the mass media in order to stir the public's conscience. Gandhi did not invent this approach to peace. Earlier, Henry David Thoreau had used civil disobedience to protest slavery and the Mexican War, and the suffragettes had used it in crusading for women's voting rights.[96] But Gandhi creatively adapted its use to his society, giving it a religious interpretation in terms of his ecumenical version of Hinduism.

30. *Inspirational.* Great leaders are morally inspiring, as well as inspired. They have moral vision and convey it to others so as to arouse moral commitment. They infuse passion for worthwhile ends; they are inspiriting. Unlike the sheer use of power, their influence is exerted through the free participation of people who are intellectually open and emotionally receptive.[97] Inspiration can take the form of charisma which excites emotions through force of personality, or it can stimulate devotion to ideals through trenchant speech, forceful writing, or exemplary conduct.

Martin Luther King, Jr., was an inspiring leader who combined deep humanity, outrage at injustice, perseverance, courage, and hope for his cause.[98] He also had a profound sense of history and was able to move things forward while putting defeats into perspective. Above all, he was an inspired speaker:

> I have a dream that one day this nation will rise up and live out the true meaning of its creed—we hold these truths to be self-evident, that all men are created equal. . . . I have a dream that my four little children will one day live in a nation where they will not be judged by the color of their skin but by the content of their character. I have a dream today![99]

King displayed the other leadership virtues as well. His creative vision was shown in advocating civil disobedience and reinterpreting it as an expression of love and forgiveness of enemies.[100] He knew that neither violent revenge nor gradual legal change could overthrow American segregation in the 1950s and 1960s. Bold and innovative confrontation through civil disobedience, however, could be used to appeal to the consciences of the majority of Americans.

King was a paradigm peacemaker, one who placed nonviolence at the core of his moral vision and who, as a sympathetic listener, could bring together people with sharply divided views. At the same time, he was a rabble-rouser. In his "Letter from Birmingham City Jail" he contrasted the violent tensions within a static racist society with the constructive nonviolent tensions that he fostered as a prerequisite for moral growth.

King accepted and responsibly exercised authority. Often he expressed the desire to step down, and he lived with daily threats on his life before being assassinated at the age of thirty-nine. During his short life he developed a remarkably balanced and comprehensive view of the American situation that enabled him to avoid fanaticism and one-sided loyalties. For example, he continued to protest the Vietnam War despite criticisms that his protests lessened public support for the civil rights movement. As he told a friend, "At times you do things to satisfy your conscience and they may be altogether unrealistic or wrong tactically."[101]

This overview of selected virtues suffices to show that philanthropy involves more than generosity. It also prepares the way for inquiring into responsibilities concerning philanthropy. Some participation virtues embody general areas of responsibility, in particular the virtues of benevolence, reciprocity, and justice (Chapter 3). In addition, the enabling virtues of respect for persons contain minimum standards of decency (Chapter 4).

3

Responsibilities to Help

A great part, perhaps the greatest part, of the intercourse amongst mankind,
cannot be reduced to fixed determinate rules. Yet in these cases there is a
right and a wrong: a merciful, a liberal, a kind and compassionate behaviour,
which surely is our duty. . . .

—Joseph Butler

Sometimes give your services for nothing, calling to mind a previous
benefaction or present satisfaction.

—Hippocrates

Are there any obligations to engage in philanthropy? This question is left
open by our definition of philanthropy as voluntary private giving for
public purposes. "Voluntary" means noncoerced, which rules out force, threats,
and legal penalties for noncompliance. It does not, however, mean nonobligatory, thereby allowing the possibility of philanthropic responsibilities which
are met (or refused) voluntarily. While much philanthropy expresses generosity
beyond all moral requirements, some is a responsibility.

One source of philanthropic responsibilities is mutual aid: the duty to
help others when they are unable by themselves to meet their basic needs
and when no significant sacrifice is involved. Another source is reciprocity:
the duty to give something back to people and communities who have shown
benevolence toward us. These general responsibilities, which are incumbent
on us all, comprise the minimum standards of decency embedded in the
virtues of benevolence and justice, to that extent making these mandatory
virtues.[1] In addition, some individuals acquire special responsibilities through
their commitments to ideals.

By "responsibilities" I mean wide-scoped obligations which allow discretion and require discernment.[2] Thus, we speak of parents' responsibilities to
support the development of their children and teachers' responsibilities to
educate students. Similarly, most philanthropic responsibilities are indetermi-
nate in their requirements and call for discretion and good judgment in deciding how to meet them.

Responding to Need

For the most part, interactions with strangers are governed by the principle of nonmaleficence—Do not harm—and the corresponding virtue of being disposed not to hurt others. This is a "negative" obligation *not* to interfere with their endeavors. There is no "positive" obligation to help others satisfy their desires, even when those desires are deeply felt or central to individuals' life plans.[3] My strong desire to buy a house places no obligation on you to help me, and a religious group's fervent desire to build a church places no obligation on us to help them. There is not even a presumption of goodness in helping others to satisfy their desires; everything depends on the situation and the kind of desire involved.

Matters are different, however, with basic human needs.[4] Basic needs are the necessities for subsistence and significant life, including food, shelter, medical care, and, in contemporary society, literacy and legal assistance in protecting civil rights. At the very least, there is a presumption of goodness in helping people who are unable by themselves to meet their own needs. It is only a presumption because other moral considerations might intervene: What if the person is Stalin or Saddam Hussein? Is there in addition an obligation, however limited, to help others meet their basic needs?

Simple decency, which is the minimal standard of benevolence, leads us to endorse the principle of mutual aid: we have a responsibility to help people meet their basic needs when they are unable to meet them through their own efforts and when helping requires little or no significant sacrifice to us. The question of when people are unable to meet their basic needs must be answered contextually, by examining particular individuals in specific settings. But what is a significant sacrifice? It is a voluntary lessening of one's overall good for the sake of someone else. One's overall good, as I understand it, is self-fulfillment—the development of talents so as to achieve happiness and meaningful life. Roughly, then, I make a significant sacrifice whenever I lower (or risk lowering) the ability to develop my talents so as to achieve meaningful and happy life.

The principle of mutual aid is vague, but not vacuous. It has numerous straightforward applications. If I can save you from drowning by throwing a life preserver, I ought to throw it. If I can prevent an infant from drinking poison by removing a bottle of Chlorox, then I ought to remove it. If I can prevent a murder by making a phone call, then I ought to make the call.

The last situation occurred in 1964 in Queens, New York.[5] Kitty Genovese was returning home at 3:20 a.m. from her job as a night manager. Moments after parking her car she was attacked and stabbed by a man she had never met before. Thirty-eight neighbors heard her screams for help. One man yelled, "Let that girl alone"; no one else did anything. The attacker walked away, then returned in a few minutes and stabbed her again. This time no one even yelled out in response to her loud cries. The attacker drove away, only to return a third time, when he finally killed her. Thirty-five minutes elapsed from the first attack to the third, fatal stabbing. When the police were finally called they arrived within two minutes, indicating that an earlier call would have prevented the murder. According to the principle of mutual aid, that call was obligatory.

Does the principle of mutual aid imply a general obligation to engage in philanthropy? Not by itself. We can imagine a world where basic needs are met without the need for philanthropy, a world of fewer hardships, as well as more effective economies and governments. Our world, however, is characterized by four glaring realities.

First, millions of people urgently require help to meet their most basic needs. More than a billion people "live in conditions of abject poverty— starving, idle, and numbed by ignorance."[6] More than thirty thousand people starve to death each day, many of them children. Second, sufficient resources are available to remedy this suffering, if only there were sufficient social cooperation. Third, huge disparities exist between the privileged and the poor, and well-off people are able to help without themselves becoming poor. Fourth, governments are not preventing the suffering through adequate levels of taxation and effective distribution of resources; often they do little beyond making politically expedient token gestures. Taken together with the principle of mutual aid, these four realities place responsibilities on us to aid destitute people by engaging in appropriate forms of philanthropy.

Governments have primary responsibility for serving the basic needs of their citizens who are otherwise unable to meet them, or so I urged in Chapter 1. Governments can marshal sufficient resources and distribute them fairly and efficiently. In addition, government commitments carry enormous symbolic importance as collective expressions of a society's concern, thereby fostering a social climate of mutual respect and caring. However, many governments are not meeting their responsibilities, and others are faced with overwhelming problems. As a result, the principle of mutual aid implies a philanthropic responsibility to help alleviate worldwide destitution.

How much is required of us? Minimum decency is owed to all human beings, not only to members of our own society. Right now you and I could save human lives by mailing a check for even a small amount to world hunger relief efforts. This gesture is seemingly as modest in its requirements as making a phone call to save Kitty Genovese. True, the latter case involved a person closer to us, not just physically closer, but a neighbor and citizen in our country. That closeness is morally significant, but the fact that suffering is more distant does not make it irrelevant. Hence, after we send one small check, it appears we ought to send another, assuming no great sacrifice is involved. And so on. At what point have we met our responsibility?

I want to approach this question indirectly, by first considering why we are not required to give even more than the principle of mutual aid calls for. According to Peter Singer, far more is required, given an act-utilitarian ethical theory: we are obligated in all our conduct to produce the most good for the most people. More precisely, Singer used a negative version of act utilitarianism, one cast in terms of preventing bad rather than promoting good: "If it is in our power to prevent something bad from happening, without thereby sacrificing anything of comparable moral importance, we ought, morally, to do it."[7] Setting aside disagreements about how to measure good and bad, it is clear that saving a person from starving to death has greater moral importance than does enjoying movies, fancy restaurants, and expensive clothes. Thus, Singer's principle implies that in order to prevent people from starving we should give up luxuries and donate large amounts of money.

How large? In his early writings, Singer argued that we "ought to give until we reach the level of marginal utility—that is, the level at which, by giving more, I would cause as much suffering to myself or my dependents as I would relieve by my gift. This would mean, of course, that one would reduce oneself to very near the material circumstances of a Bengali refugee."[8] In later writings, Singer allowed that we are permitted to maintain ourselves and dependents at a considerably higher level, in order to keep jobs that provide us with more money to give away.[9] Thus, it is morally permissible to have a car and decent clothes because they are necessary for keeping my job, but most luxuries should be sacrificed. Singer also admits that his austere doctrine might prove morally counterproductive. People might rebel against the stringent requirement and give even less than they would otherwise. For these individuals he recommends giving a more realistic percentage of their income, such as the traditional tithe, that is, ten percent.

Singer's moral perspective is grounded in an attitude of egalitarianism and strict impartiality. He thinks we should promote good, or at least prevent bad, by devoting the same degree of concern to other individuals' well-being as we devote to our own. Few of us believe that. We acknowledge that impartiality is required in some contexts: teachers should grade impartially, judges should enforce the laws impartially, and government officials should be impartial in distributing goods if that is their job. But distributing one's resources in private life is something else. We have a deeply rooted conviction that we may and often should give more to our family, friends, and ourselves than we give to a stranger. Can this commonsense conviction be justified?

Strict impartiality threatens morally significant aspects of our lives.[10] For most of us, strict impartiality would dramatically lessen prospects for self-fulfillment. It would undermine the commitments that form the core of our lives, commitments to family, friends, profession, community, and ideals—including philanthropic ideals beyond mutual aid. This is not to say that these commitments have greater moral significance than saving human lives. They do not. But the good they do have would be undermined by following Singer's impartiality principles. And we have a moral right, within limits, to give some priority to these areas of deep personal concern.

Strict impartiality would also increase insecurity and anxiety in our lives. Given the economic uncertainties in contemporary society, most of us need the safety net provided by a substantial reserve of resources. In addition, Singer's requirement of strict impartiality would lead most people to live with a continual sense of guilt for inevitable failures to live up to it. The requirements of an ethical theory should be compatible with human psychology in the sense of being roughly feasible for most people. The demand to reduce oneself to the level of a Bengali refugee may be suitable for saints, but not for most humans. The motivational structure of most people includes a substantial amount of self-partiality, and a plausible ethical theory should accept, not bemoan, that fact.[11] Here again, the claim is not that our peace of mind has greater moral importance than saving others' lives, as weighed on an impersonal scale for measuring goods. Instead, the claim is that we are not required in all areas of our life to weigh our happiness on such a scale.

Is there another ethical theory which rejects the extraordinary demands of act utilitarianism, which justifies the more modest demands made by the principle of mutual aid, and which provides some guidance concerning the limits of required giving? In fact, there are several, including the following three: (1) rule utilitarianism, (2) duty ethics, and (3) rights ethics. No agreement exists about which of these theories is most adequate. More important, each of the theories can be developed in alternative directions to yield different interpretations of what is meant by "little or no significant sacrifice" in the principle of mutual aid as it is applied to finding self-fulfillment in the United States and other wealthy countries. The interpretations range from stringent (we should give a lot) to moderate (we should give moderate amounts) to lenient (we are required to give only a little). Nevertheless, all these theories agree that mutual aid is only one responsibility which must be weighed against others. As a result, they all reject Singer's impartiality standard.

(1) Rule utilitarianism says we should act on a set of rules which produce the most good for the most people.[12] One such rule is the principle of mutual aid. Adopting this rule would provide considerable assurance that individuals caught in desperate situations are helped. It would also strengthen

social trust, mutual respect, and self-esteem by assuring that help will be available if we become unable to meet our basic needs. Conversely, we would know that we have little worth for those who are unwilling to offer us desperately needed aid at virtually no cost to themselves, and that would adversely affect the important goods of self-respect and self-esteem.

To set limits on what is required in helping others, rule utilitarians can endorse a second rule, which permits substantial preference to ourselves and our "significant others," recognizing that such a rule promotes valuable relationships and the self-fulfillment they make possible. Depending on the value placed on these personal goods, rule utilitarians will interpret the principle of mutual aid with varying degrees of stringency.

(2) Duty ethics says we ought to obey a set of duties which together delineate what it means to respect persons. It recognizes special duties inherent in intimate relationships with family and friends. It also endorses duties to ourselves to develop our talents, seek self-fulfillment, and maintain self-respect. Conceivably, a duty ethicist might understand duties to strangers as negative rules not to harm them, leaving little room for a requirement of mutual aid.[13] But most duty ethicists recognize a duty of mutual aid, "the duty of helping another when he is in need or jeopardy, provided that one can do so without excessive risk or loss to oneself."[14] As rational beings we recognize that we may need such help, and we acknowledge the duty as part of what is involved in respecting other rational beings.

How is the duty of mutual aid to be weighed against the special duties to family, friends, and ourselves? There is no consensus about how to answer this question, and different ways of setting priorities among duties results in requirements of mutual aid that have varying degrees of stringency. Even apart from questions about weighing mutual aid against other duties, duty ethicists regard mutual aid as a flexible requirement. Kant called it an "imperfect duty," to emphasize that it is imprecise in how much it requires. A perfect duty, by contrast, is specific about what it requires and to whom it is owed: for example, the duty to every human not to kill them. An imperfect duty allows considerable discretion in deciding how to meet it. While it requires us to adopt a general policy (maxim) of conduct, "it determines nothing about the [specific] kind and extent of the actions themselves but leaves a play-room for free choice."[15] In particular, "it is every man's duty to be beneficent—that is, to promote, according to his means, the happiness of others who are in need, and this without hope of gaining anything by it,"[16] but this imperfect duty does not pinpoint exactly when, how, or whom to help.

(3) Rights ethics makes human rights morally fundamental. In one version, libertarianism, all obligations are traced to negative rights *not* to be interfered with. There are no positive rights to receive aid (unless someone

promises it), and there is no positive obligation of minimal altruism.[17] By contrast, most human-rights ethicists also recognize positive rights to receive the necessities for a minimally decent life, at least when one is unable to earn them through one's own efforts and when other people have ample resources to help. Positive rights generate obligations of mutual aid: "The impoverished have rights against us," and we "meet our obligations to them . . . by providing them, as far as we are able [without great sacrifice], with what they need in order to live lives worth living."[18]

In setting limits to what is required of us, rights ethicists stress the right to autonomy: we have a right to pursue our interests by giving substantial preference to ourselves, our family and friends, and the communities in which we participate. In addition, family members, especially children, have a right to large amounts of our resources, far more than strangers do. These rights are stringent. The right to receive a quality education, for example, is not overridden by the wider good that might be achieved by distributing resources equally among starving strangers. Depending on how priorities are set among rights, the right to mutual aid places lenient to stringent obligations on us.

Each of these ethical theories, then, can be used to defend the principle of mutual aid, while allowing alternative interpretations of what the principle requires. That is not surprising, given that ethical theories are attempts to express in a systematic way our most carefully considered moral convictions. Theories unify and may somewhat reshape moral common sense, but they cannot replace it. Ultimately the theory must cohere with commonsense convictions, taken as a whole, after those convictions have undergone critical scrutiny. In this way, no one strand of common sense is self-certifying.

We have yet to consider virtue ethics in thinking about mutual aid, beyond our initial comment that the principle of mutual aid sets a minimal and mandatory level of benevolence. A familiar complaint made against virtue ethics, usually by defenders of the three theories above, is that it does not provide sufficiently precise guidelines about what is required of us. This complaint needs to be reconsidered in light of how any type of ethical theory can be developed in alternative directions. Perhaps, after all, the rough guidance offered by the virtues may be all we can hope for in many situations, including applications of the principle of mutual aid.

An appreciation of the virtues can be as helpful as any of the three theories in steering us between callous selfishness and guilt-ridden excesses demanded by Singer. A keen sense of justice and a compassionate heart, combined with practical wisdom in dealing with specific situations, provide as much guidance as any abstract set of rules about utility, duties, or rights. Moreover, they convey a good deal more inspiration by keeping before us ideals about the kinds of people we aspire to become.

In applying those virtues, however, we need to be aware of a further complexity. Philosophical discussions of world hunger and related issues about helping people to meet basic needs have tended to focus exclusively on the clash between the responsibility of mutual aid and partiality toward oneself and individuals with whom one has a personal caring relationship. Yet there are other important philanthropic responsibilities beyond mutual aid— responsibilities of reciprocity which are not automatically outweighed by the principle of mutual aid.

Giving Something Back

Good should be returned for good. In particular, we ought to reciprocate in appropriate ways for benevolence shown to us. This principle of reciprocity is contained as a minimum standard in the virtue of reciprocity, just as the principle of mutual aid is a minimum standard of benevolence to strangers. In particular, the virtues of reciprocity embody obligations to do one's fair share and to show gratitude in appropriate ways. Sometimes those obligations are best met through philanthropy.[19]

Reciprocity is a cross-cultural moral principle. Anthropologists have documented its role in an enormous variety of societies, primitive and modern alike, which have markedly different conceptions of goodness and customs for reciprocating.[20] Aside from philanthropy, here are three of many examples: the ancient practice of making offerings to the gods in return for their gift of the harvest; the Kula, which is a ceremonial exchange of arm shells and necklaces in circular patterns over years, as practiced by the Trobrianders in the South Sea islands; exchanging presents on holidays such as Hanukkah and Christmas.

Like the requirement of mutual aid, the principle of reciprocity is only a rough guideline, and attempting to render it precise would be futile. We could, of course, begin a long list of examples and rules of thumb about appropriate ways to reciprocate, and another list of caveats and permissible exceptions. Thus, reciprocal gifts should be apt, but they need not be of the same kind. They should take into account the amount and importance of the original gift, but they need not be equal in amount. In some situations, prompt reciprocation is desirable; in others, promptness insults by suggesting that the initial gift was a burden to be quickly repaid. And so on. This list could never be completed, however, because reciprocity functions in too many different settings and interacts with too many other moral principles to allow a tidy formulation of its requirements. Everything depends on context: on the nature of the received gift, its importance to us, our relationship with benefactors, their attitudes and needs, our desires and resources, and so on. Customs provide some guidance, but reciprocity is a matter of sensitivity and good judgment, not rule following.

Reciprocity is a fundamental norm which contributes to meaningful and rational life in five ways identified by Lawrence C. Becker.[21] First, reciprocity provides necessary help, not only in particular instances, but also by reinforcing helping behavior in general. The vagaries of misfortune ensure that we all need help sometimes. Patterns of reciprocity encourage further helping so that on balance everyone benefits.

Second, reciprocity is crucial for maintaining social equilibrium. As social creatures, our ability to be productive depends upon supportive interactions with other people. These interactions require stable practices of give and take. Mere taking upsets the balance. So can mere giving when it is wholly one-sided and when benefactors refuse to accept expressions of appreciation or in other ways place themselves above recipients. Both the selfishness of egoists and the occasional elitism of helpers disturb the sense of equality that underlies everyday exchanges. Hence, there must be ways for recipients to reciprocate, if only by showing appreciation or engaging in subsequent philanthropy of their own.

Third, patterns of reciprocity form part of the wider bedrock of shared expectations. Patterns of reciprocal conduct are inculcated in early childhood training (of course, with many cultural variations). Once instilled, the patterns generate expectations that other people will return good for good. This framework of social expectation enables us to approach each other with shared understanding about the prospects for mutually supportive interactions.

Fourth, reciprocation affects self-respect. When socially ingrained expectations of reciprocity are not met, self-esteem and self-respect are put at risk. ("What's wrong with me that others fail to acknowledge my kindness?") Conversely, when the social expectations are met, they strengthen a sense of equal worth.

Fifth, reciprocal giving is usually pleasurable. Not always, since there is the occasional annoyance in receiving an unwanted kindness or feeling a burden to reciprocate. Yet, overall, reciprocity offers a more satisfying mode of interaction than one-sided relationships.

Reciprocity is so important that it is a mandatory virtue, one that each of us ought to acquire. As Becker writes, "We ought to be *disposed*, as a matter of moral character, to make reciprocity a moral obligation."[22] We should be inclined to engage in beneficent acts in return for beneficence and benevolence, and we should be prepared to do so with the spontaneity of habit, rather than with a formal sense of duty.[23] In addition, if we fail to exercise the virtue of reciprocity on appropriate occasions we should acknowledge the appropriateness of guilt, shame, and blame.

With these general reflections in mind, we can note that sometimes philanthropy is the best way to reciprocate. In fact, reciprocity pertains to a much wider range of voluntary service than mutual aid does. Virtually all types of philanthropy, not just humanitarian aid serving basic needs, offer appropriate ways to "give something back" in return for benefits we receive from communities.

Several aspects of reciprocity are noteworthy in generating obligations that are often best met through philanthropic giving: (1) gratitude, (2) fairness within cooperative ventures, and (3) fairness in conserving and advancing public goods received from previous generations.

(1) Gratitude is the emotionally richest form of reciprocity. Its core is an attitude of appreciation for benevolence shown toward us.[24] This attitude generates emotions (of appreciation) and desires (to express appreciation) which serve as motives for giving something back to communities, whether through schools, hospitals, museums, art galleries, environmental projects, or in any number of other ways.

If gratitude involves emotions and desires, which are not directly under our control, can it be a genuine obligation?[25] As Kant said, "Ought implies can": we are only obligated to do what we can. "Ought" judgments are designed to guide conduct, and hence they have no meaning when applied to things beyond our control. Notice, however, that ought judgments are also used to identify obligations, including those which would be under our control if we had taken appropriate measures. Drug addicts and drunk drivers might render themselves incapable of meeting their obligations, but their obligations do not thereby vanish. Now, the obligations of gratitude are primarily obligations to be (or become) a certain kind of person (over time), rather than to perform specific actions. We ought to be caring, honest, and appreciative; that is the kind of character we should develop. Furthermore, gratitude is somewhat under our direct control through reflection on the reasons that make it appropriate on particular occasions. Thus, gratitude can meaningfully be called obligatory, and ingratitude a vice.

It may be undesirable or impossible to give back directly to the individuals who helped us. Perhaps they are dead. Or perhaps we do not know who they are and it would be too complicated to find out. All of us, after all, have benefited from the cumulative benevolence of innumerable strangers who made possible the culture we live in. Those strangers were not entirely motivated by benevolence in making their contributions to culture, no more than any of us are, but benevolence was usually an aspect of their motivation. At the same time, it may be reasonable to believe that these benefactors would be pleased to know we engaged in reciprocal voluntary service, perhaps just as they did in helping us. Voluntary service offers numerous avenues for suitable reciprocation. Sometimes the giving back in gratitude is targeted

directly toward institutions from which we have benefited, and other times
it is a more symbolic expression of gratitude for benefits received from a
community.

Gratitude can be shown toward institutions and groups as well as toward
individuals.[26] For example, we feel grateful to a college or university for the
education we received. The gratitude is toward the school as a whole, as well
as toward specific teachers, in part because the school enabled those teachers
to influence us in the ways they did. Since we can never directly repay the
anonymous donors and taxpayers who made our education possible, our gratitude is appropriately expressed through alumni giving.

Are all alumni obligated to give to their alma maters? No. Perhaps they
received a poor education, or perhaps their well-endowed alma mater needs
less support than other schools which are in financial trouble. Such giving
is appropriate, for it supports institutions engaged in the same practice (education) from which one benefited, and perhaps like the alma mater is supported in part by public funds. At the very least, there is an obligation for
alumni to give to their school when it is worthy of support, when it is in
financial trouble, when they should feel grateful for the valuable education
they received, and when they have ample resources to help.

(2) Fairness is a more impersonal form of reciprocity. It has both a focused and a wider-scoped form. In the focused form, fairness is the willingness to do one's share when participating in cooperative endeavors from
which one benefits, motivated (at least in part) by respect for people. There
is an obligation to show this willingness. More fully, participants have an
obligation to contribute their fair share to cooperative practices in which they
receive shared benefits worth more than their cost, when the practice is just
and divides burdens equitably, and where recipients either voluntarily accept
benefits or are necessarily provided with public goods (a possibility I will
discuss in connection with wider-scoped fairness).[27]

An example of voluntarily accepted benefits is regularly watching American public television, a nonprofit institution substantially supported by private donations. People who voluntarily enjoy substantial amounts of public
television have a responsibility to pay their share of expenses, assuming they
have the resources to do so.[28] Here are some other examples: parents doing
their share within scouting organizations to which their children belong;
pitching in to do one's share in neighborhood organizations that directly
benefit oneself; and service within churches or synagogues that one attends.
In all these cases, philanthropic contributions function much like "user fees"
for services, except that the fee is expected to be given voluntarily. In each
case, too, "free riders" act unfairly when they accept benefits without making
contributions they can easily afford.

(3) In its wider-scoped form, fairness concerns doing our share within
communities, as well as specific practices. Each of us is a steward charged

with conserving and (if possible) advancing public goods which we have received from our predecessors.[29] We have benefited from a vast web of altruism (mixed with self-interest) from past generations. That web generated the communal goods which make civilized life possible. We are entrusted to preserve those goods, and we have a reciprocal obligation to pass them on to new generations. Some goods are environmental: clean water, breathable air, wilderness areas open to the public. Others are cultural: public architecture, museums, accumulated knowledge. Still others are political: laws, effective government. Along with our contemporaries, we share responsibility to do what we can, at least without significant hardship, to extend communal goods into the future.

Philanthropy offers an array of opportunities for meeting this responsibility. For example, each of us has benefited from research in science and technology. We have also benefited from health organizations, schools, museums, the arts and humanities. Philanthropy has played a key role in all these areas. Most of today's government-provided services had their origins in philanthropic endeavors. Universal public education had its origin in Horace Mann's nineteenth-century crusade to have government assume responsibility for education. Community libraries proliferated when Andrew Carnegie gave seed money for several thousand public libraries. And so on. We did not ask for these benefits, nor did we voluntarily accept them. They represent a vast heritage of public goods generated largely through the beneficence of thousands of people and transferred to us through the stewardship of millions of other people.

Of course, we cannot give back to the original benefactors. Most are dead, and many gave anonymously in the first place. Nevertheless, philanthropy provides suitable ways to give something in return. Recall one of the primary overall points of reciprocity: to sustain practices and institutions. Just as past benefactors gave to sustain practices and institutions, we reciprocate in a fitting way through the same kind of giving. Moreover, most philanthropic giving has an indefinite intention: it is directed toward large groups of people rather than specific individuals. It is a fitting return for us to give in a similar way to benefit individuals unknown to us. In doing so, we participate as members of communities that are cross-generational, stretching from past to present and into the future.[30]

Personal Callings

The responsibilities of reciprocity and mutual aid are universal: all of us have them. In addition, some philanthropists are motivated by a strong sense of personal responsibility—a "personal calling" which neither they nor we regard as a matter of universal duties. How is this sense of responsibility to be understood? Is it merely an interesting subjective experience which has nothing to do with obligation? Or are there genuine responsibilities involved in personal callings? I believe there are. The responsibilities are supererogatory, in that they are beyond the general call of duty incumbent on everyone, but they are responsibilities nonetheless.[31]

To begin with, individuals often *believe* they have a special responsibility to engage in particular philanthropic activities which they do not think are incumbent on everyone in their circumstances. Here are several examples; there are many others.

(1) As a university student, Albert Schweitzer resolved to pursue his interests in philosophy, religion, and music until he turned thirty, at which time he would devote his life to humanitarian service, in some form not clear to him at the time. He felt a strong sense of responsibility to make this commitment as a way to give something back in return for his privileged upbringing, his unusually happy childhood, and the exceptional talents he found in himself. By age thirty he was a distinguished professor with considerable fame as a scholar in several disciplines, yet he kept his resolution. In order to equip himself for the kind of service which then seemed to him most inviting, he returned to school to earn a medical degree. Initially he planned to offer his services to prisoners. When that idea did not work out, he saw an opportunity to go to Lambarene, a French missionary site in equatorial Africa. There he served during the next fifty years until his death in 1965.

At one level, Schweitzer felt he was acting on a duty incumbent on anyone with a comparably fortunate upbringing. "Whoever is spared personal pain," he wrote, "must feel himself called to help in diminishing the pain of others. We must all carry our share of the misery which lies upon the world."[32] Yet he did not believe that all similarly privileged people are required to devote themselves so completely to helping others. In fact, he would often discourage others from service as demanding as his:

> Only a person who can find a value in every sort of activity, and devote himself to each one with full consciousness of duty, has the inward right to take as his object some extraordinary activity instead of that which falls naturally to his lot. Only a person who feels his preference to be a matter of course, not something out of the ordinary, and who has no thought of heroism, but just recognizes a duty undertaken with sober enthusiasm, is capable of becoming a spiritual adventurer such as the world needs.[33]

In short, Schweitzer believed he had a responsibility which was not incumbent on everyone, at least not in the same degree.

(2) Saints comprise a large and varied set of examples. As a rough generalization, saints experience a focused sense of obligation to God and responsibility to humanity. As A. I. Melden suggests, often they "take

themselves to be under an obligation to *any* human being, whoever and whenever he or she may be, an obligation of the order that parents have for their children."[34] Thus, Saint Francis of Assisi cared for sick and starving strangers as if they were his own children, and Father Damien cared for lepers as if they were members of his own family.

(3) Bob Geldof will never be canonized, at least by mainstream churches, though he was knighted by the British government in recognition of his service. In 1984 he watched the televised scenes of famine in Ethiopia—emaciated adults, malnourished children with swollen bellies, crying mothers whose children died in their arms. "I felt disgusted, enraged, and outraged," he wrote, "but more than all those, I felt deep shame" and guilt for complicity in having allowed the tragedy to happen.[35] Geldof felt he must do more than write out a check. Within days he organized a large group of rock stars who, working at a frantic pace, produced the Band Aid record, "Do They Know It's Christmas," which raised millions of dollars of aid for Ethiopia. Later he helped create Live Aid, the seventeen-hour live television concert which set a record for a single fundraising event.

(4) On May 3, 1980, Candy Lightner returned from shopping to be told that her thirteen-year-old daughter, Cari, had been killed. Cari had been walking with a friend to a church carnival when a drunk driver swerved off the road and hit her. The driver had been convicted three times before of drunk driving. Lightner's first impulse was to kill the man; after obtaining a gun, she set about to do just that. Yet, as she later wrote, "I promised myself on the day of Cari's death that I would fight to make this needless homicide count for something positive in the years ahead."[36] She explored the possibility of donating Cari's organs so that other lives might be saved, but the body was too damaged from being hurled forty yards by the car that struck her. Days later, Lightner resolved to form an organization: MADD (Mothers Against Drunk Driving), which now has 300 chapters and 600,000 donors, and which has successfully lobbied state legislatures to pass tougher laws against drunk drivers. In forming MADD, Lightner had multiple motives: love, grief, a desire to honor her daughter, and a felt responsibility to prevent further death and suffering.

Lightner, Geldof, Schweitzer, Damien, and Saint Francis all believed they had a responsibility to engage in their voluntary service. But were their beliefs justified? *Belief* in a responsibility is one thing; actually having one is something else. A critic might object that these individuals were simply mistaken in their beliefs. Unquestionably they felt a sense of responsibility, but that feeling was illusory since there was no real obligation involved. Thus, according to J. O. Urmson, in his discussion of heroic and saintly individuals, such individuals are either unduly modest, confused, or excessively conscientious when they portray their actions as morally required. They experience an illusory feeling of obligation: "Subjectively, we may say, at the time of action, the deed presented itself as a duty, but it was not a duty."[37]

An additional explanation concerns the deep caring shown by individuals with a sense of personal calling. Deep caring often generates a "volitional necessity" in which we cannot bring ourselves to act in ways inconsistent with what we care about.[38] We are physically able to do otherwise, but doing so would violate our own "will." That is because our will (and commitment) is constituted by what we care deeply about. Hence the force of Martin Luther's remark: "Here I stand; I can do no other." Luther was not coerced by external forces; he was constrained by his own free will. While Luther represents an extreme case, it is typical for personal callings to be accompanied by a similar sense of "I must." This important psychological symptom, however, does not establish a genuine moral responsibility. Indeed, the same sense of necessity may accompany patently immoral commitments, as with a terrorist who feels called to a radical cause.

Now, these attempts to explain away these responsibilities will not do. It is true that the general commitments to ideals and the specific services performed by Schweitzer and the others were supererogatory in the sense of being beyond the general call of duty. Yet they were not beyond *their* call to duty, their calling. They were both supererogatory and a responsibility.

At first glance, this talk of supererogatory responsibilities sounds self-contradictory. After all, obligations and supererogatory conduct have traditionally been defined as mutually exclusive. This traditional dichotomy, however, needs to be rethought. Consistent with its colloquial usage, "supererogatory" retains its meaning of beyond the general call of duty, beyond the requirements incumbent on everyone, such as to keep promises and to pay debts, as well as duties attached to social roles, such as parenting and professions. Even so, there are supererogatory responsibilities.

What, then, is the source of supererogatory philanthropic responsibilities? What kinds of moral considerations generate them and justify them as genuine responsibilities? I offer a four-part answer.

(1) The most straightforward part of the answer concerns how philanthropic commitments generate responsibilities. Once a philanthropist makes a pledge to donate money or a commitment to serve in a particular way, responsibilities are created. Promises to make a philanthropic gift create obligations in the familiar way that all promises do. At least, they do so when the promise is made to other persons who then depend upon and trust us to keep our commitment to them.

Of course, many service commitments are open-ended. One might agree to serve for an unspecified number of years on the board of directors of a service organization and remain free to withdraw one's commitment at any time, at least following reasonable notification of one's resignation. In this respect, many service commitments are like commitments to jobs. Upon taking a job one acquires responsibilities, but one can permissibly end one's responsibilities by resigning, after giving proper notice. Even Schweitzer was free to abandon his service after giving due notice to his patients.

If this were all that is involved, however, there would be a mystery about how personal callings are experienced. Schweitzer and the other individuals felt a responsibility to make their commitments to voluntary service. That is, their sense of responsibility preceded their specific commitments. Schweitzer said that his general sense of responsibility to help others led to his specific service commitments, not vice versa. In his eyes, the commitment did not create the responsibility; the commitment was evoked, motivated, directed, and sustained by his sense of responsibility.

(2) Ethicists have tended to be preoccupied with universal principles of obligation, including the general duty to keep one's promises. Yet it seems doubtful to me that moral obligations can be understood in isolation from individuals' beliefs about the world and their place in it, especially their religious beliefs. Without lapsing into the insidious form of relativism that reduces morality to whatever a group or individual happens to believe, we can acknowledge the relevance of world views to morality.

In this connection, Melden draws attention to the special religious roles that saints believe they have, beliefs which others may believe are accurate. Saints believe they are God's intermediaries who are called upon by God to act as surrogate parents toward other humans. Most people have no such calling, hence no such obligations. But that does not mean "the *saint* is not morally required to act as he does, that he was not meeting *his* moral obligation" in displaying extraordinary benevolence.[39] Furthermore, while ordinary mortals are in no (morally appropriate) position to criticize saints when they fail to meet their extraordinary responsibilities, saints may appropriately criticize themselves for their failures.

I would recast Melden's point this way: Saints usually believe that their personal relationship with God is such that they have been assigned a special responsibility. The relationship involves love, submission to authority, and joyous appreciation for having the privilege to serve in the special way assigned or invited by God. *If* their beliefs are true, then they would indeed have special responsibilities—moral as well as religious responsibilities. People who share the saints' beliefs will share their belief in these responsibilities, whereas the rest of as who live outside that faith will understand that the sense of responsibility is conditional on the faith, but not the merely illusory feelings mentioned by Urmson.

Melden emphasizes the uniqueness of saints, saying they have "a radically different sort of life" and that most of us would be foolhardy to seriously imitate them (as distinct from being inspired by them).[40] By contrast, I would emphasize the continuity between saints and ordinary people. Most saints embody unusually high degrees of certain virtues which many other people embody in lesser degrees. In addition, other individuals experience special callings akin to those of saints, albeit on a more modest scale and with or without a religious foundation.

(3) Next consider the idea of devoting oneself to a philanthropic ideal, that is, an envisioned perfection which is more general than the specific philanthropic projects it inspires. Nicholas Rescher attempts to understand this devotion in psychological terms which carry no suggestion of actual responsibilities:

> Nobody has a *duty* to his fellows to become a saint or hero; this just is not something we *owe* to people, be it singly or collectively. Such "duty" as there is will be that of "sense of duty"—an inner call to be or become a person of a certain sort. Here we are not, strictly speaking, dealing with a matter of duty at all but with a dedication to an ideal, the inner impetus to do one's utmost to make the world into a certain sort of place—perhaps only that small corner of it that consists of oneself.[41]

Rescher is correct in saying there is no duty to become a saint. It does not follow, however, that individuals cannot have and pursue responsibilities which, as it turns out, others regard as saintly or heroic. Responsibilities, like intentions, depend upon how they are described. "Become a moral hero by serving the medical needs of Africans" is not Schweitzer's responsibility, but "serve the medical needs of Africans" may be. Again, "we" do not owe people supererogatory conduct, but perhaps Schweitzer and the others did.

Dedication to ideals requiring supererogatory conduct is morally optional. But once that devotion arises, whether through an explicit or a spontaneous commitment, could supererogatory responsibilities arise? In my view, supererogatory responsibilities are generated by commitments to valid ideals beyond what is morally required together with particular situations. Strong commitments to ideals place demands on individuals to engage in particular types of service implied by the ideal and taking into account our circumstances and resources.

Ideals are not impersonal abstractions; they embody ways of caring about other individuals, practices, and communities. Those ways of caring interact with immediate situations. This explains the focused sense of obligation: "I must help—here and now, in this way—or else betray my ideals." Thus, a person with religious ideals of humanitarian service is confronted by the unmet needs of Africans (Albert Schweitzer) or lepers (Father Damien). A person devoted to the ideal of world community is faced with mass starvation in Ethiopia (Bob Geldof). A mother devoted to her daughter and to the ideal of preventing suffering envisages the prospect for a campaign to reduce the highway slaughter caused by drunk drivers (Candy Lightner).

Supererogatory responsibilities arise only when the ideals involved are themselves morally desirable. Moreover, the ideals must be (reasonably) seen as applicable to one's situation, construing that situation broadly to include membership in a world community. Failure to act will lead to further harm or loss of an important good.

In short, supererogatory responsibilities are grounded in the devotion to valid (desirable) ideals together with the claim those ideals make on us in practical circumstances. This is schematically expressed as follows: Strong commitment to a justified ideal + Accurate perception of an urgent situation to which the ideal applies + Ability to help —→ Personal responsibility to help in a particular situation —→ Commitment to a specific course of helping. As this scheme indicates, supererogatory responsibilities to engage in particular service activities derive from prior commitments, but the commitments are to ideals rather than to the service activities themselves.

Philanthropic ideals usually embody a vision of worthwhile communities. This was the central point made by George Herbert Mead in "Philanthropy from the Point of View of Ethics." According to Mead, philanthropy is prompted by an "inner obligation," or what I have called a supererogatory responsibility, even though "charity implies both an attitude and a type of conduct which may not be demanded of him who exercises it."[42] The philanthropist, Mead says, glimpses an ideal community and senses an opportunity to move toward it by assuming "a duty which he lays upon himself."[43] The ideal community, which is felt to be "implicit" in this world, "haunts the generous nature, and carries a sense of obligation which transcends any claim that his actual social order fastens upon him. It is an ideal world that lays the claim upon him, but it is an ideal world which grows out of this world and its undeniable implications."[44]

For example, philanthropists who feel obligated to contribute to higher education may be tacitly committed to an educational ideal that would be realized in an ideal society. Again, individuals who donate to humanitarian causes may be tacitly committed to an ideal society where people are connected by deeper ties of caring than at present.

(4) Russell Grice suggests that supererogatory responsibilities, or what he calls "ultra obligations," arise from the requirements for personal fulfillment. Ultra obligations are obligations to "do more than is required by the basic obligation of beneficence" (minimum decency) and to do so from altruistic motives.[45] These obligations are grounded in considerations of self-fulfillment. Some people find self-fulfillment in becoming poets, and others by engaging in philanthropy. "When a man's fulfilment consists in the de-

votion of his own capacities to the interests of others, the judgement that he ought to adopt this life is one of ultra obligation."[46]

Grice does not explain how self-fulfillment creates moral obligations to others, and that is puzzling. How can reasons concerning one's own good generate moral obligations to help others beyond the ordinary standards of morality? Perhaps there is a moral obligation to pursue our self-fulfillment, and this obligation generates ultra obligations for those individuals whose self-fulfillment is found in voluntary service. Perhaps surprisingly, ultra obligations to others would then derive from obligations to ourselves.

Whether or not this is what Grice had in mind, it can only be part of the justification of supererogatory responsibilities. For the entire spirit of supererogatory responsibilities is other-centered, not self-directed. The concern for self-fulfillment, and I would add self-integrity, is secondary; it derives from keeping faith with a responsibility that is owed to others. Though secondary, however, it constitutes a supplementary justification of supererogatory responsibilities.

Insofar as one is strongly committed to the ideal, one must sometimes undertake particular service commitments or else betray one's integrity, as well as betray the ideals to which one is committed. Expressed schematically: Devotion to ideals + Obligations to maintain integrity ⟶ Personal obligation to promote ideals in practical situations ⟶ Commitment to a specific course of helping.

Professional Ideals

We have distinguished two categories of philanthropic responsibilities: (1) general responsibilities derived from the principles of mutual aid and reciprocity, and (2) supererogatory responsibilities derived from commitments to ideals beyond minimum requirements. The professions offer an interesting context for thinking about the interplay between these categories. On the one hand, professional ethics largely consists of general moral principles applied to professional settings. On the other hand, personal callings are often connected with professions, as in the case of Schweitzer's voluntary service as a physician. Indeed, some professions promulgate philanthropic ideals, and perhaps more should.

Professions are those forms of work which demand expertise grounded in sophisticated theory and which promote important public goods. Today they include far more than the four traditional vocations of law, medicine, teaching, and the ministry—for example, the professions of engineering, innumerable specialized sciences, accounting, and counseling. In order to serve the public good, individuals and organizations must meet minimum standards of professional conduct, such as obligations to maintain confidentiality, to be truthful, to respect clients' autonomy, and to exercise due care in serving the interests of clients. In addition, some principles call for *pro bono publico* work: service for the public good at no fee or at a reduced fee, whether in serving basic human needs of individuals unable to pay full fees for service or in improving the profession's overall effectiveness in promoting public goods.

Do *pro bono* principles specify supererogatory ideals which are morally optional or general obligations incumbent on all members of a profession? If they are obligations, should they be enforced, either with legal penalties or through self-regulation within professions?

These questions arise with respect to professions, but not to other forms of work, for an important reason: professions tend to develop monopolies over important services.[47] This occurs during the emergence of professions. As services become increasingly specialized, practitioners convince society that they are most competent to provide them and that unqualified workers put the public at risk. In response, government authorizes the profession, through its professional societies, to exercise a substantial degree of autonomy in setting standards, overseeing certification and licensing requirements, and accrediting educational programs. The upshot is a monopoly.

Governments grant monopolies on the basis of a tacit "social contract" that the profession will make adequate services available to the public. The profession has a collective (shared) responsibility to make sure that occurs. The responsibility can be met in several ways, but one of the most important is to encourage philanthropy. Thus, a professional society might formally endorse an ideal of philanthropic service, make the ideal prominent in its code of ethics, establish forms of recognition for outstanding voluntary service, and develop support mechanisms such as a computerized system which matches community needs with the desires of interested professionals. The profession may also endorse some *pro bono* service as obligatory, and perhaps enforce the obligation.

Consider law, which has a long tradition of encouraging philanthropic service. Since the fifteenth century in England, officers of the court have been required to carry out a judge's assignments to defend indigent defendants at no fee or at substantially reduced fees.[48] Moreover, while attorneys are not required to seek out needy clients to whom they offer free services, they are expected to accept some clients who are unable to pay full fees without great hardship. Do lawyers, then, have obligations to engage in *pro bono* service? If so, should the obligations be mandatory, that is, enforced by penalties for noncompliance? These questions have been vigorously debated recently within the legal profession.

Proponents of mandatory *pro bono* service argue that it is the best way to meet the profession's collective responsibility to make adequate services available.[49] A mandatory obligation ensures that the needs of the poor are met without conscientious lawyers having to do additional work because of slackers. The most discussed form of free service is a set amount of time, perhaps forty hours per year, throughout a career. Another idea is two years of service at the beginning of one's career, comparable to a military draft, that would ensure legal services in parts of the country where they are most needed.[50] Such requirements are also defended as fair forms of reciprocation for the privilege to practice law and for the government funding that subsidizes most law schools. They also promote a positive image of the profession.

Opponents of mandatory service insist that citizens, not attorneys, are responsible for providing legal services for the poor through government-supported legal clinics or funding programs comparable to Medicare and Medicaid.[51] Government, for example, should expand the federally funded Legal Services Corporation, which provides civil-law aid for the indigent. Mandatory *pro bono* service threatens the spirit of voluntary service, especially since enforcing obligations results in legalistic restrictions on permissible kinds and amounts of free service.

At present, the American Bar Association's Model Rules of Professional Conduct regard *pro bono* service as a nonenforced responsibility that can be met in several ways: "by providing professional services at no fee or a reduced fee to persons of limited means or to public service or charitable groups or organizations, by service in activities for improving the law, the legal system or the legal profession, and by financial support for organizations that provide legal services to persons of limited means."[52] According to critics, this statement amounts to window dressing. It creates the appearance of a profession committed to service while allowing professionals to avoid service whenever they choose. Others argue that this is a reasonable compromise. By foregoing enforcement and being flexible in its requirements, the Rules allow service to be genuine philanthropy.

There is no abstract resolution to this debate. Government certainly has the right to negotiate with professions reasonable conditions for granting the privileges that go with monopolies (such as high salaries). Those conditions depend on the situation, especially on the extent of unmet needs for professional services and the options available for meeting them.

If government and the legal profession do not find solutions, consumer groups will. One recent consumer response is to the failure to make sufficient services available at reasonable costs is the recent movement to de-professionalize some legal services. For example, simplified language and forms have been developed to enable individuals to write their own wills, and no-fault laws have made it easier to get a divorce and to deal with minor auto collisions. This movement has included some courageous voluntary service by lawyers—courageous, because of the strong opposition from the wider legal profession which saw its self-interest threatened.

Another example is the community board movement. Ray Shonholtz is an attorney who was frustrated with how his profession's virtual monopoly over dispute resolution made people feel powerless, not to mention the waste involved in flooding the courts with minor disputes.[53] He envisaged alternative forums for conflict resolution based in local communities. These community boards rely on volunteers who receive training in communication and conflict resolution techniques. Instead of having to confront a costly and forbidding court, disputing neighbors appear before panels of volunteers who help them work out their problems. From a modest beginning, the community boards spread to two dozen neighborhoods in the San Francisco area, and eventually to many communities around the United States.

Having focused on law, I should emphasize that attorneys have done far more than most professionals to encourage voluntary service. Perhaps only the ministry has done more. Given the need for improved medical care for the poor in the United States, it comes as a surprise to learn that the American Medical Association (AMA) does not now promulgate a strong voluntary service ideal, even though many physicians do make voluntary service an important part of their professional lives. In its first, 1847, code of ethics the AMA urged (as did Hippocrates) that gratuitous services should be freely accorded to indigent patients. Today, however, only in life-threatening emergencies are physicians expected to care for people who cannot pay full fees. The emphasis in the AMA Code of Ethics is on the rights of physicians, not those of the poor: "A physician shall, in the provision of appropriate patient care, except in emergencies, be free to choose whom to serve, with whom to associate, and the environment in which to provide medical services."[54] To be sure, the code says "A physician shall recognize a responsibility to participate in activities contributing to an improved community," though that vague statement can refer to involvement as a citizen. And in fairness, the recent flood of law suits against physicians has made it difficult for concerned individuals to provide free services.

To mention just one more example, the engineering profession has not embraced a *pro bono* ideal, even though some engineering professional societies regularly offer awards and other recognition for members engaged in voluntary service. Disadvantaged groups among the rural and inner-city poor, the elderly, and Native Americans have needs for basic engineering services that provide running water, sewage systems, energy sources, and transportation.[55] Yet for many years codes of ethics forbade offering engineering services on a free basis or at below normal fees. Supreme Court rulings led to the removal of such statements as improper restrictions of free trade, but there has not been a movement to encourage *pro bono* service. Yet engineering involves a complication. The scale of modern technology requires that the vast majority of engineers work for large corporations, rather than as independent consulting engineers. Prospects for *pro bono* work center on the corporation. That raises the more general question about philanthropy in business.

Business and the professions are often contrasted. Professionals are expected to serve the public good, whereas business people are supposedly free to devote themselves to seeking profit within the bounds of law. This distinction is artificial, however. Most professionals are also business people. When professionals, like engineers and accountants, are primarily employed by profit-seeking corporations it becomes difficult to foster strong *pro bono* ideals. Difficult, but not impossible.

The primary responsibility of corporations in a free enterprise economy is to stockholders to maximize their profits. When corporations engage in philanthropy, typically below one percent of their pretax income, their aims (and motives) are primarily to promote corporate interests.[56] Education receives the largest share of corporate philanthropy, about 40 percent, which is not surprising given businesses' interest in recruiting a qualified labor force. Giving for cultural and community purposes is usually tailored to enhance a corporation's image.

There is no reason to bemoan the primary focus on self-interest in corporate philanthropy. The concern for corporations to be perceived as socially responsible provides opportunities for individuals to engage in philanthropy. Consider a director of public relations for a large manufacturing company in Suffolk, Massachusetts.[57] His job naturally leads him to become engaged in community activities, yet he does far more than his company requires. He uses his assigned work as a springboard for greater involvement, such as accepting numerous requests to organize community events. The genuineness of his community involvement is reflected in the fact that he turns down promotions that require leaving the town.

Not-for-profit corporations offer even greater opportunities for voluntary service during the normal course of work. Service-oriented professionals, for example, might choose jobs that are low-paid or in poor areas. Or they provide services well beyond what they are paid for, as do many health professionals, lawyers, and teachers. Often their efforts are not seen as supererogatory because their work has built into it high ideals that do not sharply distinguish between the mandatory minimum and supererogatory service.

One example is Jaime Escalante, the nationally recognized math teacher at Garfield High School in East Los Angeles.[58] Escalante defied the stereotype that Hispanic students lacked the motivation to succeed in Advanced Placement math courses which he created. He set unusually high standards and helped his students meet them by holding additional classes before and after school and during lunch breaks. Within a few years his classes accounted for one-fourth of all Hispanic students in the country who passed the Advanced Placement Tests, which gave them college credits, thereby encouraging them to enter college.

It would be naive to expect professionals to solve the extraordinary problems confronting society. Government has the primary responsibility for meeting the basic needs of disadvantaged citizens. Yet the magnitude of social problems makes it highly desirable for professions to promulgate ideals of *pro bono publico* service, understood broadly to include service to disadvantaged people and on behalf of other civic-oriented goals connected with a given profession. In turn, it is highly desirable for individual professionals to adopt those ideals as a matter of personal responsibility. In doing so they display the virtue of public-spirited commitment to making society better.[59] Wherever possible, it is desirable that individual professionals exercise this virtue freely and in ways that allow the exercise of discretion.

Discretion and Good Judgment

Philanthropic responsibilities, whether personal or general, are usually vague in their requirements. The general obligations of mutual aid and reciprocity do not tell us exactly how to help others and how to give back to communities. Again, Schweitzer eventually arrived at a focused sense of responsibility to serve in Africa, but that focus was not present years earlier when, as a college student, he committed himself to pursuing an ideal of humanitarian service upon turning thirty. Aristotle noted long ago that neither morality nor ethics (the philosophical study of morality) admit of the precision of mathematics.[60] Nowhere is this truer than concerning philanthropic responsibilities, which leave large areas for exercising discretion.

What is moral discretion? In part, it alludes to the right to decide, without interference, how to meet responsibilities. In part, it alludes to situations where there is a range of morally permissible options, some of which are preferable to others but none of which is "right" in the sense of morally obligatory. Discretion is the exercise of good judgment in selecting one of the better options.

Exercising discretion responsibly in making philanthropic decisions is no easy matter. We must estimate consequences and set priorities in response to a large number of considerations. Here are ten general factors, in addition to many factual uncertainties in particular situations.[61]

(1) Philanthropy and other service. Philanthropy is only one way to meet the responsibilities of mutual aid and reciprocity. It is part of a continuous spectrum of service to family, friends, work, citizenship, and voluntary service. How can I, right now, best help others and meet my responsibilities to give something back to the communities from which I have benefited— through work, through voluntary service, or through which combination thereof? Some individuals have little time or money for voluntary service because they select low-paying and time-demanding service careers, yet they generously give back to communities through their careers.[62]

(2) Public purposes. Should we emphasize humanitarian aid or cultural patronage? Which humanitarian purposes: world hunger, homelessness, child abuse, crime prevention, or research on AIDS and care for AIDS victims? Which cultural purposes: education, the arts, the humanities, or scientific inquiry? Should we give to the young or elderly, to environment preservation, or to a scholarship fund for aspiring scientists and engineers? Within each of these general categories, precisely where should we focus our efforts?

(3) Strategies. With respect to humanitarian giving, should we emphasize immediate disaster relief or long-term aid to prevent suffering? If the latter, should we emphasize economic development which applies present technology or programs in basic research that promise longer-term solutions? Should we give directly to relief organizations or to political organizations that lobby governments to expand their humanitarian commitments? With respect to cultural patronage, should we emphasize successful organizations or promising but struggling groups?

(4) Forums for giving. Should we link our voluntary service to our professional activities or in ways independent of our careers? Should we give through large organizations (such as United Way) or more focused organizations (such as the American Cancer Society). Should we support an existing foundation or help to create a new one? Occasionally there are obligations to give to particular organizations, as when reciprocity demands giving to the public television corporation from which one directly benefits. But in contemporary society there are far more worthy organizations than we can possibly support. I can meet my responsibility of mutual aid by giving to CARE, OXFAM, UNICEF, or the Red Cross, to name only a few of many effective organizations. The organizations I select will reflect my interests and personal history, including past opportunities to investigate particular organizations.

(5) Form of gifts. Should we give money, items of economic value, time and talent, or which combination of these? Sometimes hands-on volunteering is needed and reveals a greater depth of concern than "just" sending a check. Yet other times money is the appropriate gift, for example, when a well-

staffed but underfunded intermediary organization is effectively situated to know the specific needs of beneficiaries.

(6) Timing. When should we give? Should volunteering be spread throughout a lifetime, or postponed until late in our career and during retirement when more time is available? Should monetary gifts be spread out over a lifetime, or made primarily toward the end of our lives, perhaps through a will? For the most part (setting aside disasters in our immediate communities), the duties of mutual aid and reciprocity allow considerable leeway over time. Some people do best to give many small amounts throughout the year, others to give several large donations over longer periods of time, and still others to leave very large amounts in their wills. By "do best" I mean give in a manner that is personally satisfying, compatible with other commitments, and most effective in helping.

(7) Quantity: macroallocation. How much should we give, whether in terms of total quantities or of percentages of our available resources? Should we perhaps change our lifestyle to leave more time for volunteering? It is impossible to quantify with even rough precision the amounts of giving required of an individual.

(8) Quantity: microallocation. Should giving be spread thin so as to help many people a little, or concentrated so as to help a few people a lot? How much should we give on this occasion to this cause? Some individuals find it preferable to make one or a few large donations, rather than many small ones to a wider variety of causes, believing they make a greater difference in this way. Other people will give many small amounts, realizing that such gifts add up. The March of Dimes, for example, with its emphasis on many people giving small amounts, funded the research that discovered a cure for polio.[63]

(9) Proximity. Concerning spatial proximity, should and may we give more to communities physically closer to us, emphasizing local over regional, national over international? Concerning temporal proximity, how should we weigh the claims of people living today against the claims of future generations? Regarding social proximity, how far are we justified in giving within our particular social groups, rather than to "outsiders" who may have greater needs? Is there anything wrong with devoting exclusive attention to religious and ethnic groups to which we have special loyalties?

Proximities are relevant as they bear upon caring relationships. An ethic that takes seriously caring relationships must appreciate giving to groups which evoke our strong loyalties. Morally desirable loyalties carry with them special responsibilities,[64] and the obligations of reciprocity are greater toward groups from which we have personally benefited.[65] At the same time, it is desirable to have caring relationships beyond the narrow bailiwick of our everyday lives, especially within our increasingly cross-cultural world. Exclusively clannish giving may reveal a failure to appreciate the moral status of human beings who have value beyond their membership in narrow groups.[66]

John Kekes opposes clannishness, but he criticizes generalized benevolence toward strangers. He raises three main criticisms: (i) General benevolence is unrealistic: we care deeply only about people to whom we are tied by personal loyalties and shared customs.—This charge overlooks our significant, albeit limited, capacities to care for strangers. (ii) General benevolence is impractical: effective helping requires knowing about people we seek to help; to avoid wasting resources we should focus on helping people close to home. —Even though we may lack detailed information about distant cultures, we can identify and give to trustworthy intermediate organizations that have and act on such information. (iii) General benevolence is immoral: "It directs our attention away from intimacy and toward universality and impartiality. The more successful it is, the less there is left for everyday moral relationships" where our responsibilities are clear and demanding.[67] —Instead, we should seek to balance everyday relationships and responsibilities to strangers. The former can be met with a substantial, but not exclusive, emphasis of resources in their direction.

(10) Private and public priorities. How should philanthropic responsibilities be weighed against obligations to family, friends, employers, and colleagues? How far is it permissible to give preference based on personal ties, especially when our resources might do greater good if directed toward the survival needs of strangers? It is often easy to identify abuses, such as the person who neglects personal ties and the person oblivious to wider loyalties. But it is anything but easy to identify the golden mean.

Listing these ten areas of vagueness barely hints at the complexity and the variety of permissible ways of exercising discretion in making philanthropic decisions. Most of the questions above are too abstract to answer with any precision, and certainly they reveal large areas for exercising discretion. Even when the questions confront us in structured moral dilemmas, discretion plays a major role.

Moral dilemmas are situations where several moral reasons come into conflict and point toward incompatible actions. The reasons may be cast in terms of obligations, responsibilities, rights, goods, or virtues. As an illustration of discretion in responding to dilemmas, as well as a springboard for commenting on the role of moral reasoning in exercising discretion, consider the following illustration. It is borrowed from Jean-Paul Sartre and involves setting private and public priorities.

During World War II, one of Sartre's students sought his advice concerning a dilemma between staying home to help his mother and volunteering to help liberate Nazi-occupied France.[68] Good reasons favored going to war: defense of human liberty, loyalty to country, making amends for the treason of his father who was a Nazi collaborator, and acting in memory of a brother killed by the Nazis. Good reasons also favored staying with his mother: love for her, her need for special care, and her complete emotional dependence on him. We can say that the student had a public, philanthropic responsibility grounded in loyalty to his country and commitment to the cause of freedom. He also had a private responsibility grounded in love for his mother. How should he proceed in balancing these responsibilities? I will consider four approaches.

First, Sartre's approach was to reject the possibility of reasoning about moral dilemmas, beyond being honest in confronting them. By honesty he meant avoiding self-deception about relevant facts and about our radical freedom to choose the values we live by, unguided by objectively defensible values. He did not mean truthfully weighing valid moral reasons, because he did not believe such values exist. In Sartre's view, solving a dilemma means committing ourselves to a course of action without guidance by objectively justified moral reasons. Hence his advice to the student: "You are free, therefore choose—that is to say, invent."[69] Sartre says we are responsible for our choices, but only in the sense that we are authors of them, not that we are accountable for them according to justified moral reasons.

Sartre's approach is grounded in skepticism about justifiable values, yet that skepticism makes nonsense of his own example. The student experiences a moral dilemma precisely because he acknowledges his prior responsibilities to his mother, his country, and the cause of human liberty. Reconciling these responsibilities requires sensitive deliberation, not sheer invention. At the very least, the student must reject patently unjustified responses to the dilemma. A decision to run away to Switzerland or Southern California for a long vacation would be irresponsible, whether or not it was prompted by self-deception.

Second, we might search for a priority rule that ranks conflicting reasons in order of importance. Unfortunately, that search is futile. No general ranking is possible among love for parents, loyalty to country, and respect for freedom. Sometimes one should take preference, and sometimes another. Even if we believe that the student should give priority to his mother or to his country in this situation, the opposite emphasis may be best in different circumstances.

Over two millennia of philosophical disagreement strongly suggest there is no one canonical way to set priorities among moral principles, no one moral perspective that would be embraced by all ideally rational moral agents who are clear-thinking, fully informed, and caring about other people.[70] Even if there were, it would probably be too abstract to yield only one permissible answer to difficult dilemmas such as the student confronted. Some general principles can be ranked: "Save an innocent life" has priority over "Tell the truth." But most principles cannot be neatly ordered until they are applied to specific situations.

Third, we might appeal to intuition. David Ross argued that we know basic moral rules with certainty, as a matter of direct intuition. These rules include: Show gratitude for unearned services; Make amends for past wrongs; Do not injure others; Help people in need; Keep promises; Be fair; Develop one's talents. These rules, however, all are *prima facie* duties: they are duties that are sometimes overridden when they come into conflict with other duties that are more pressing in a given situation. Applying them requires context-sensitive judgment. Thus, the student has one obligation to respect and show gratitude toward his mother and another to help protect his country; the two come into conflict. Which should have priority? There is no general answer.

How should we proceed in resolving dilemmas? Ross says we should immerse ourselves in the situation, so as calmly and fully to consider all relevant facts and moral reasons. Eventually we arrive at a considered judgment about our "actual duty"—what we ought to do, all things considered: "When I am in a situation, as perhaps I always am, in which more than one of these *prima facie* duties is incumbent on me, what I have to do is to study the situation as fully as I can until I form the considered opinion (it is never more) that in the circumstances one of them is more incumbent than any other."[71]

Despite his insight into the contextual nature of moral reasoning, Ross's procedure makes a mystery of moral decision making. Calmly mulling over moral reasons apparently causes a judgment simply to pop into consciousness. Surely moral reasoning involves more than that. In emphasizing that all such judgments are fallible, Ross provides no way to distinguish sound moral judgment from arbitrary preference.[72] In addition, his procedure carries a risk: by immersing ourselves in the immediate situation we may lose perspective. Moral reasoning is contextual, but we need a more robust notion of good judgment that connects immediate contexts to wider and richer perspectives—richer than an abstract list of duties and wide enough to include all our moral ideals and commitments.

A fourth approach, then, is to grant the importance of contextual reasoning, but to balance it with an emphasis on achieving proper perspective—seeing the immediate context within a morally illuminating framework. Proper perspective has a personal dimension: it interprets situations in light of our full set of personal ideals, especially those most important in our lives. Proper perspective also has a social dimension: it attempts to relate situations to the wider society in which we live. In both ways it seeks to balance and sustain relevant moral considerations, albeit without a neat set of priority rules. How do we achieve proper perspective?

To begin with, moral reasons must connect with ourselves—with our ideals, our sense of life's meaning, and with what we care about most deeply within the spectrum of morally permissible acts. Considered separately, the student's options of helping his mother and fighting Hitler are each desirable. Yet quite possibly one of those options will best sustain what he cares about most deeply—not just at that moment, but in terms of his overall life. Sartre would say that what he most cares about is established by the decision he makes in the situation. On the contrary, his decision should be guided by his reflection about his prior caring. This is shown by the fact that the student can make a mistake, and deeply regret the decision he makes if it fails to accord with what is most important to him.

As Harry G. Frankfurt wrote about the student, "the resolution of the young man's dilemma . . . requires that he really care more about one of the alternatives confronting him than about the other; and it requires further that he understand which of those alternatives it is that he really cares about more."[73] Caring more means having a pattern of emotions, desires, beliefs, and commitments. This pattern is discovered rather than "invented" on the spot. While reflecting on dilemmas within the full context of our lives and ideals, we often discover that our will is already shaped in a certain direction. Hence volitional necessity: we must act in one direction rather than another, or else do violence to who we are. That does not make our decision coerced. Our caring is self-imposed; it is who we are.

Of course, what we care about most deeply may be a product of prejudice, naiveté, and narrowness. Hence, moral dilemmas also need to be understood in light of what we *should* care more about—when that can be understood with any clarity. Good judgment means finding a reasonable way to relate immediate moral demands in a situation to a justified wider social perspective. But we should allow that there are a variety of such perspectives.

Abstract philosophical theories only provide a framework for reflection. Practical wisdom must be exercised in seeking to illuminate a dilemma using both a grasp the possibilities in the immediate situation and the resources offered by wider perspectives—moral, religious, social, and historical. In the case of the student, these include perspectives that reveal the threat of fascism to democracies, but also perspectives on the importance of family and other intimate relationships in an increasingly impersonal world.

Most likely, relating the details of a situation to wider personal and social perspectives will enable the student to reasonably select a course of action. In a rare case it may not, and then the decision does involve some arbitrariness. Even so, the student should try to give the fullest possible expression to all his areas of caring. If he decides to go to war, can he find a way to help reconcile his mother to his decision, and can he find a friend to support his mother while he is away? If he decides to stay with his mother, is there some war-related activity that will enable him to do his share in fighting fascism? Similarly, most decisions involving philanthropy do not require severing entire areas of moral concern.[74]

The diverse functions of moral reasons, as well as their multiplicity, explain why moral dilemmas arise in the first place. As James D. Wallace explains, moral reasons that arose in one setting, to deal with one set of problems, enter into new contexts where their application may not be straightforward.[75] Thus, moral reasons linked to love for one's parents suddenly enter into a context of war. Solving dilemmas requires adapting moral reasons to new situations. That means reflecting on their wider role in our lives while finding ways to relate them to fresh possibilities.

Novel situations generate agonizing dilemmas concerning philanthropy. For example, in recent decades the mass media have placed us in a much more direct relation with world suffering. Not only are we better informed; we also witness starvation as it happens, watching on television the sunken cheeks and distended bellies of starving children. In addition, the disparities between rich are poor are more extreme than before, and the rich can help far more than was ever possible. These global changes make unprecedented demands on us. Moral virtues of beneficence and loyalty which developed in local communities are now thrust into the context of a worldwide community. It is not surprising that we are unclear about our responsibilities, and that consequently a certain amount of self-doubt and guilt seem inevitable.

We should not be overeager to criticize ourselves and others harshly, yet not just anything goes. The participation virtues, together with the general and personal philanthropic responsibilities, provide some basis for evaluating ourselves and other people, focusing on character rather than on each occasion of giving or not giving. While we cannot precisely gauge what is required of a given individual at a particular moment, nevertheless we can discern blatant patterns of selfishness and callousness (in ourselves and others).

I have suggested there are responsibilities to engage in philanthropic giving, albeit ones that leave wide areas for discretion and good judgment. According to a time-honored ideal, however, philanthropic giving should be caring, joyous, and freely engaged in. Doesn't this talk of responsibility threaten to make giving an onerous moral burden, thereby destroying the true spirit of philanthropy?

Note that there is a difference between (a) having and acting to meet a responsibility, and (b) being motivated to act primarily by a sense of duty. In meeting many obligations, ironically, we should be prompted by more than a sense of obligation. Thus, it is highly desirable for spouses and parents to be motivated primarily by love, caring, and delight in meeting their obligations rather than by impersonal conscientiousness. The same is true of philanthropy.

At the same time, on some occasions a strong sense of responsibility is desirable, in philanthropy as in parenting. Overstressed parents who contemplate abandoning their children do well to have an active sense of responsibility. Likewise, a sense of responsibility is surely one legitimate motive for engaging in philanthropy, and it need not threaten other desirable motives. As one aspect of a genuine spirit of caring, a sense of responsibility is deeply personal rather than an impersonal "duty for duty's sake."

Finally, I have tried to show that discretion involves ample freedom to make specific philanthropic decisions. In prizing good judgment in selecting from a range of good options, we should renounce the heavy-handed moralizing that insists every caring person must give to this or that cause. We should also oppose all forms of coercion that undermine autonomy in meeting philanthropic responsibilities.

4

Respect for Autonomy

Act so that you treat humanity, whether in your own person or in that of
another, always as an end and never as a means only.

—Immanuel Kant

Be just before you are generous.

—Proverb

PHILANTHROPY CAN BE ineffective for many reasons: bad luck or poor
judgment, unrealistic faith or lack of hope, excessive generosity or insufficient courage. When philanthropy is ugly and demeaning, however, as
well as ineffective, usually the primary cause is a failure to respect persons.

In this context, respect is recognition of the moral worth of all people,
rather than admiration for exceptional individuals. Kant suggested that to
respect persons is to respect their autonomy—their rational and moral self-
governance. Difficulties arise concerning how he developed this suggestion.
For one thing, in exalting reason he downplayed other value-bestowing aspects of human life, such as capacities for sympathy and loyalties to communities. This is part of a wider failure to understand respect in more personal
terms which take into account individual differences and particular contexts,
rather than to treat persons as instances of an abstract rational being. For
another thing, he relied on a simplistic view of moral reasoning as grounded
in absolute or exceptionless moral principles, failing to appreciate how often
rules conflict in ways that force exceptions. Nevertheless, Kant's emphasis on
autonomy has fundamental importance in understanding respect for persons.

Autonomy has three aspects: rights, capacities, and competencies. *Rights
autonomy* is possessing moral rights to pursue one's legitimate interests without unjust interference from others. People are morally equal in the sense
that they all have these rights. *Capacity autonomy* means having the general
capacities to reason, exercise self-control, identify with and affirm healthy desires, and care for persons, practices, and organizations. Infants, young children, and some adults lack these capacities in varying degrees. *Competence
autonomy* means exercising these capacities skillfully so as to meet morally

permissible goals. Competence autonomy is a moral achievement, at least when it becomes a steady pattern.

Respect for autonomy, accordingly, implies respect for rights and respect for people's efforts at self-determination. In philanthropy, failures of moral respect take many forms, sixteen of which I will discuss under the following headings: Freedom to Harm, Tyranny of Gifts, Manipulation of Givers, Exploitation of Women, and Incentives to Give. Taken together, these examples suggest that as philanthropists we do well to heed Hippocrates' advice to physicians: Above all, do no harm.

Freedom to Harm

1. *Harm to Third Parties*. Democracies not only tolerate but also foster pluralism, that is, the acceptance of alternative moral perspectives. Within generous boundaries, democracies also tolerate mistaken and harmful conduct, including that which occurs through philanthropy. Often the harm is done to third parties, that is, to individuals other than philanthropists and their intended beneficiaries.

According to a sanguine picture, philanthropy is a set of practices in which well-intentioned people choose to promote different but complementary public goods, no doubt making errors along the way, but overall promoting the common good. This picture is accompanied by slogans urging blanket support for particular areas of philanthropy. Support education, we are told, by giving to the college or university of our choice, even though not all schools are worthy of support. Worship God as you choose and contribute accordingly, even though some religions are morally objectionable. Support the arts, even though some art has little worth. And so on.

According to a more somber picture, philanthropists do enormous harm to third parties. Viewed from the trenches, philanthropy is a battlefield in which rights are assaulted and defended, where "the other side" constantly threatens the public good, and where for every good cause there is a bad one. For example, the National Rifle Association sees itself as defending basic Constitutional rights against enemies of freedom; gun control groups charge the NRA with callous disregard of the rights of victims of crime. Environmentalist groups attack industry for violating rights to a livable environment; pro-industry groups charge environmentalists with violating rights to jobs and profit making. The American Civil Liberties Union defends pornographers' rights of free speech; anti-pornography activists, including both some feminist and some conservative groups, defend restrictions on violent pornography as necessary protections for the rights of women and children. Euthanasia advocates defend the right to die with dignity; anti-euthanasia groups reject euthanasia as an assault on the sanctity of life. Pro-choice abortion activists defend the rights of women; pro-life activists defend what they view as the rights of unborn persons. Groups promoting peace and pluralism promote multicultural education; hate groups promote ethnic supremacy and xenophobia. Gay and lesbian activists defend sexual freedom and challenge homophobia; opposing groups try to suppress homosexuality.

There is additional indirect damage. Because opposition groups contribute so much money and human resources, we feel the need to join battle with our money and energy. As a result, precious resources are deflected away from vital humanitarian and cultural needs. Thus, we hear speakers on both sides of the abortion controversy decry the waste of resources that could help alleviate problems of world hunger, drug abuse, and desperately underfunded schools. If only the other side had better moral judgment, how much good could be done!

Sanguine observers make several rejoinders.[1] They point to the good in allowing people to express their honestly felt convictions, even when the convictions are misguided. Integrity is a key value promoted as individuals give according to their vision of worthy causes, assuming they do so with genuine moral concern. Then, too, there are the valuable ties of caring that emerge through loyalty to both good and misguided causes. ("My country, right or wrong.")

Optimists also remind us that democracies thrive on controversies. So long as the opposing sides avoid violence, and so long as the political-legal process does its job in forging reasonable compromises, vigorous debate backed by philanthropic funding tends to produce good results—certainly better than those of authoritarian societies which prevent such conflict. To celebrate democracy is to affirm moral pluralism and its philanthropic expression.

Truth is elusive. As John Stuart Mill emphasized in *On Liberty*, none of us is infallible. It is always possible that we, rather than our opponents, are in error, and the opposition may have at least part of the truth on their side. Even with respect to abortion, where absolutes clash, seemingly without hope of compromise, perhaps someday we will find a way to reconcile elements of truth on both sides. Even when our views are correct, vigorous challenge to them enables us fully to grasp their meaning and justification. However true our view may be, "if it is not fully, frequently, and fearlessly discussed, it will be held as a dead dogma, not a living truth" that influences feeling and conduct.[2] Philanthropy helps make possible lively debate and dialogue.

These sanguine rejoinders are important, yet they complement the somber picture rather than refute it. Much philanthropy does contribute to complementary aspects of the public good; much supports integrity and furthers caring relationships; philanthropic practices are vital to democracy; and living truths emerge through vigorous controversy. None of this, however, removes the harm done by misguided philanthropy.

Let us acknowledge the truth in both the sanguine and the somber views, each of which must enter into a sober, realistic picture of philanthropy. Or to shift metaphors, let our map of philanthropy display many roads leading to aspects of the common good, but also numerous battlefields in which rights are threatened and harm is done. What follows?

It follows that this will be a short section. It would be long if I defended my views on the aforementioned controversies, or on many others. Instead, I will simply acknowledge a truth that Pollyannas deny and pessimists exaggerate: Philanthropy can support or harm third parties.

Tyranny of Gifts

Ideally, gifts augment autonomy. They empower recipients by providing them with resources to pursue their interests. In general, an underlying long-term aim of philanthropy is to support competence autonomy, especially with regard to humanitarian support for basic needs.

Maimonides, the twelfth-century Jewish philosopher, distinguished eight "degrees" of philanthropy. Moving from less to more admirable forms of philanthropy, the degrees are to give (1) grudgingly, (2) meagerly, (3) in response to a request, (4) before being asked, (5) without the donor's knowing the recipient's identity, (6) without the recipient's knowing the donor, and (7) without either the donor's or the recipient's knowing the other. The highest form (8) is "to take hold of a Jew who has been crushed and to give him a gift or a loan, or to enter into partnership with him, or to find work for him, and thus put him on his feet that he will not be dependent on his fellow-men."[3] In my terms, the best form of philanthropy is to restore or to augment competence autonomy.

Maimonides had in mind humanitarian giving, and that will be my focus here. Cultural giving usually has different aims, such as uniting benefactors with creative artists and thinkers in a shared pursuit of excellence. At the same time, Maimonides' emphasis on self-reliance is sometimes applicable to cultural giving. An example is Andrew Carnegie's practice of giving money to build libraries with the stipulation that local communities assume responsibility for book acquisition and maintenance.

TechnoServe, a voluntary organization currently involved in a hundred projects in eleven countries in Africa and Latin America, is a paradigm of how philanthropy effectively supports autonomy.[4] Edward P. Bullard founded TechnoServe in 1968 after leaving his job as chief production engineer for a manufacturing company in order to help people in Africa and Latin America. Bullard knew suffering first hand. Six years earlier he had spent a year in Ghana managing a hospital while on a mission funded by his church. There a three-year-old girl had died of starvation as he held her hand. Bullard also knew that, in addition to immediate disaster relief, long-term solutions had to be found, solutions that would enable individuals to meet their own needs.

TechnoServe adopted as its motto the Chinese proverb that giving people a fish feeds them for a day, but teaching them how to fish feeds them for life. The organization provides expert advice about farming techniques, market research for developing new products, finance and accounting skills, construction, transportation, and technology appropriate for the groups it serves. After several failures, it learned to select farmers who saw their personal and group self-interest promoted by contributing their own labor and resources. Unrestricted handouts were less effective than requiring farmers to invest their funds, however meager, including payment of a small service fee to TechnoServe.

A time limit is set at the outset for involvement with each group. Typically, projects last two or three years. Then TechnoServe moves on to new projects, while showing support by staying in touch to monitor the group's autonomous progress. One project was the Drumvale Ranch in Kenya. TechnoServe worked with 1,500 Kenyans in turning a 15,000-acre cattle ranch into a profitable venture. Years after TechnoServe's involvement, the ranch was able to survive the devastating drought of 1984–85 by employing the long-term management learned from TechnoServe.

A second paradigm of effective support for autonomy is National Women's Employment and Education, founded by Lupe Anguiano.[5] As a civil rights specialist working for the Department of Health, Education, and Welfare, Anguiano had listened to Latino women express the desire to get off welfare and became self-supporting. When her efforts to change government priorities toward finding jobs for women were unsuccessful, she moved to San Antonio to work with the Catholic Church on welfare reform issues. In 1979, drawing on her experience in government and nonprofit organizations, she founded National Women's Employment and Education.

The organization emphasizes job placement, job preparation, and childcare for women on welfare. It collects and makes information available about job opportunities. Then it provides training in skills at the level specified by prospective employers. Equally important, it helps women find childcare and transportation. Anguiano has also formed a consulting firm to help other communities to develop comparable programs. Her long-term goal is national welfare reform modeled on these community-based programs, rather than on the "soup-kitchen" model that was appropriate during the depression, when national welfare programs began.

Not all philanthropy works as well as in these paradigms. When it involves unequal power relations there is the danger that givers and gifts might erode the autonomy of recipients. Money is power, and so is voluntary service, especially in leadership roles. That power is easily misused to harm recipients or others. When that happens, to invert a scripture, it becomes less blessed to receive than to give.[6]

I will discuss five types of harm to recipients: pauperism, damaged self-respect, paternalism, coercion, and manipulation. In addition, I will discuss how nonrecipients can be harmed by losing a fair opportunity for acquiring resources.

2. *Pauperism*. Pauperism occurs when poverty and undesirable forms of dependency become a way of life. Becoming too comfortable in receiving charity or government welfare, individuals may lose the desire to be self-reliant—a crucial psychological prerequisite for competence autonomy. As a result, they fail to pursue opportunities for education and work that would enable them to earn their own way.

Pauperism was a concern long before it became an objection to contemporary systems of welfare and foreign aid.[7] For good reasons, the history of philanthropy is filled with practical advice about how to avoid pauperism. Insofar as the goal of humanitarian giving is to empower beneficiaries, rather than to glorify benefactors, pauperism makes philanthropy self-defeating as well as wasteful. Along with the Golden Rule we need the Iron Rule of Giving: "Don't do for others what they can do for themselves."[8]

One way to avoid pauperism is to create a context of cooperation between donors and recipients who work toward a shared goal.[9] Cooperation promotes a sense of equality even when the relative contributions are unequal in quantity. TechnoServe is one paradigm. Another is Habitat for Humanity, an organization founded by Millard Fuller and made famous by the participation of former President Jimmy Carter and Rosalynn Carter. Operating in hundreds of U.S. cities and two dozen foreign countries, the organization builds homes for individuals whose needs are not met by governments and private funding. Costs are kept very low by using volunteer labor and inexpensive designs. For example, in 1986 Habitat for Humanity was able to build homes in Nicaragua for families of ten people at a cost less than $500.[10] The beneficiaries are required to spend hundreds of hours in helping to build their homes and to pay for building materials, typically by paying a small monthly mortgage to Habitat.

Pauperism is a complex phenomenon which is open to alternative explanations. Conservatives see it as the result of sloth. Liberals see it as the result of behavioral conditioning. No doubt both are partly right. So are more radical critics who argue that upper-class giving to pauperized classes helps maintain class supremacy. America's upper economic class comprises about

one percent of the population, yet it owns the major share of economic resources—about half of the U.S. corporate stock and one-fifth of the national
wealth.[11] Its patterns of giving function in part to maintain the power that
goes with wealth.

For example, most voluntary service by upper-class women consists of
fundraising, leadership on community boards, and participation in exclusive
groups such as the Junior League, whose membership is by invitation only.[12]
When benefits go to the poor, they are usually palliative rather than aimed
at fundamental economic reform. Susan A. Ostrander argues that the primary
function of voluntary service by upper-class women is to maintain the status
quo. It is an "exercise of class power: power of volunteer boards over paid
professionals, power to keep clients and consumers from gaining significant
representation on community boards (which might result in their changing
things), and power to maintain private, class control over institutions that
might otherwise be run by the government."[13] In addition, the service helps
make the extraordinary privileges of a rich minority palatable to the majority
of citizens who might otherwise lessen it through tax laws. At the same time,
enormous good is accomplished by upper-class philanthropy. Here, as so
often in thinking about philanthropy, there is a genuine moral ambiguity:
actions which considered by themselves produce good are embedded in wider
social patterns that have problematic consequences.

Whether class dominance is objectionable depends, of course, on the requirements of justice. One need not be an egalitarian who favors economic
equality to condemn the failure of societies to provide an adequate "safety
net" for people at the lower end of the economic spectrum. Having political
rights is one thing; having the economic ability to exercise them is another.
Poverty disenfranchises people, or at least it silences their voices when privilege and money dominate.

3. *Damaging Self-Respect.* Assaulting the self-respect of recipients is one
way to pauperize; it is also a distinct category of harm. Self-respect is a
psychological prerequisite for self-assertion, for positive social interaction, and
in general for exercising competence autonomy. Gifts can threaten self-respect
in several ways. To begin with, merely perceiving one's benefactor as having
more power, because more money, is thereby to perceive oneself as having
less power. That perception need not be bad; it may even stimulate effort.
But when one lacks opportunities for effective effort, the perception tends
to increase feelings of inferiority and powerlessness.

Matters are worse when benefactors and observers are condescending toward recipients, or when recipients believe they are. Tact and sensitivity are
called for. Kant even recommended moral pretense when engaging in face-
to-face philanthropy: "[W]e shall recognize an obligation to help a poor man;

but since our favour humbles him by making his welfare dependent on our generosity, it is our duty to behave as if our help is either what is merely due to him or but a slight service of love, and so to spare him humiliation and maintain his self-respect."[14] This tactic may or may not be sound in a given instance, but instead of pretense we do better to rely on structures of giving and types of aid designed to promote mutuality and to minimize self-righteousness.

Self-respect and self-esteem can be threatened when there is no way to reciprocate appropriately. For example, when kidney transplants first became possible, donors and recipients were allowed to know each other. That proved debilitating to many recipients and even to some donors. Recipients felt an enormous debt, with no way to reciprocate. This occurred even when the kidney was taken from a corpse.[15] To counterbalance this effect, health professionals now routinely maintain anonymity of organ donors.

A parallel situation arises with foreign aid, both philanthropic and governmental. American foreign aid tends to cause hostility when it is given directly, rather than through intermediary groups such as the Red Cross.[16] Bitterness increases when aid is accompanied by rigid restrictions on how money is spent, bureaucratic accounting procedures, and surveillance. Distrust intensifies when political and economic purposes guide humanitarian giving, as they usually do, or when there is a suspicion of attempted ingratiation—using gifts to establish oneself in the favor of recipients in order to gain some advantage.

International gifts are most appreciated when they convey a spirit of moral equality. It is often preferable to offer loans rather than outright gifts and to require repayment when it is within a country's means, though without requiring usual interest rates (which is perceived as exploitive usury). The exception is disaster relief in which accepting aid does not create a sense of inferiority.[17]

4. *Paternalism.* Paternalism, or parentalism, is the attempt to promote the good of other people by interfering with their liberty. Paternalists act on their own view of what is good for recipients, whether or not it matches the recipient's view. Hence, paternalism may cause harm in two ways: (i) interfering with autonomy and (ii) producing consequences that are undesirable from the point of view of recipients.

Some paternalism is justified, especially "weak paternalism" aimed at preventing self-harm by recipients with lessened capacity autonomy, such as children, mentally disabled adults, and adults whose competence autonomy is temporarily impaired. For example, intervening to prevent the suicide of a temporarily depressed individual is usually justified. In general, weak paternalism is justified when it is intended to prevent serious harm and when it is done with the reasonable hope that the person will later agree with our action (or would agree if they could).[18]

Only rarely, however, is there a justification for "strong paternalism," which is interfering with the liberty of individuals competent to guide their own lives.[19] At best it is patronizing, offensively condescending. At worst it violates rights to liberty. Strong paternalism demeans people by underestimating or undervaluing their capacity for self-governance. Often it is mixed with cruelty: witness southern slave owners who acted "kindly" toward black people whom they regarded as incapable of guiding their own lives. Even when mixed with compassion, paternalism can be damaging: witness the often well-intentioned missionaries who treated "heathens" as unqualified to know their own good.

Paternalism is a risk whenever donors rather than recipients shape the use of gifts. The solution is to acknowledge that mature adults have the capacity to discern their own needs. This implies, for example, that foundations serving communities should include community representatives on their boards of directors, in significant numbers rather than as tokens.[20] An experiment along these lines is the Haymarket People's Fund, created in 1974 in Boston.[21] Major seed money for the Fund came from young people with inherited wealth, such as George Pillsbury, the heir to the food company fortune. The use of the money was entirely under the direction of a board of community activists, not the donors. Most other "alternative fund" foundations that have emerged during the past two decades use combinations of community representatives and donors on their boards. At present they represent only a beginning in that they amount to .01 percent of giving by the wealthy.[22]

5. *Coercing Recipients.* Coercion can mean physical restraint or violence, but here it means threat of harm unless a course of action is followed. The threats may be explicit or tacit, and they may be present at the time gifts are made or subsequently. Harm includes both moral harm in violating rights and harm by lowering people's economic or psychological well-being.[23] Obviously, differences in values are reflected in disagreements about when harm and coercion occur.

The history of missionary movements contains many instances of coercion in pursuing voluntary service, including some rather ingenious ones. For example, the London Missionary Society was formed in 1795 with the initial focus of proselytizing in the islands of the South Pacific, beginning with Tahiti.[24] The early missionaries found the Tahitians welcoming but uninterested in their dogmas. In response, they formed a contract with a local chief, who was an alcoholic enamored of the "spirits" brewed by the missionaries. The missionaries supplied the chief with firearms to use in his wars with competing chiefs on the condition that he would force the conversion of the natives after he won the war. The agreement was kept. Following his victory, the chief passed laws requiring profession of the Christian faith and abandonment of local religious customs. Missionaries helped enforce the laws by turning in violators who were punished by prison, hard labor, or even death in the case of overt rebels against the faith. Within a few years, Tahitian religious culture was destroyed. The tactic was repeated in other South Pacific islands.

A more recent example concerns philanthropy scholarship. When foundations give grants to scholars to study foundations they are sometimes surprised to discover they have funded publications critical of themselves, in particular of their conservative ideologies which stifle social experimentation. Upon publication of his second book critical of foundations, one prominent scholar was unable to find further funding. Another distinguished researcher became the object of hostility in philanthropic circles after presenting a carefully researched paper critical of grant makers for serving economically privileged groups.[25] It takes only a few well-publicized examples like these to create a climate of intimidation hurtful to unbiased scholarship.

6. *Manipulative Strings.* Attaching strings (conditions) to gifts enables benefactors to maintain control over how their gifts are used. Doing so may be desirable. Responsible giving implies having reasons for believing that gifts will be put to good use. Strings are unobjectionable when they express a shared understanding of the purpose of the gift and require reasonable accountability. But when strings constrict freedom in harmful ways, they invite the metaphor of puppeteers manipulating puppets.

That metaphor may seem too strong, since what is at stake is making offers rather than coercing by threats. People are free to refuse offers, even extremely attractive ones. Overwhelmingly attractive offers, however, can be psychologically seductive—resistable only with extraordinary effort or sacrifice.[26] Suppose that a sadist offers an impoverished individual several thousand dollars on the condition that he or she will do some depraved act. In this case the seduction comes against a background of poverty; in other instances people do not want to be given large amounts of money that would pressure them to change their lives in ways they find undesirable.[27] Sometimes this amounts to "undue influence": making an offer that seduces someone into performing morally objectionable acts. It is precisely the large gift which tends to come with conditions, and large donors may take for granted that their gift buys them influence. As one wealthy philanthropist remarked, "If I make a large gift to an organization I would expect to have some influence if change really was necessary."[28]

Raising questions about manipulation is one thing; settling them is an-

other. Perhaps everyone understands in advance that money is being ex-
changed for influence, so that the exchange is based on a shared understanding. The problem is that open discussions of influence buying rarely occur.
In part this results from the pressure of need: recipients are eager to get
resources, hence not eager to challenge donors' motives and aims. In part it
derives from the halo effect: philanthropy is assumed to be altruistic until
shown otherwise.

Value-based estimates of harm enter into judgments about manipulative
offers as well as about coercion. Some years ago my university received several million-dollar gifts which came with the condition, agreed upon by the
president, that the donors would remain anonymous. The editor of the student newspaper learned the donors' names and sought to publish them. He
argued that students had a right to know the identity of individuals whose
gifts might buy influence in directing the school, hence that the condition
of anonymity was unacceptable. Despite this, the president prevented publication of the names. In his view, anonymity was necessary to honor his promise, to prevent withdrawal of the much-needed gifts, and to avoid future
fundraising difficulties.

Consider, too, a philanthropist who offers twenty million dollars to an
all-male private college if the college begins admitting women students.[29] The
offer may be seductive to college officials, especially if the college is seriously
pressed for funds. If we value the goal of coeducation, perhaps because the
college is located in an area where women do not have equal opportunities
for higher education, we will speak of "influence" being exerted, but not
manipulation. If instead we object to the goal, we will speak of manipulation
in a derogatory sense.

Now reverse the case. A women's college is being pressured to accept
men, and a donor offers twenty million dollars if it does. If the college is
the only women's college in a region of the country where we see a need
for such institutions because of the special opportunities they offer to women, then we will see elements of manipulation. Otherwise we might emphasize that the college is at liberty to accept or reject the offer. In practice,
of course, colleges and other nonprofit organizations have varied constituencies with conflicting value perspectives. That makes it difficult to form a
consensus about when manipulation occurs.

7. *Harming Nonrecipients.* Helping some people implies not helping others. That is inevitable, given limited resources and unlimited problems. Problems arise when help for some people comes at the expense of undermining
the autonomy of others.

A case in point is the philanthropically funded reformation of medical
education during the first two decades of this century. Carnegie and Rocke-

feller money, under the guidance of Abraham Flexner and Frederick T. Gates, singled out some medical schools for support and thereby undermined the ability of others to compete. Students applied to the well-funded schools, which had the resources to provide a better education. Enormous good was accomplished by raising educational requirements and improving faculty and facilities. However, great harm was done too. Racism and sexism influenced the foundations, so that schools for women and black people were not funded.[30] Nearly all of them were forced to close, thereby worsening professional opportunities for women and minorities and also eroding medical care for minorities.

Any act of helping has the potential to make nonrecipients feel left out and angry.[31] Sometimes the anger derives from unjustified envy, but other times it is rooted in justified resentment of society's indifference. Philanthropy is often caught in the middle since some efforts, unlike the medical school case, are legitimately aimed at particular groups based on race, sex, or ethnicity.

Manipulation of Givers

Givers are the victims as well as the agents of manipulation. Ideally, development officials and volunteer leaders serve as facilitators, offering benefactors opportunities to pursue their ideals. Their chances of success turn on whether they are trusted to respect the good will and autonomous purposes of benefactors. This fiduciary relationship is abused by infringing philanthropists' rights autonomy and undermining their competence autonomy. Abuses range from the unabashed greed of the charlatan to the incompetence and overzealousness of the nobly intentioned. Tactics include deception, coercion, duress, violating privacy, and exploiting individuals with lessened competence autonomy.

8. *Deception.* To deceive is to mislead intentionally. Usually deception implies success in creating false beliefs or ignorance, although here I will expand it to include attempts to mislead. Deceivers employ a variety of methods: lying, exaggeration, understatement, pretense, withholding pertinent facts, creating misleading impressions, and deflecting attention from important information. Not all deception is dishonest. There is, however, a moral presumption against deception, which only a pressing reason can override, because it violates autonomy by interfering with self-governance based on a grasp of facts.[32]

Corrupt charities use deception as their primary tool. Well under 5 percent of charities are corrupt, yet they cause a disproportionate amount of damage, and not only to their immediate victims. Once uncovered, cases of charity fraud tend to be widely publicized. That makes some people more prudent in giving, but it makes others cynical and lessens the public trust essential for philanthropic practices to flourish.

Dishonest panhandlers deceive in the way they characterize the needs of recipients, whether themselves or others.[33] Most often they seek funds for themselves by pretending to have a legitimate need which cannot be met through their own efforts: begging for food money becomes a ruse for acquiring drugs. Charity racketeers, by contrast, typically appeal to a genuine need or legitimate cause, which they then subvert.

Abraham L. Koolish belongs on any list of infamous charity racketeers. His scams included the ingenious Ident-O-Tag, a key-ring-size personalized license plate.[34] The tags were mailed to drivers with an accompanying invitation to donate a dollar or more to the Disabled American Veterans. The ploy was to evoke feelings of appreciation for the ingenious gift, as well as to evoke guilt for hesitating to reciprocate with a donation. It worked. More than $21 million was raised during the first four years of the program, none of which went to disabled veterans. Eventually Koolish sold the Ident-O-Tag operation to the veterans association for $1.3 million, even though the veterans could have used the idea for free since it was nonpatentable. Koolish conducted a variety of other lucrative charity capers before he was finally convicted of fraud in 1963 at the age of seventy-three.

Abuse is compounded when children are used to evoke people's sympathies. An insidious example is "Children's Wish," which solicited funds to grant terminally ill children their wish for such things as a trip or a special toy. The name "Children's Wish" mimicked "Make a Wish," the name of an honest and well-run organization that has helped many children and their parents. Only 10 percent of the money raised by Chidren's Wish was used to help children. The rest provided a lavish lifestyle for the husband-and-wife managers of the organization.[35] Benefactors' aims and autonomy were subverted, needy and deserving children were denied gifts intended for them, and other worthy charities were hurt by the adverse publicity when the ruse was exposed on national television.

Well-intentioned charities, devoted to good purposes, are sometimes tempted to deceive in order to conceal their inefficiency or other activities the public might find offensive. Occasionally they mislead the public by withholding information about their success, in that they have ample funds to accomplish their goals. In both cases, deception prevents philanthropists from putting their money and time where it can do the most good. Nor will it do to rationalize deception with the attitude that what donors don't know won't hurt them and will even make them happy. ("Ignorance is bliss.") That attitude demeans persons by reducing them to mere pleasure-seeking organisms. Philanthropists want more than happiness; they want to help.

Deception can be dangerous as well as exploitive. Deceiving volunteers in experiments exposes them to harms which only they have the right to accept or refuse on the basis of informed decisions. They must be given all information necessary for making a rational assessment of the risks they undertake. The importance of this norm has been clear since the Nuremberg trials revealed the horror of Nazi experiments on Jews, yet it has not always been heeded. During four decades, beginning in the 1930s, the U.S. Department of Public Health and Tuskegee Institute conducted studies of advanced syphillis in poor and uneducated black men. The men believed they were receiving the best available medical care. In fact they were given no treatment or substandard treatment. Nor were they informed of risks and alternative treatment. At least forty men died, and all were denied available therapy.

9. *Coerced Giving*. Giving is coerced when it is accompanied by force or threats of harm. For example, someone threatens to reveal embarrassing information about a wealthy philanthropist unless a large donation is made to a particular charity.[36] Coerced giving is extortion rather than voluntary philanthropy.

Coercion is often difficult to identify. It is obvious when a manager, frustrated by low participation in a United Way fund drive, threatens employees with penalties unless they contribute. More often, however, there is a more ambiguous climate of intimidation. Employees receive a memo stressing the importance of United Way and alluding to the corporation's image as a responsible member of the community. Follow-up reminders about the value of United Way programs are sent to nonresponsive employees, and a chart is posted itemizing the contributions of specific company divisions. As a result, employees feel forced to give as a condition of job security. In other instances, employees experience an unspoken, but palpable, pressure to please employers by giving to their favorite charities.

Does coercion occur when a minister warns members of a congregation in a threatening tone that if they fail to tithe they will suffer God's wrath? Assuming that the minister is acting on sincere religious beliefs, that the money is used for legitimate purposes, and that members of the congregation freely respond according to their own religious convictions, there is no coercion. Even though we are repelled by this fundraising tactic, a threatening tone is not a threat. Yet what about the following case?

In 1987 Oral Roberts told his television congregation that God would "call him home," presumably cause his death, unless $8 million in donations was raised by a certain deadline. Roberts believed he was reporting a revelation from God. To some members of his congregation, however, the appeal may have sounded like a threat: "If you do not contribute, you will be partly to blame for Oral Roberts' death." Related cases occur when religious or political leaders, like Gandhi, engage in life-threatening fasts unless others engage in a certain line of conduct. If we hesitate to call these cases of coercion, we must at least acknowledge an unusual degree of pressure and perhaps duress.

10. *Duress.* Duress is something less than coercion but more than usual pressure. In duress, rational decision making is threatened by manipulating "negative" emotions such as guilt, fear, and anxiety.

Perhaps all fundraising involves some pressure. Consider the following excerpt from a handbook for fundraisers:

> By their very nature, personal appeals or even telephone appeals for contributions involve pressure and are extremely difficult for most people to resist. . . .
>
> Although you may wish it were otherwise, pressure is essential in raising money. Just as you cannot make an omelet without breaking eggs, you cannot raise money without applying pressure. You must believe enough in your cause to ask directly, forcefully and convincingly. . . . True, you will probably offend someone at some point along the way. One fund-raising pro shrugs this off with the observation, "The dogs bark, but the caravan moves on."[37]

With refreshing candor, the author reminds us that some pressure may be necessary and inevitable. At the same time, the offensive concluding remark reminds us of the temptation, inherent in fundraising, to reduce people to moneybags. There is pressure and pressure. Autonomy is subtly affected when pressures lead us to give with annoyance and subsequent regret rather than with identification with a cause.

Peers and acquaintances exert subtle pressures, if only with a gaze, as when a collection plate is passed through an audience. If the context is a church or a fundraising event where the practice is expected, the pressure is acceptable and perhaps desirable, assuming the cause is good. If the context is a public lecture, the fundraising activity may be repugnant because it introduces an element of duress.

Much fundraising is legitimately conducted among friends. If I respond to your invitation to contribute to a cause, it is understood that I may call upon you to give to mine. There are limits, however. Asking a nonreligious friend to contribute to a religious cause, or a nonenvironmentalist friend to contribute to a wilderness preservation organization, reveals insensitivity to both autonomy and friendship. If there is any hint that the donation is a condition for continued friendship, the friendship is already devalued.

11. *Violating Privacy.* Autonomy is linked to privacy. Intimate activities preclude an audience, and we seek control over information about ourselves.

Privacy is increasingly threatened by computerized records containing sensitive information: credit ratings, medical and counseling records, income, purchasing habits, education records, and so on. Some fundraising techniques pose additional threats.

Specialists in "prospect research" have become familiar on university and hospital development staffs. Their job is to uncover personal information about possible contributors. In addition, lists of past donors to specific causes are available for purchase by groups seeking to target their fundraising efforts.

Once information about specific donors is collected in files, it can easily be misused. Strict confidentiality about this information is an understood obligation among development officers. Yet no shared understanding has yet emerged concerning donors' rights of access to this information. In a 1989 study, prospect researchers were asked this question: "A large donor to your institution calls and asks to review the file you have created on him. What do you do?"[38] Fifty-eight percent said they would show the file; 5 percent would refuse to show the file; 24 percent would show part of the file, allowing the donor to believe it to be the entire file; 13 percent would show parts of the file and divulge that there are other parts accessible only to the development staff. That means that nearly half would withhold sensitive information, such as negative comments made about the donor.

12. *Exploiting Lessened Autonomy.* It is easier to exploit people who have lessened competence autonomy, as with children and some elderly people. Some senior citizens have diminished competence autonomy beyond physical impairments. Mental disabilities weaken capacities to make reasonable choices, and emotional vulnerabilities cause exaggerated fears and naivete. Con artists are ready to take advantage, but so are less patently dishonest groups. For example, some nonprofit corporations make mail requests for funds to lobby for programs for the elderly, such as maintaining social security and medical benefits, and then use most of the money for overhead costs and further mailing.

Whereas the elderly may have diminished competence autonomy, young children are just beginning to develop it. With wide latitude, parents have a right and a responsibility to instill their fundamental values in their children, including the values of voluntary service. That makes children the most vulnerable category of volunteers. Extreme abuse, for example, occurs in service within dangerous cults. Members of the Jim Jones cult brought their children into practices that eventually resulted in the 1978 mass suicide at Jonestown in Guyana. Among the 913 people who died, 276 were children.[39]

Such extreme abuses warrant government intervention, but that carries its own risks. Majorities are always ready to impose their attitudes on unfavored groups, and the courts have not always set appropriate limits. The Supreme Court, for example, once upheld a Massachusetts law preventing Jehovah Witnesses' children from distributing religious pamphlets on public streets.[40] It interpreted the Massachusetts law as a legitimate attempt to ensure that children not be hurt by the negative public reactions of scorn, pity, or indifference toward the children's voluntary service in an unpopular church. In my judgment, this ruling violated the religious freedom of parents.

In the abstract, the central responsibility of parents is clear: caringly to serve the interests of their children until they reach maturity. In practice, parents have responsibilities which may conflict: to protect their children from physical and psychological harm; to convey values; and to help them develop capacity autonomy, responding to their rights to "an open future" in which, as adults, they can shape their own lives.[41] In the case of the Jehovah Witnesses, the teaching of values led to children's being exposed to negative public responses. Critics view religious training as restricting later freedom to choose, whereas sympathizers interpret it as laying a foundation for adult autonomy.

Further conflicts arise from responsibilities to more than one child. It seems clear, for example, that parents should not allow their children to undergo risky medical procedures that have no health benefit to them, but what if a procedure helps another child?[42] In 1979, the nine-month-old son of Mr. and Mrs. Altenback, living in Pennsylvania, was dying of Wiskott-Aldrich Syndrome, a rare blood disease curable only by a bone-marrow transplant.[43] The parents authorized a transplant from their other, two-year-old child. A more dramatic case occurred a decade later.[44] Abe and Mary Ayala were parents of a seventeen-year-old daughter suffering from leukemia. A bone-marrow transplant would give her a 70 percent chance of cure, but no suitable donor had been found. They decided to have another baby, hoping for a suitable bone-marrow match, and their hopes met with success. In 1991, their fourteen-month-old girl underwent the transplant of bone marrow into her nineteen-year-old sister. In my view, the parents in both these cases acted responsibly, because the procedure was only mildly painful and minimally risky. Nevertheless, such cases raise concerns about potential abuse. Suppose that parents pressure their children into similar donations for persons who are not family members?

Exploitation of Women

13. *Sexism.* Philanthropy is not a refuge from the sexism that pervades society. According to a recurring criticism by some feminists, traditional forms of philanthropy exploit women. I emphasize *some*: feminist perspectives are multiple and varied, and there is no consensus among feminists on

this issue. Most dramatic, in 1971 the National Organization of Women (NOW) called on women to stop providing unpaid social services, such as food, education, and health services.

To exploit is to use unfairly, in this case to use women unfairly to serve the interests of males. Exploitation takes many forms. It can be episodic or systemic, that is, expressed in social practices, institutions, and stereotypes.[45] It can be conscious or unconscious, and deliberate or unintentional. It can be nonconsenting or consenting, whereby exploited individuals agree to the exploitation.[46] While feminists have explored all these forms, they have devoted special attention to unconscious systemic exploitation in connection with philanthropy, in both deliberate and unintentional forms.

NOW contrasted two categories of voluntary service: "traditional, or service-oriented," and "political, or change-oriented." Service-oriented volunteering, NOW charged, is exploitive because it uses women's unpaid labor to provide welfare benefits which government (hence all citizens) should provide through taxation. By contrast, change-oriented political volunteering advances worthy causes which conservative governments cannot be expected to fund.

According to NOW, service-oriented volunteering harms women in a variety of ways when it is used to replace government funding. It adds to women's traditional economic disadvantages, given that volunteers are unpaid and use time that could be devoted to paid careers. It reinforces stereotypes of women as unpaid helpers in the home and community, and hence it encourages the traditional role differentiation based on that stereotype. Since it usually has low social status and little authority, it does not increase and may lower self-esteem, especially since positions of leadership in philanthropy have traditionally gone to men. Service volunteering reinforces the status quo and deflects women's energies away from challenging sexism through the political process. Finally, it mitigates rather than solves social problems, especially those harmful to women and children: voluntarism provides a chaotic "hit-or-miss, band-aid, and patchwork approach to solving massive and severe social ills which are a reflection of a social and economic system in need of an overhaul."[47]

Men, by contrast, benefit from a system that encourages women to feel fulfilled through family and low-prestige community service. Their competition at the workplace is reduced, and they benefit from stable families and communities. In addition, their greater monetary resources give them power, including dominance within philanthropy. Therefore, welfare-oriented volunteering should be shunned in favor of political-oriented activism.

NOW's critique of philanthropy has been beneficial in several respects. It added pressure on government to meet its responsibilities; it encouraged women to explore valuable new options; and it prompted significant improvements in service organizations that previously put men in authority and rel-egated women to menial tasks.[48] Nevertheless, the conclusion that all women should shun service volunteering is unwarranted, even in the eyes of feminists who agree with NOW's general criticisms.

Wendy Kaminer, for example, rejects NOW's equation of traditional with service-oriented philanthropy. Volunteering in a rape crisis center or a shelter for battered women is both service-oriented and nontraditional in ways that do not reinforce traditional sex stereotypes.[49] Ideally these services should be funded by government, but we should not disregard present needs while seeking eventual reform. The same is true for underfunded programs in such traditional service areas as medicine, care for the elderly, and food and hous-ing for the poor. Alleviating immediate problems is compatible with actively seeking change; indeed, people involved in service often have a stronger voice in the political process. Kaminer recommends integrating paid professional work with part-time volunteering, as male philanthropists have done.[50] She identifies a tendency in this direction, caused by the economic necessity for women to work in order to support themselves and their children, as well as by new career opportunities for women.

Herta Loeser, developing similar views, agrees with NOW that women have been exploited in philanthropy by political agendas that regard philan-thropy as a substitute for essential welfare programs.[51] Nevertheless, it is short-sighted to reject traditional forms of service. NOW's argument is anal-ogous to concluding that women should not become teachers or nurses be-cause in the past they have been exploited by low wages and little prestige in these careers. In both cases women do better to seek change by working within the system. As reform comes gradually, voluntary service will continue to offer women opportunities to enrich their lives, including women with careers. It also offers to women preparing for careers the chance to gain work experience. Loeser implies that volunteering as a primary vocation will in-creasingly become left to the past, as the legacy of such women as Clara Barton, Jane Addams, and Eleanor Roosevelt, or else be a "compromise" for wealthy women. In this connection, she makes a "plea for tolerance" by fem-inists toward middle-aged and older women who have been "molded" by sexist stereotypes.[52]

Loeser's talk of compromise, tolerance, and molding suggests that wo-men do not autonomously choose traditional roles and instead are condi-tioned into them. This suggestion is made explicit in feminist critiques of philanthropy which are even more radical than NOW's critique. Thus, Doris B. Gold contends that "from a feminist and/or progressive unionist point of view, voluntarism is clearly exploitative—in its implication that social justice for all classes can be achieved through the moral 'service' of some who are expendable, albeit out of [so-called] 'free choice.' "[53] According to Gold, society "manipulates" women's uncertainties, playing on their "conditioning to serve" and their general uncertainties about work. "Why do women volunteer? Powerful social disapproval, coupled with their own psychological conditioning of self-negation and ambivalent self-realization, compels women to regard themselves as marginal jobholders except in times of family crisis or poverty."[54] In this way, women are alienated from their own philanthropic activities, even when they do not consciously feel alienated.[55]

As many other feminists have also argued, social exploitation relies on a stereotype widely held by both men and women. According to the stereotype, women's "natural" dispositions and "appropriate" virtues are to be "moral, modest, attentive, intuitive, humble, gentle, patient, sensitive, perceptive, compassionate, self-sacrificing, tactful . . . religious, benevolent, instinctive, and mild.[56] Women "ought always to give the interests of others more weight" than their own.[57] More than men, they should display the virtues of charity and self-sacrifice.[58]

Gender molding guided by this stereotype begins early. From infancy on, girls are trained to put others' interests before their own, whereas boys are raised to assertively pursue their interests. The result is a "compassion trap" in which women are conditioned to be more sacrificing than men.[59] Cast as "the helping sex," women are perceived as ready-made for traditional service roles, whether in philanthropy or elsewhere. Then, by participating in those roles, women inadvertently reinforce the stereotype.

In response, feminist leaders have urged women to set themselves against this stereotype and the lopsided upbringing based on it. In the nineteenth century, Elizabeth Cady Stanton urged women to embrace the attitude that "self-development is a higher duty than self-sacrifice."[60] In the twentieth century, Simone de Beauvoir warned that "to identify Woman with Altruism is to guarantee to man absolute rights in her devotion."[61]

While I find these critiques incisive, I see a danger in overstating them in ways that deny women's capacity autonomy to choose freely. Isn't it possible to make an autonomous decision to adopt traditional roles centered in family and community service?

The answer turns on what is meant by "autonomous." Some definitions of autonomy stress independence, so that by definition to be family-dependent and service-oriented is not to be autonomous. There are good reasons, however, to reject definitions which place an unqualified emphasis on independence, definitions which are the basis of the male-dominated mode of life that is itself suspect. Accordingly, recent feminists have begun to develop new conceptions of autonomy which do not clash with the mutual dependency, or rather interdependency, involved in caring relationships.

My conception of autonomy is of the latter kind.[62] According to it, autonomy involves rights to pursue one's life without coercive interference and the competence to exercise those rights rationally. Then, within a framework of rights, the focus is on competency and skills, not on independence per se. Competence autonomy means exercising the skills of reflective decision making, self-control, and uncoerced identification with the desires one acts on. This conception leaves open the possibility that some individuals will exercise the requisite skills in choosing traditional roles of interdependency and service.

Dependency can mean different things. It may be economic (relying on another person's income), emotional (needing the affirmation of others for one's sense of self-worth), intellectual (being influenced by the views of others), and volitional (allowing others to influence one's choice of activities). Caring relationships often involve all these types of dependency, in healthy or unhealthy forms. With parents and children the dependence is one-sided, and with adults the dependence is mutual in varying degrees. In some traditional relationships, dependence (in all forms) becomes excessively lop-sided in favor of men. The woman is oppressed even though she consents to a form of servitude, or, in other cases, her competence autonomy has been too subverted by social conditioning to speak of free consent.

How are we to tell the difference between women who choose autonomously (in varying degrees) and women who are essentially conditioned into accepting traditional lifestyles? We study their lives—as individuals. If, for example, a woman espouses sexist stereotypes, or if her lifestyle reveals exceptional passivity, there are grounds for suspecting conditioning. If, instead, a woman has reflected on NOW's arguments and provides reasons for preferring a traditional lifestyle, there is a presumption of autonomous decision making. As we consider other relevant evidence, we do so without presuming that choices are conditioned simply because of their content—that traditional choices are wholly conditioned and nontraditional choices are liberated. After all, we are all conditioned to some extent, and that very conditioning can foster the capacities and skills that make autonomy possible.

According to Kaminer's extensive interviews with women, voluntary service is rarely the product of mindless passivity, though occasionally it is. For example, Kaminer interviewed Martha Standish, a sixty-five-year-old woman who for two decades volunteered in a natural history museum. Standish began volunteering because "it was either that or staying home and doing housework . . . or doing something along the social line . . . bridge clubs, that sort of thing."[63] She described her work as "mostly routine idiot work" which was "just a way of filling time that was a little more interesting than playing bridge."[64] For Standish, volunteering seems to have reinforced passivity, fear of change, an unwillingness to think seriously about the roles of women, and a failure to value her own self-development. There was no autonomous reflection in entering into or maintaining her volunteer role.

Women are often pressured into voluntary service by their family, especially their husbands. In a study of volunteer civic leaders, Arlene Kaplan Daniels reports women's feeling pressured to move into prominent leadership roles for the sake of promoting their husbands' careers. A physician's wife, for example, said, "I loathed being president of the auxiliary; but I was a doctor's wife. I did it for my husband, of course."[65] Another woman commented, "My husband wanted me to be in volunteering. He felt it accrued to his prestige to have me [be] president of the Junior League."[66]

When such pressures become intense, they pose obstacles to women's autonomy. Nonetheless, the studies by Kaminer and Daniels suggest that most women make thoughtful responses to family and social pressures. While they may be uninformed about some wider ramifications of volunteering—how it may indirectly maintain the status quo among economic classes—they are not mere pawns of their husbands. The majority of the civic leaders, according to Daniels' study, feel called upon to engage in philanthropy from gratitude and a sense of *noblesse oblige*, together with a view of service as a form of self-expression.[67]

To sum up, philanthropy is not immune to sexism, giving women additional reasons for caution when engaging in voluntary service, but it does not follow that traditional forms of service should be avoided. We need to find ways to overthrow sexist stereotypes while respecting both traditional and new forms of voluntary service.

Incentives to Give

Incentives for philanthropy are personal benefits, other than altruistic satisfactions, offered as motives for giving. Usually the benefit is directly for one's own good, such as stipends for volunteers, tax deductions for charitable contributions, prizes in charity raffles, extra academic credit for community service, recognition in entrance decisions for college applicants, or a scholarship (that one funded) named in one's honor. Occasionally the benefit is a good for one's family, such as having a building named for one's parents, or receiving a credit toward blood free for one's relatives in return for making a blood donation.

Incentives seem innocent enough, and most are. They are even desirable when they encourage worthwhile giving. Some incentives, however, raise issues concerning respect for persons, for example, marketplace incentives that threaten philanthropic ideals, incentives within coercive contexts, and incentives which function as penalties.

14. *Erosion of Philanthropic Ideals.* The marketplace has increasingly influenced voluntary service. It has become acceptable, for example, to recruit

volunteers by advertising economic benefits, such as work experience that can be listed on resumes, prospects for business contacts, and economic "perks" for volunteers. Another example is widespread corporate experimentation with "cause-related marketing" in which consumers are promised that a percentage of the purchase price on products will be given to charities.

Certain marketplace influences raise concerns about the erosion of philanthropic and humanitarian ideals, as with the following examples from medical philanthropy: giving blood and organs, volunteering in medical experiments, and surrogate motherhood for people outside one's circle of family and friends. The concern is that putting a price tag on the body degrades persons, whereas voluntary service avoids the problem. I will argue that sometimes the objection is valid and sometimes not.

(i) In the United States, blood donation began as a philanthropic practice and later become increasingly commercialized. Richard M. Titmuss argues that commercialization "represses the expression of altruism, erodes the sense of community."[68] Voluntary blood-donor systems, by contrast, "represent one practical and concrete demonstration of fellowship relationships institutionally based in Britain in the National Health Service and the National Blood Transfusion Service. It is one example of how such relationships between free and equal individuals may be facilitated and encouraged by certain instruments of social policy."[69]

Specifically, Titmuss suggests that commercialization of blood violates the right to give blood voluntarily: "private market systems in the United States and other countries . . . deprive men of their freedom to choose to give [voluntarily] or not to give."[70] Taken literally, this remark is false. Freedom to donate blood voluntarily is violated only when one is required to receive payment, not when payment is one option among others. Titmuss' main point, however, concerns symbolism. England's purely voluntary system bestows on a blood donation a clear public meaning as "the gift of life." America's partly voluntary and partly commercial system blurs that symbolism as blood becomes a commodity to be bought and sold.

This argument is forceful, but not fully convincing. The value of symbols needs to be weighed against other goods, such as assuring an adequate blood supply and recognizing economic freedom to sell marketable items. Moreover, partial commercialization may increase understanding that blood is an economically valuable gift, as well as a lifesaving one. Even donated blood has a market value; the Red Cross sells much of it to hospitals. And if putting a price tag on a life-giving substance is a step toward treating persons as commodities, it is at most a small step.[71]

Titmuss' arguments are more persuasive when used to prevent healthy individuals from selling body parts, such as kidneys or corneas. A healthy person can live with one kidney, and see with one eye, and if you can save the life of someone you care for by donating a kidney, your act may be both permissible and admirable. However, we should not allow healthy people to sell a kidney to strangers for profit.

Why? One reason concerns risks and actual harm. Loss of organs does impose risks, unlike blood donation. With kidneys there is the increased risk in losing renal functions if the one remaining kidney is damaged. With some organs, such as corneas, transplants destroy important body functions. Another reason concerns symbolic meaning. Allowing healthy individuals to sell organs would encourage people to use their bodies as money-making devices. Of course, in a way, so does dangerous work, such as jobs in coal mines and chemical plants. Yet there is a difference between meaningful work that requires undergoing risks and procedures which treat health and bodily integrity as a commodity to be bought and sold. Admittedly the difference is a matter of degree, but it is important to draw lines here.

(ii) Medical experimentation raises similar issues. Consider the testing of new drugs (though we could also consider new forms of surgery and other therapies). In order to gain approval by the Food and Drug Administration, all drugs must be tested on healthy individuals to identify safe dosages and undesirable side effects. Ideally the subjects in these experiments voluntarily undergo risks on behalf of humanitarian goals. In reality, fees must be offered as incentives to attract a sufficient number of volunteers.

Is this practice degrading? It does seem to put a price on human health, or more precisely, on the use of one's body for the purpose of putting it at risk to gain knowledge. Thus, Marx Wartofsky compares paying incentives to volunteers in risky experiments to prostitution. Putting a price on sexual intercourse robs it of the dignity and love it expresses when engaged in voluntarily. In prostitution, "just as in participation in experimentation for money, what is being bought and sold is something which is taken to be so intimate to one's person, that there is something disturbing in the notion that it is alienable, as a commodity."[72]

Wartofsky is not objecting to voluntarily taking health risks in medical experiments. His point is that medical volunteering should be a free act of self-sacrifice to help others. It is dehumanizing only when it becomes saleable, as a commodity with a price. Wartofsky admits that paid volunteers are at present necessary, since not enough unpaid donors are willing to take the risks essential for valuable research, but he hopes that public education about the need for volunteers will end the practice of paying volunteers.[73]

Like Titmuss, Wartofsky overstates the problem. Let us distinguish between incentives and inducements. Incentives are usually intended to provide motives that supplement altruism, whereas inducements are intended to provide sufficient motives for engaging in activities. Wages are inducements, and paying a wage to medical subjects means they are not engaged in philanthropy. By contrast, compensation for costs (for example, travel) and inconvenience is an incentive which provides a supplemental motive for volunteering. Moreover, there is a rationale for the practice of paying incentives, even though a few individuals may regard the intended incentives as inducements.

We can also distinguish between inducements and awards which are intended as recognition for service and which for some individuals also serve as incentives. Peace Corps volunteers receive several thousand dollars at the end of their service. The money is intended as an award, that is, as recognition for service achievements, although it also helps individuals readjust to life outside the Peace Corps. Medical and other volunteers more often receive other kinds of rewards in the form of certificates, plaques, or publication of their names.

The goal is to attract volunteers willing to take health risks primarily because of moral and medical interests, such as a desire to help others, intellectual interest and curiosity, or a desire to gain experience in test techniques. To meet this goal, monetary compensation and awards should be kept low, well below minimum wage, to prevent them from becoming inducements. This generates a dilemma. Economically disadvantaged people form a large percentage of subjects because they are desperate. By keeping compensation low, with the purpose of attracting certain kinds of volunteers, don't we just exploit them further? As Wartofsky argued, the only adequate solution is to provide jobs or adequate welfare programs for the poor. Here again, a difficulty for philanthropy can only be removed by solving wider social problems.

(iii) A similar dilemma arises concerning surrogate mothers. Medical technology has spawned several possibilities, including artificial insemination and embryo transfer, such that a woman carries a baby to term and then gives it to someone who pays her a fee. Surrogacy raises a host of perplexities.[74] For example, who is the mother: the surrogate who gives birth to the baby, the supplier of the ovum, the woman married to the man who donates the sperm, the eventual adopter of the child? What are the psychological effects on the children brought into the world through surrogacy? And, turning to the issue of particular interest here, does surrogacy exploit women, especially where the surrogacy helps people beyond one's immediate circle of family and friends so as to qualify as philanthropy?

Typically, a surrogate mother is paid a fee of about $10,000, with hospital and legal costs also paid by the individuals seeking the baby. Should society allow this fee to rise to whatever the market will pay? Is keeping the price relatively low exploitive of disadvantaged women for whom this money represents a sizable income? Is the money an incentive which compensates the surrogate mother for her inconvenience and pain, or an inducement which essentially buys a baby and rents her body for nine months? If it is an inducement, surrogacy seems to violate the traditional ban on baby selling and buying—a ban grounded in attitudes about the sanctity of a human life and the integrity of families. Equally bad, it seems to put a price on a woman's reproductive capacities in a way that could easily be exploited in a society with a long history of sexism. Suggestions that legal contracts can solve the problem mistakenly presume that business arrangements can overthrow values surrounding parenthood and respect for women.

A simple solution would be to forbid all surrogacy arrangements, but that is too extreme. Infertile couples may have a profound and fully legitimate desire to be biological parents, and surrogacy can satisfy that desire. Certainly there are acceptable paradigms: for example, an altruistic woman voluntarily chooses to be a surrogate for her married sister, producing joy all around and a loving family for a newborn. But there are also disturbing prospects: for example, a wealthy and fertile couple pays a stranger to have their child in order to bypass the inconvenience and pain of childbearing, and then refuses the child when genetic abnormalities appear.

There is no easy solution to the surrogacy controversy. At stake are genuine moral dilemmas that will continue until we see some abatement of wider trends of depersonalization, sexism, and erosion of families. Once again, solving philanthropic issues is linked to solving wider social issues.

15. *Coercive Contexts.* Coercive contexts are defined by unusual degrees of behavior control affecting all areas of life. In particular, prisons control every aspect of inmates' lives. That makes prisoners ideal subjects in medical experiments: random variables can be controlled with relative ease, incentive costs are low, prisoners are available any time of day or night, and they provide a large pool of experimental subjects. Critics contend, however, that the prison environment systematically coerces in ways that preclude informed consent.

Informed consent is central to the ethics of human experimentation. The right of autonomy entails a right to decide what will happen to one's body and in particular the (avoidable) risks one undertakes. In turn, that implies a more specific right to decide whether to engage in risky experiments by giving informed consent (or refusal), which means choosing voluntarily on the basis of information needed to make a rational decision. Prisons pose substantial risks to voluntary consent. Always there is the hint, even when explicitly disavowed by officials, that participation will increase prospects of early parole. According to critics, that incentive is so compelling that it coerces individuals into taking unreasonable risks. Paying them to participate adds a further inducement that is coercive, given the absence of other opportunities to gain money.

I disagree. Punishment for crimes does not ban all opportunities for service, nor should it prohibit the same incentives offered outside prisons. Using prisoners as subjects calls for exceptional care in obtaining consent and avoiding abuses, but it does not automatically cancel voluntariness.[75]

To see this, let us distinguish between two types of medical experiments: therapeutic and nontherapeutic. Therapeutic experiments are used to test new drugs on patients who have a chance of having their health improved by them. Nontherapeutic experiments are performed on subjects who have no likelihood of medical improvement from the procedure. It would be inhumane and a violation of autonomy to deny prisoners the chance to participate in therapeutic experiments that might restore their health. But then the same conclusion should hold for nontherapeutic cases, since autonomy is at stake in both cases in the same way. This suggests that the real concern is not over whether informed consent is possible, but over how to secure the special safeguards needed to prevent abuse in the prison setting.

16. *Incentives as Penalties.* Incentives that seem to be positive benefits for voluntary service may actually function as coercive penalties. This concern has been raised with regard to recent proposals for a national service program. The proposals have come from both ends of the political spectrum. On the liberal side, Charles C. Moskos articulated the basis for the 1989 Nunn-McCurdy bill, which would offer "national-service vouchers" worth about $10,000 in return for volunteering in either military or civilian service at subsistent wages.[76] The vouchers could be used for college, job training, or housing. On the conservative side, William F. Buckley, Jr., defended an analogous program, although he preferred a guaranteed tax deduction for $10,000 after completing the service, rather than an outright cash payment.[77]

The proposals are not overtly coercive, as they would be if they mandated a period of service accompanied by penalties for noncompliance. In this respect they differ from William James' proposal for a mandatory period of service as the "moral equivalent of war." James thought that conscription would assure fairness between rich and poor (though he probably meant only young men, not women). Hardihood, self-discipline, and a sense of community could be fostered, he believed, by conscripting youths to civic service and a "war against nature," sending them "to coal and iron mines, to freight trains, to fishing fleets in December, to dishwashing, clothes-washing, and window-washing, to road-building and tunnel-making, to foundries and stoke-holes, and to the frames of skyscrapers."[78] Mandatory service like this, however, might provide more service than the country needs, displace workers who need jobs, and create a huge government bureaucracy. There is also a chance it might violate the prohibition of "involuntary servitude" stated in the Thirteenth Amendment to the Constitution.

Current plans for national service sidestep these problems by avoiding outright conscription. In addition, they have much to recommend them. They would provide an enormous number of currently needed social services for childcare, environmental conservation, education (teachers' aides, tutors), care for the elderly, criminal justice (police staff support, civilian patrols), book preservation in libraries, and so on. They would benefit volunteers, not just through the incentives provided, but by strengthening their sense of community and providing them with a tangible way to fulfill their civic responsibilities. They would strengthen a sense of social unity, balancing the many forces toward excessive self-seeking. Moreover, other educational plans may be worse.[79] For example, Ronald Reagan's presidency stimulated a move away from grants toward government loans. The result was a drop by about one-fifth in the percentage of college students from working-class families, not to mention the large default rate in paying back loans. Much can be said, then, for proposals of national service with strong incentives attached, assuming they prove sufficiently attractive to the public to be politically feasible.

At the same time, the proposals contain coercive elements. Funding for the programs would come from denying financial aid, both grants and loans, to college students who do not volunteer. Given the importance of college education, this amounts to a form of coercion for students who could afford college only through the service program. Other penalties for nonparticipation are even more clearly coercive. Buckley recommends a long list of sanctions at the state level, including the denial of drivers' licenses to nonparticipants in the program.[80] Any such plan which essentially undermines the ability to function in modern society is coercive. That does not by itself mean the plans are unjustified, any more than coerced taxation is necessarily bad. If some of the programs are sufficiently valuable, and assuming students do not have rights to a free college education, coercion may be justified.

There is, however, a deeper objection to the proposals: they are unfair by being selectively coercive. Children of rich families would be able to opt out of the service, whereas poorer youths would feel pressured into volunteering in order to obtain a college education. This would make "the educational aspirations of the poor hostage to public service, while excusing the affluent."[81] The nonwealthy would be forced to postpone their college education, while the rich would retain the option of beginning it immediately. Government grants and loans for college were created in the first place to help give equal opportunities to less-advantaged students. If we believe in rights to equal opportunity, or if we simply find it desirable to integrate disadvantaged persons into society, we will view the so-called incentives for national service as camouflaged forms of coercion. Mandatory service bypasses this difficulty and would ensure fairness. Yet it is hoped that the voluntary plans can be formulated to allow students to engage in service during summer months or following college, so as not to be placed at unfair disadvantage.

The topic of incentives connects with wider issues about motives for philanthropy. I have been assuming, for example, that mixing altruism and self-interest is unobjectionable. It is time to examine that assumption.

5

Mixed Motives

The structure [of human feeling] must consist of a number of motives which
are genuinely distinct and autonomous, but which are adapted to fit together,
in the normal maturing of the individual, into a life that can satisfy . . .
as a whole.

—Mary Midgley

No man [or woman] does anything from a single motive.

—Samuel Taylor Coleridge

CARING RELATIONSHIPS IMPLY altruism, but altruism is not the only reason for entering into them. Regard for our own well-being is an additional potent stimulus. Philanthropic giving usually springs from a
combination of altruism (caring for others for their sake) and self-interest
(caring for one's own well-being). I refer to this type of multiple motives as
"mixed motives." Of course, self-interest and altruism have varying degrees of
motivational strength for particular individuals on different occasions. A motive is a desire—often embedded in an emotion, attitude, or commitment—
together with beliefs about how to satisfy the desire. It is a reason an agent
acts on, whether or not it is a sufficiently good reason to justify the act.

The thesis that virtually all philanthropy springs from mixed motives
raises four objections. *Consequentialists* insist that results are all that matter
in philanthropy, and as a result they tend to downplay the interest in philanthropists' motives. *Psychological egoists* deny altruism and assert that all motives are variations of self-seeking; hence, there are no mixed motives. *Cynics*
insist that people are essentially selfish; even if altruism is possible, it is too
rare to be important. *Purists* find mixed motives objectionable on the
grounds that philanthropy ought to be purely altruistic. In response to these
objections, I will argue that mixed motives for philanthropy are not only
ubiquitous but also usually acceptable and even desirable.

Diverse Motives in Unified Lives

Why do people engage in philanthropy? The inspirational and advocacy
literature accents altruism as the key motive. Gordon Manser and Rosemary

Higgins Cass, for example, praise voluntary service in glowing terms as "the unfolding of humanity's highest and noblest impulses":[1]

> The enlivening principle which has kindled efforts at social reform has been the Judeo-Christian concept of love of one's neighbor. Without it social reform is stunted and cut off at its roots, having only self-interest as its motivating force. . . . The idea of one common humanity, of the basic dignity and worth of all persons without exception, has been the inspiration for countless legions to give of themselves in service to others.[2]

Manser and Cass acknowledge that occasionally philanthropy is engaged in for personal gain, but they dismiss such anomalies as violating the spirit of "true philanthropy." They present us with a dichotomy between altruism, which is typical and appropriate, and self-seeking, which is atypical and inappropriate. Is this dichotomy sound?

Identifying the motives for voluntary service is a scientific task rather than a topic for speculation. Early studies in the social sciences provided support for the inspirational model, but only because a flawed methodology was employed.[3] Investigators simply asked philanthropists why they donated their time or money. Not surprisingly, the answers emphasized benevolence. After all, we like to think of ourselves as kind and compassionate, and it is especially flattering to interpret our giving as generous and noble. In addition, we want to appear admirable to investigators who come to us wrapped in the mantle of scientific authority. We might even assume that investigators are interested in hearing about human decency, and hence we unconsciously emphasize that aspect of our giving. Moreover, both investigators and subjects are influenced by conventional beliefs that giving is good, thereby creating a further presumption concerning the motives under investigation. Clearly, the reasons we offer for our actions, even when sincerely stated, are not always those which actually prompt us to act. The absence of self-knowledge is commonplace, unconscious motives are familiar, and there is a natural tendency to exaggerate our altruism.

More rigorous scientific studies of philanthropists during the past two decades sound a different note (or chord) than the inspirational model. They suggest that mixed motives are the rule rather than the exception.

Jon Van Til found that twenty studies of volunteers and donors published over a twelve-year period in the *Journal of Voluntary Action Research* consistently revealed that "motivational multiplicity is the usual pattern among volunteers."[4] Altruistic desires are certainly important, but so are desires for personal benefits: self-expression, developing talents, gaining work skills, and having rewarding associations with other people. Here are four sample studies.

In a study of bottle and can recyclers, the vast majority of research subjects claimed to be recycling for the sake of the environment, hence implicitly to help people maintain a livable environment.[5] It was discovered, however, that many of these subjects engaged in recycling only once or a few times when given the incentive of gaining a small cash return. This does not mean they cared only about the money, which they might have earned more easily in other ways. But it does suggest that usually an element of self-interest was mixed with altruism.

A second study of volunteers engaged in low-complexity activities found that "in order to be satisfied, a volunteer needs, above all, a task in which self-expression is possible—a task which gives the volunteer the opportunity to develop abilities and skills, a task which is seen as a challenge, a task where achievements can be seen."[6] This study reinforced the testimony of volunteer coordinators: altruism is not enough to keep most people licking stamps, stuffing envelopes, xeroxing, and doing other menial tasks over a long period of time. At some point, personal challenge is needed to sustain interest and commitment.

A third study, of women volunteers in a range of settings, concluded that "altruism and self-actualization were about equally important motivators" for groups as a whole.[7] The study showed that both played some role for most individuals, though in different combinations. About three-fifths of the women studied engaged in volunteer work as a supplement to their careers. In their case, three desires were equally represented: to serve the community, to associate in rewarding ways with others, and to grow in personally satisfying ways. The other women used volunteering as their primary work activity or to prepare for a new career, and in their case mixed motives were also found in various combinations.

A fourth study, of Canadian social service volunteers, found that while "the humanitarian motive—to help others—and the desire to feel useful and needed quite consistently outweigh other reasons," self-fulfillment and personal development were also very important.[8] The investigators added, "It is likely that altruistic concerns and the desire to obtain self-fulfillment are closely interrelated motivators and find congruency through the Judeo-Christian Ethics (which equates 'righteousness' with good works)."[9]

These few studies cannot prove generalizations about mixed motives, especially since some of them focused more on the motives present in groups, rather than precisely delineating the configurations of mixed motives in individuals. Nevertheless, the studies raise an interesting question: Do philanthropists ever act solely from altruism, without any admixture of self-interest? I suspect they occasionally do, though far less often than we are inclined to believe. However, I want to consider the possibility that no one ever acts ✓ from pure altruism without any admixture of self-concern.

This possibility is asserted by David Horton Smith, a sociologist who has conducted numerous studies of volunteers. He defines altruism as finding satisfaction directly from satisfying other people, rather than from expecting some further benefit in return. Based on his own studies and a review of the literature, he concludes that "there is literally no evidence to justify a belief in some 'absolute' form of human altruism, in which the motivation for an action is utterly without some form of selfishness."[10]

In stating this conclusion, Smith confuses self-interest with selfishness. In its most common usage, "selfishness" is a pejorative term which means immoral self-seeking. It implies disregard of others and inappropriately or excessively seeking personal advantages at their expense. As a scientist, Smith does not intend to make a value judgment. Instead, he is claiming that human acts are always promoted in part by self-interest, that is, desires for things perceived as good for oneself in some respect. (In related senses, "self-interest" refers to one's overall good, to the desire for that good, or to desires for things that promote that good.) Most self-interested motives are permissible or desirable. For example, it is good to be prompted by self-interest to brush one's teeth, eat healthy food, and earn money to support oneself. Selfishness occurs when I steal your toothbrush and food or prefer dependency over working for a living.

With this clarification in mind, let us return to Smith's conclusion. He is not denying there are altruistic motives for philanthropy, but he is claiming that altruism intermingles with elements of self-concern. Is there anything surprising in this claim?

We have mixed motives for other interpersonal activities such as work, conversation, interactions with family, spending time with friends, making love. Multiple desires, emotions, commitments, and interests stir within us at any moment and seek expression. Many of them, such as desires for self-esteem, for moral decency, for fun and sexual pleasure, are expressed across an array of daily activities for which we have other motives as well. If we are to act effectively in satisfying such diverse interests, our motives must tend to converge.

Social, personal, and biological pressures systematically favor integrating motives in order to express several in tandem. Society molds us into consistent and constructive patterns of conduct. Personal ambition in seeking all major goals requires self-discipline to restrain and redirect desires. Sometimes the integration requires effort, but more often it is automatic. Indeed, biology has provided us with a complicated motivational structure which had to evolve in the direction of integration in order for us to survive. Human nature is structured by "a number of motives which are genuinely distinct and autonomous, but which are adapted to fit together, in the normal maturing of the individual, into a life that can satisfy" the individual as a whole.[11]

In addition to providing coherence, the networking of motives yields power. Freud made us familiar with sublimation in which psychological energy is transferred and rerouted from one motive to another. We are equally familiar with how commitment to an activity is reinforced by having multiple reasons for it. Shifting to a value judgment, it is often desirable that self-interest supports altruism in philanthropy. Vulnerable to discouragement and burnout, volunteers do well to combine their altruistic desires with a sense that their own good is interwoven with helping others. Here as elsewhere, self-interest is too powerful a motive not to be harnessed for moral ends.

The constant interweaving of motives is easy to overlook because motives are embedded in gestalt configurations. At any moment, some reasons are in the foreground of attention and others in the background. For example, a student regularly attends class. Why? On a given day, the foreground motive might be enjoyment of the subject matter or wanting to see a friend. Background motives, which are acted on without thinking of them, concern how the class fits into her wider plans: the desire for a good grade, both for itself and for its contribution to getting her degree, which in turn will help entrance into graduate school, which will lead to an advanced degree, making possible a challenging career, a comfortable living, and the ability to help others through a profession. Like waves, these motives reinforce each other, and their entire pattern would need to be sorted out in order fully to explain the structure of the student's motives in going to class.

The gestalt metaphor reminds us that complexes of motives can be viewed in different ways. Other observers might see as prominent what we see as secondary, both in terms of motivational force and the value of motives. In addition to shifts in perspective, the potency of motives in the gestalt pattern itself shifts. Of a half-dozen overlapping motives the student might have for attending class, any one may be prominent on a given day. The same is true regarding patterns of voluntary service and individual acts of giving. Usually present is a shifting mixture of altruistic and self-interested motives that function in tandem and with varying degrees of motivational strength and significance.

Consider Marti Stevens, the founder and director of the Cornville Players, an amateur theater group in a small town in Maine. After ending a brief career in the theater in New York, Stevens moved to Maine intending to pursue a new career as a teacher. A serious automobile accident modified her plans, but she was able to begin tutoring people in addition to holding a half-dozen other part-time jobs. Two years later a local elementary school principal learned of her background in theater and asked her to direct a school play. Thus began a series of volunteer activities which eventually led her to found the Cornville Players.

What were her motives for volunteering? Not the love of children, whom she claims (not without hyperbole) to loathe. Caring about her neighborhood was one motive. She felt gratitude and a desire to reciprocate: "I thought, hey, you're in a community . . . you owe them something, they've been okay to you. They haven't hustled you out. . . . I was treated well; suspiciously, but well. You owe something."[12] In part, she sought further acceptance from the community, and in part she needed to enrich her life: "I felt a dissatisfaction that I couldn't identify. I wasn't sure where I was going. I was teaching . . . and very happy with that, but there was still part of my life that was empty."[13]

Later, as she began directing plays on a regular basis for adult and teenage actors in the community, her volunteering was supported by further mixed motives: delight in training people to act, love of directing, and appreciation from the community. She also made community contacts which indirectly led to work: "I've gotten jobs out of this, because I've given somebody a part in a play."[14] The more involved she became in the community, and the more her well-being became tied to the well-being of the community, the more impossible it becomes to pry apart her motives into categories of self-concern and concern for others.

Results and Reasons

So long as volunteers such as Marti Stevens contribute to their communities, does it really matter what ultimately motivates them? In fact, if motives are inextricably mixed, and hence their precise configurations are unknowable, why be concerned with them? Aren't results all that matter, not reasons?

According to consequentialist ethical theories, morality begins and ends with good results. Right action is a matter of maximizing good consequences, and people should be judged by their deeds, not by their desires. Consequentialism has a pragmatic, hard-headed ring to it. It urges us to stop worrying about motives in order to get on with the urgent task of helping, and to remember that philanthropy is a response to the world rather than an exercise in character building. Starving people need food, not friendly feelings; cultural endeavors need support, not splendid intentions. In a world crushed by poverty and violence, where communities are fragile and excellence difficult to achieve, philanthropy should focus on effective helping. Preoccupation with motives leads to self-absorption and deflects us from the task of making the world better.[15]

These points are well taken, but they neglect much that is valuable in philanthropic giving. Motives do matter. They shape the spirit in which we give, thereby affecting the kind of people we are, the kind of relationships we have, the significance of our lives for others, and indeed the results of our actions.

To begin with, motives are central to character. Our interests include moral interests to care for others for their sake—that is an important feature of the kinds of persons we are.[16] Admittedly, the final measure of caring is the willingness to act on behalf of others, but caring as an attitude is not reducible to actions. It implies desires, emotions, sensitivity, and reasons for acting.

Not surprisingly, a concern for knowing one's motives permeates philanthropists' autobiographies. For example, Armand Hammer, the Occidental oil magnate, portrayed himself as wanting to help others even more than wanting money and influence. He begins his memoirs by recalling his childhood prayer and how it remained a theme throughout his life:

> I asked God, then, that I might be given the strength to help deserving people as much as I was able. . . . If my main motive had been to make myself rich, I could have been numbered among the multi-billionaires of the world. I am not. All my life I have given away a large part of my fortune, more money than I could count. . . . My childhood creed has always been my guide.[17]

Hammer gave many tens of millions of dollars to innumerable causes. One priority was the promotion of world peace, especially through building ties between America and the U.S.S.R. He promoted business with the Soviets, funded peace conferences, encouraged summit meetings, negotiated diplomatic ties, and financed emergency medical aid for the nuclear disaster at Chernobyl. Another priority was finding a cure for cancer. His major gifts included many direct gifts to cancer researchers and a five-million-dollar gift to Columbia University's research center. He also served as chairman of the president's cancer panel. A further priority was promoting the arts, again through major gifts and by serving on the board of trustees of the Los Angeles County Museum of Art. In all these areas his autobiography makes the case for admiring him as extraordinarily generous, peace-loving, and visionary.

Hammer's critics portray him differently. They see him as "domineering, shrewd, egotistical, selfish, scheming."[18] They point to his use of tens of millions of corporate dollars for projects that brought more recognition to him than to Occidental. For example, he spent $100 million corporate dollars to create the Armand Hammer Museum of Art and Cultural Center to house his collection of art. The collection, which most critics judged as too mediocre to warrant a separate museum, had been publicly promised for seventeen years to the Los Angeles County Museum of Art. Hammer peevishly broke his pledge when he could not secure a guarantee for a separate wing of the museum to bear only his name, rather than to include the name of one other donor. In addition to the concern for prestige and his place in history shown in his large gifts, critics point to his $54,000 illegal donation to Richard Nixon's campaign and the subsequent use of his influence to win a presidential pardon following his conviction.

No doubt the truth lies somewhere between Hammer's rosy self-portrait and his critics' denigration. Few philanthropists have a perfectly lucid grasp of their motives, but observers can be just as blinkered in their judgments. It is a treacherous enterprise to delineate precisely what prompted a particular gift or patterns of giving, itemizing and weighing elements of altruism, business benefits, power motives, and concern for reputation. But it is an enterprise in which we are legitimately interested insofar as we want our character fairly assessed by ourselves and others.

Furthermore, motives shape relationships. The caring relationships created and sustained through philanthropy are defined in part by motives—by caring for others for their sake, rather than acting solely from ulterior motives of self-seeking. Self-interested motives may be present, but they are not enough to create caring relationships. If I contribute to United Way solely to please my employer and gain a pay raise, I am not entering into caring relationships with the people my money helps.

We degrade philanthropists, whether ourselves or others, when we view them as mere resources for other people. We degrade recipients when we assume they are uncaring and ungrateful toward people who help them. Insofar as we construe philanthropy as an impersonal transaction, rather than as an expression of caring, we fail to appreciate its moral importance.

Our motives also matter to others. In particular, the motives of givers matter to recipients. Lawrence A. Blum offers the example of giving support to farmworkers who are striking against fruit growers because of low pay and poor working conditions. The support might mean participating in pickets and sympathy strikes, boycotting growers' products, or sending money and food. These actions help to put pressure on growers and also contribute to a political climate favorable to the farmworkers. In addition to prompting these actions, however, motives have further importance:

> At least some of the striking workers will value and appreciate the support, not only for this concrete assistance, but also for the human sympathy which they take it to express. For it shows that other citizens, unknown to them personally and remote from their situation, support them and their cause, agree with their position in the dispute, care enough to give something of themselves even though they themselves do not (typically) benefit, etc.[19]

Technically it is the motives-as-perceived (by the farmworkers) that have this effect, but perceptions and reality are not entirely disconnected. The actual motives both lead to the acts of support and influence how the farmworkers perceive that support. Moreover, recipients want accurate perceptions of why people help them because they value caring and resent pity and contempt.

Caring relationships are sustained by altruism, but altruism need not be the sole motive. In fact, altruism and self-interest become increasingly interwoven as caring relationships deepen. Intimate love relationships are defined by shared conceptions of self-interest, such that one individual's good includes actively supporting the beloved's good. Maintaining the caring relationship is central to the well-being of the participants because it focuses and adds meaning to everything else.[20]

Similarly, caring philanthropists join their lives with others in ways that expand self-interest. When volunteering creates close working relationships, as with Marti Stevens and her theater group, friendships emerge from the networks of caring relationships linking the interests of participants and beneficiaries. When giving is to strangers, caring relationships express the conviction that our well-being is tied to the well-being of other members of communities we participate in, including the world community. Rather than viewing philanthropy as hurting us by wasting our resources, we see it as a personal expression that enriches us. We give for *us*, for the recipient *and* ourselves, rather than just for them.

Both philanthropists and their beneficiaries want altruism to play a prominent role, even when it is mixed with self-interest, but prominent in what sense?

Consider several types of mixed motives.[21] (1) Sufficient altruism: Altruism is enough by itself to motivate giving, with self-interest serving as a supplementary motive. (2) Sufficient self-interest: Self-interest is enough to motivate philanthropy, with altruism as supplementary. (3) Doubly sufficient motives: Altruism and self-interest are each by themselves sufficient to motivate giving. (4) Jointly sufficient motives: Altruism and self-interest combine to motivate the giving, though neither by itself would suffice to prompt giving. As a special case of the last type, (5) Substantial altruism: Altruism is present in a significant degree. The substantial altruism is primary when it is present in a higher degree than the self-interest.

As a simple illustration, consider a woman who makes a substantial year-end gift to her favorite charity from mixed motives: an altruistic desire to help people and a self-interested desire for a tax deduction. Five combinations are possible: (1) The desire to help sufficed to motivate the gift, with the desire for a tax deduction supportive. (2) The desire for a tax deduction sufficed to motivate the gift, with the altruistic desire supportive. (3) Each desire sufficed by itself to motivate the gift. (4) Together the two desires sufficed to motivate the gift, though neither by itself was sufficient. (5) The desire to help was present in a significant degree, perhaps a primary degree.

According to an ideal shared by many of us, it is desirable that altruism tend to be either a sufficient or a substantial motive for humanitarian giving, just as we want it to be a substantial motive for the good done within love relationships.[22] Our sense is that caring should be enough or at least primary in moving us to prevent starvation or to provide shelter for the homeless. Let us dub this the ideal of *moral authenticity*.

Usually we are content with something less for cultural giving, where the pursuit of excellence plays a more prominent role. That pursuit is driven by a concern for achievement, such as in the arts and humanities, which in turn is a mix of commitments to practices and the need for personal expression. Yet even there we find it desirable for altruism to be present as a significant contributing motive, at least if we are to morally esteem philanthropists.

Patterns are usually what matter in understanding a person's character, not the motive for every particular action. Similarly, in assessing philanthropists, what matters is that altruism be a significant motive for giving throughout a series of gifts, though not necessarily with respect to each act of service.

I began this section by saying that most consequentialists dismiss motives as unimportant. Most, but not all. Consequentialists can accommodate the importance of motives by modifying their theory in one of two ways. One way is to emphasize their usefulness, their instrumental value in producing other good results. We are incapable of doing the right thing unless we have the appropriate motives, and that means fostering altruism from childhood on. The other way is more interesting. According to consequentialists, right actions are those that produce the most good overall, but that view becomes concrete only when a theory of goodness is provided.[23] Classical utilitarians construed goodness as pleasure or happiness, but more recent utilitarians offer a pluralistic theory of goodness. They offer a list of inherently good things: (most) pleasures, happiness, wisdom, aesthetic appreciation, and so on. Adding altruism and the virtues to this list is one way to acknowledge the importance of motives.

These adjustments will seem ad hoc, however, from the point of view of virtue ethics. An adequate ethical theory, and certainly applied ethics, should give balanced attention to consequences and character. Motives, attitudes, and relationships are as important as good results in understanding the moral life.

Psychological Egoism

Psychological egoists deny that there are altruistic motives, that is, desires to promote the good of others for their sake, hence tacitly deny that there are mixed motives.[24] The name "psychological egoism" is apt: "psychological" because the theory attempts to describe motives and explain conduct; "egoism" because it portrays people as exclusively self-seeking. Thomas Hobbes, writing in the seventeenth century, put it this way: "Of the voluntary acts of every man, the object is *some good to himself*."[25] More precisely, people are always and only motivated by what they believe is a benefit for themselves in some respect. Benefits to oneself include one's pleasure, absence of pain, wealth, power, fame, good reputation, safety, freedom, self-development, and self-esteem.[26]

Until recently, nearly all social scientists accepted psychological egoism. Psychologists adopted it largely as a procedural assumption, designing experiments to identify which, not whether, self-interested motives determine conduct. Economists took for granted that producers and consumers only seek benefits for themselves as they satisfy their preferences in the marketplace. And sociobiologists, who explain social behavior in terms of genetic inheritance, have explained away altruism as a disguised form of self-seeking.

Psychological egoism should not be confused with cynicism, the view that all people are selfish or egotistical. "Selfish" is a pejorative term which refers to immoral self-seeking at the expense of others, and "egotistical" refers to objectionable forms of self-absorption, such as arrogance and narcissism. Psychological egoists attempt to describe motives, not criticize people as selfish. Their theory allows that only certain instances of self-seeking are selfish, for instance, stealing, cheating, and cruelty, while most instances are not.

Nor should psychological egoism be confused with the assertion of universal prudence: people always pursue their self-interest, that is, what is best for them in the long run, or at least what they believe is in their self-interest. That assertion is obviously false. As everyday experience testifies, and as Joseph Butler observed in the eighteenth century, people "daily, hourly sacrifice the greatest known interest, to fancy, inquisitiveness, love, or hatred, any vagrant inclination."[27] At times we do not even make an effort to be prudent. Because of laziness, carelessness, or stupidity, we fail to adopt a long-term view of what is good for us. Even when we know what is good for us, we are weak of will in using dangerous drugs, gambling excessively, overeating, or entering into degrading sexual relationships. Most of us care, not too much, but far too little about our own best interests.[28]

Psychological egoists are well aware of all this. Their claim is that people always pursue what they *think* is good for them *in some way*, not that they always discern and deeply care about their long-term good. Indeed, disturbed by human folly, psychological egoists frequently embrace *ethical egoism*: people ought always to maximize their long-term self-interest.[29] Ethical egoism is a claim about values, about what ought to motivate us, whereas psychological egoism is a theory about what actually does motivate us. The doc-

trines are different but complementary. If by nature we cared only for benefits to ourselves, then perhaps it would be sound advice to focus on our
long-term best interests in order to avoid the harm to ourselves and others
caused by imprudence. I will not discuss ethical egoism here, however, since
in rejecting the desirability of caring about others for their sake, it amounts
to a skeptical rejection of the moral values which provide the foundation for
this book.

Whereas ethical egoism rejects the desirability of altruism, of caring for
others for their sake, psychological egoism rejects the possibility of altruism.
Why would anyone accept such an alarming view? No doubt one reason is
simplicity. It reduces the vast multitude of human motives to one category.
But that is not an adequate reason: simple theories can be simplistic and
obfuscate more than they elucidate. On the surface, at least, psychological
egoism is indeed simplistic. It denies a fundamental, commonsense conviction
that we sometimes do care about other people for their sake, rather than
solely for some ulterior benefit for ourselves.

Consider a woman who makes a substantial contribution to alleviate
world hunger. Common sense tells us she might be motivated in part by
altruism, and the studies about mixed motives bear this out. How might the
psychological egoist argue against this possibility? I will consider five arguments, each of which is unsound but fruitful in that it leads us to draw
distinctions important for thinking about human motivation. The distinctions are simple but slippery. Like most philosophers, I believe that psychological egoism is appealing largely because these distinctions are not kept
clear.

Argument 1. We can always imagine a self-seeking motive for what initially appear to be altruistically motivated actions. For example, the world-
hunger donor might be motivated by external rewards, such as social
recognition (praise, awards, enhanced reputation) or religious gains (answers
to prayers, salvation and avoiding eternal punishment, believing that God
loves a cheerful giver).[30] She might also be motivated by internal rewards:
pleasure in helping, self-respect from living up to ideals, avoiding guilt in
seeing people suffer when she could help, or relieving the anguish caused by
seeing others suffer. If she thinks she is motivated by altruism, perhaps she
is deceiving herself, given an understandable desire to think well of herself
as being altruistic. Therefore, psychological egoism is true: people are motivated only by what they think is good for themselves in some respect.

—*Possible versus actual motives.* We can *imagine* a motive of self-seeking,
and perhaps she is deceiving herself—of course! No category of behavior is
immune to self-interest, so that only altruistic motives could produce it. Even
saving another person at the cost of one's own life may have self-interested

motives, such as posthumous glory or masochism. However, nothing follows from these abstract possibilities about what actually motivates people. Imagined motives may be only imaginary. With a little ingenuity we can also imagine an altruistic motive for almost any action, but that fancy hardly supports a belief in universal altruism.

Argument 2. Close scrutiny of acts of helping always turns up an element of self-concern. The world-hunger donor, for example, probably knew she would feel better about herself after she made the donation, given her value commitments. Even if the self-satisfaction was not conscious at the time, it was embedded as an expectation in the full motivational structure (gestalt) which led to her donation. Therefore, psychological egoism is true.

—One motive versus the only motive. I doubt that empirical scrutiny always turns up an element of self-concern, but suppose it does. That supposition would be consistent with the studies which reveal mixed motives as typical in philanthropy. However, it lends no support to psychological egoism. Saying that self-concern is one motive for each human act does not mean it is the only contributing motive. Between *one* motive and *only* motive lies ample room for elements of altruism, including those which are sufficient to motivate philanthropy.

Argument 3. People always act on their own desires. Even if the world-hunger donor has a desire to help other people, she still acts on her desire. Therefore, we only seek things good for ourselves, namely, the fulfillment of our own desires.

—My desire versus my desire for my good. Of course, we always act on our own desires; that is true by definition. Unlike muscle spasms, digestion, and other involuntary processes, actions are motivated by desires, together with beliefs about how to satisfy them. And by definition, my actions are always motivated by my desires. However, psychological egoism asserts something vastly different, something not entailed by mere definitions. It asserts that all our desires are for benefits for us only. Desires are distinguished according to their objects, according to what they are desires for. Self-seeking desires are for things beneficial to us in some respect; altruistic desires are for things beneficial to other people for their sake; and mixed motives are desires for things beneficial both to oneself and to others.[31] In each case the desire is one's own. The world-hunger donor acts on her desires, but that does not imply she desires only a benefit for herself.

Occasionally we do talk as if we acted without a desire, but that talk is more clearly expressed in ways that reveal the presence of a desire. We say, for example, "I didn't want to keep the promise (pay the debt, risk my life), but I had to because it was my responsibility." This means I was motivated, not by pleasure, but by a desire to meet an obligation. Again we say, "I acted

on whim, without any desire or motive whatsoever." But there was a desire—a spontaneous desire to break a boring routine (ditch a class), do something fun (go to the beach), try something different (buy a lottery ticket),
or be adventurous (ride a New York subway). Finally, the world-hunger
donor might say, "I acted to make someone else happy, to fulfill their desires,
not mine." This means she desired to give a benefit to someone other than
herself. In general, then: to act is to act on a desire; our actions are prompted
by our desires; desires differ according to what they are desires for, with
self-seeking desires aimed at benefits for oneself and altruistic desires aimed
at benefits for others. None of this implies psychological egoism.

Argument 4. People always and only seek satisfaction (pleasure, enjoyment), including the satisfaction of avoiding dissatisfaction (pain, suffering).
Even the world-hunger donor hoped to gain satisfaction from helping others.
Perhaps she also wanted to escape anguish or a guilty conscience from failing
to alleviate human suffering. Therefore, psychological egoism is true: people
seek only their own satisfactions.

—My satisfaction versus my satisfaction from obtaining my benefit. Suppose
we do always seek to gain satisfaction and to avoid dissatisfaction, immediately or in the long run. We still need to distinguish different sources of
satisfaction, just as we distinguished different objects of desires. Here are two
general sources, and there are others: (1) pleasure from obtaining a benefit
for oneself, and (2) pleasure in giving a benefit to someone else. The former
goes with self-seeking; the latter characterizes altruism. Altruistic acts bring
pleasure because we first have a desire to help others for their sake and then
act on that desire.

In particular, assume the world-hunger donor wants pleasure from giving, in addition to wanting to help other people. That is fully compatible
with altruism. In fact, one mark of altruists is their capacity to derive pleasure from helping and from seeing others prosper. Again, assume the donor
is in part motivated to lessen her own anguish in seeing others suffer and in
part to avoid feeling guilty for not helping. In healthy degrees (setting aside
neurotics), these emotions manifest altruism. The anguish derives from compassion, from being sympathetically moved by the suffering of others. The
guilt reveals a sense of responsibility to help, such that failing to help would
generate a painful sense of having wronged others.

—Finding versus seeking satisfaction. Even when we hope to gain satisfaction, we do not always aim explicitly at it. Most of the time we desire other
things: cars, homes, jobs, professional achievements, helping a friend or a
stranger. Satisfaction comes as these desires are fulfilled, as a consequence
rather than as a direct aim. There could be no satisfaction unless we first
had these desires. In fact, often our chances of finding satisfactions improve

as we forget about ourselves and our pleasures and become engrossed in activities and relationships (a theme important in the next chapter).

Argument 5. All desires arise from a combination of biology and environment, genetics and conditioning, nature plus nurture. These forces, operating amid a fierce struggle for survival, have led us to evolve as creatures who find pleasure in satisfying our desires. Therefore, we are caused to desire only what we perceive as satisfying our desires and as good for us.

—*Origins versus objects of desires.* This argument is a variation on the previous two arguments. Even if we are completely caused to seek the satisfactions we do, and of course that is open to challenge, it wouldn't follow that we find satisfaction only from obtaining benefits for ourselves. There is an additional flaw, however. The argument slides from a claim about the origin of desires to a claim about what the desires are for. We should be suspicious of any theory which purports to explain away altruistic desires. Scientific theories which purport to establish universal self-seeking are quickly forced (by the facts) to allow the possibility of altruistic motivation. Sociobiology is a notable example.

Sociobiology seeks biological explanations for social behavior. From the perspective of modern biology, with its foundation in Darwin's theory of evolution, there is a puzzle about why animals behave in ways that benefit others more than themselves. Ethology reveals numerous examples of helping behavior, such as caring for young, sharing food and shelter, and defending groups at great risks to oneself. On the surface, self-sacrificing behavior should lessen chances of survival, and hence over millions of years of evolution it should disappear. Yet it continues to be found in generation after generation of organisms. Why? What evolutionary purpose is served by helping behavior?

The standard answer is twofold: kinship selection and reciprocity. Animals, including humans, share genes with members of their kinship groups, both their immediate family and their wider circle of relatives. Helping behavior toward kinship members tends to increase the survival of the group which shares many of one's genes. Thus, kinship behavior tends to propagate one's genes. By contrast, reciprocity explains helping outside kinship groups, as well as adding a further explanation of helping within them. In the sense used by sociobiologists, reciprocity is a behavioral concept: I help you and you help me, and as a result we both increase our chances of surviving. As a result, animals willing to enter into reciprocity relationships have a better chance of having their genes propagated.

Nothing in all this entails psychological egoism. Sociobiology is a theory about the origins of helping behavior, about its emergence and propagation in terms of its evolutionary function. It is not a theory about motives. Unfortunately, sociobiologists have confused claims about the origins of behavior patterns and motives for specific acts, and as a result they have asserted psychological egoism for reasons unsupported by their own theory.[32] Especially in their popular writings, they write metaphorically about animals being determined by "selfish genes" which determine self-seeking behavior, and then talk as if those genes also generate self-seeking motives for helping behavior. Their theory about the origins of helping behavior slides surreptitiously into an assumption about motives.

For example, Edward O. Wilson, often called the father of sociobiology, distinguished two forms of alleged altruistic motives, and then reduced both to egoistic forms of behavior. The first form, hard-core altruism, refers to acts "unilaterally directed at [the good of] others" and represents "a set of responses relatively unaffected by social reward or punishment beyond childhood."[33] It operates primarily within kinship and tribal groups where there is "group narcissism as a form of compensation."[34] That is, when people act wholly for the good of others, they are motivated solely by rewards from the group, including self-centered gratifications based on identifying with the group. Surely, however, human gratifications from identifying with a family and community are not reducible to self-seeking. Interwoven with the self-seeking is caring about others—seeing their good as important, not only for our benefit, but in part because we value other people for their sake.

The second form of alleged altruism, soft-core altruism, consists in helping beyond the kin group. Wilson says it is completely "selfish," but he means self-interested or self-concerned. "The [alleged] 'altruist' expects reciprocation from society for himself or his closest relatives. His good behavior is calculating, often in a wholly conscious way, and his maneuvers are orchestrated by the excruciatingly intricate sanctions and demands of society."[35] This is a half-truth which at most accurately portrays some cases. Not all reciprocal helping is reducible, without remainder, to "calculating" self-interest.[36] Nor does Wilson's genetics of reciprocal behavior imply that it is.

Reciprocal behavior has many different motives. In particular, it can spring either from self-interest or from mixed motives. Here is a case of self-interested reciprocity: I help you because I seek reciprocal benefits for me sufficient to outweigh my inconvenience. By contrast, here is a case of mixed-motives reciprocity: I help you because I care about your well-being and also because I hope you will show reciprocal concern for me. Spouses, parents, and friends usually have mixed motives; they hope for and even expect reciprocal help and care, but that is not their sole motive.

Altruism can be a motive even when continued giving is conditional on reciprocity. In fact, altruism usually is conditional, with tacit conditions and expectations in the background. We care for one another genuinely and deeply, but if that care is spurned or never returned, despite ample opportunity for reciprocation, we have reason to limit or withdraw caring.

To sum up, psychological egoism looks less and less plausible as we attend to pertinent distinctions—possible versus actual motives, contributing versus sole motives, different objects of desires, different sources of satisfaction, finding versus seeking satisfactions, and origins versus objects of desires. Scientific theories of human motivation should take these distinctions into account at the outset. Theories such as sociobiology are insightful when they help explain the origins and survival value of helping behavior, but not when they try to explain away altruistic motives.

Nothing I have said minimizes the importance of self-seeking in human affairs, indeed its predominance. The distinctions noted above are compatible with what Gregory S. Kavka calls *predominant egoism*, a view he defines with five generalizations:[37] (1) Most people are capable of making sacrifices on behalf of others, though usually the sacrifices are small compared with the gains for others. (2) Only a small number of people are regularly more altruistic than self-interested. (3) Most people occasionally allow altruism to override self-interest. (4) When altruism overrides self-seeking, it is usually on behalf of a small number of people, such as friends, family, and groups to whom one feels a special devotion. (5) People tend to become more altruistic after they reach (what they believe to be) a secure level of well-being. Let us add a sixth generalization: People tend to continue in general patterns of conduct (as opposed to individual actions) only when the patterns are perceived as benefiting them in some respect.[38] Thus, when patterns of philanthropic involvements are perceived as either harmful to oneself or simply not satisfying, the odds are high that the patterns will be altered or discontinued.

These are sober, realistic claims. By acknowledging that self-concern is extensive but not exclusive, they leave room for mixed motives in philanthropy. Indeed, they suggest that patterns of helping will tend to be sustained insofar as we see our good connected with the good of others.

Cynicism

Cynicism is the attitude that people are in general selfish, including when they help others. It differs from psychological egoism in several ways. Cynicism is primarily a negative attitude toward human nature, whereas psychological egoism is a descriptive psychological theory. Cynics emphasize selfish, not merely self-seeking, motives. They view people as egotistical, cruel, hypocritical, and driven by hurtful motives in gaining power and self-elevation at the expense of others. By contrast, psychological egoists do not specify which self-seeking motives are most common, nor do they highlight harmful forms of self-seeking and downplay prospects for positive human interactions. Finally, cynicism is a matter of degree depending on how much selfishness is ascribed to human beings, whereas psychological egoism is an all-or-nothing assertion of universal self-seeking.

Cynicism generates an unmasking approach to philanthropy which uncovers hypocrisy and underscores such motives as vanity, self-aggrandizement, and snobbery. Extreme cynics dismiss the (so-called) virtues in giving as sentimental fluff and disguised forms of self-seeking. By contrast, such moderate cynics as La Rochefoucauld, Thoreau, Hawthorne, and Hobbes qualify and focus their criticisms historically, offering criticisms that contain insights, despite their one-sidedness.

François duc de La Rochefoucauld aimed his famous maxims at the superficialities of French aristocratic society during the seventeenth century. "What is called generosity," he wrote, "is most often just the vanity of giving, which we like more than what we give."[39] Again, "what passes for generosity is often merely ambition in disguise, scorning petty interests so as to make for greater."[40] Notice the caveats "most often" and "often" which prevent these barbs from becoming sheer hyperbole. Even today, in a world where philanthropists sometimes flaunt their wealth to gain praise or social prominence, La Rochefoucauld's maxims are forceful.

Mid-nineteenth-century American literature produced several stinging critiques of philanthropy which conceals corruption. Henry David Thoreau protested how philanthropy disguises cruelty and moral complacency. In *Walden* he wrote:

> There are a thousand hacking at the branches of evil to one who is striking at the root, and it may be that he who bestows the largest amount of time and money on the needy is doing the most by his mode of life to produce that misery which he strives in vain to relieve. It is the pious slave-breeder devoting the proceeds of every tenth slave to buy a Sunday's liberty for the rest.[41]

Thoreau acknowledged that philanthropy does some good, but he objected to the exaggerated claims made on its behalf. Citizens in Concord, Massachusetts, touted it as the primary forum for virtue, ranking the contributions of local philanthropists above those of Shakespeare and Newton. "I would not subtract any thing from the praise that is due to philanthropy," Thoreau wrote, "but merely demand justice for all who by their lives and works are a blessing to mankind."[42] He urged his peers to devote more attention to their own moral development rather than to be so eager to help others: "Do not stay to be an overseer of the poor; but endeavor to become one of the worthies of the world."[43] Given the historical context of his assault on parochialism and anti-intellectualism, Thoreau's epigrams are insightful, albeit one-sided.

Far more than Thoreau, Nathaniel Hawthorne sought to unmask corrupt motives. In *The House of the Seven Gables* he describes how Judge Pyncheon's vast philanthropic activities made him a paragon of virtue in the eyes of his community: "his devotedness to his party . . . his remarkable zeal as president of a Bible society; his unimpeachable integrity as treasurer of a widow's and orphan's fund; . . . his efforts in furtherance of the temperance cause . . . the smile of broad benevolence wherewith he made it a point to gladden the whole world."[44] But darker traits lay buried beneath this "sculptured and ornamented pile of ostentatious deeds."[45] Pyncheon's wealth came through causing the death of his uncle, allowing an innocent cousin to go to jail for the crime, and fraudulently acquiring the cousin's inheritance. Pyncheon then built his fortune through shady business dealings which exploited his neighbors.

Pyncheon is a hypocrite, someone who culpably pretends to be more virtuous than he really is—"culpably," because unlike an actor or a joker, his pretense constitutes dishonesty and generates unfairness. He is also a self-deceiver who evades nasty truths and uses rationalization to maintain a flattering self-image.[46] Self-deception about his faults compounds his wrongdoing, adding a second level of dishonesty in his reasoning.

Hypocritical and self-deceiving philanthropy may conceal attempts to domineer and exploit. In his most searing indictment of philanthropists, *The Blithedale Romance*, Hawthorne portrays Hollingsworth as an idealist obsessed with a plan to reform criminals through moral teaching. In order to obtain the funds for his ill-conceived project, he is willing to dominate and cheat his followers at a utopian commune (a fictional variation of Brook Farm, the experimental socialist commune in Massachusetts where Hawthorne lived for a while). Hollingsworth's fanaticism reveals how "godlike benevolence has been debased into an all-devouring egotism" that misuses philanthropy as a tactic for gaining power over other people.[47]

With or without hypocrisy, philanthropists sometimes exert power they already have in order to gain praise and to augment self-esteem. As Hobbes observed, "There can be no greater argument to a man, of his own power, than to find himself able not only to accomplish his own desires, but also to assist other men in theirs: and this is that conception wherein consisteth *charity*."[48] Inspired by Hobbes, one recent psychologist suggests that helping behavior "defines a *power hierarchy*; the donor is cast in the role of a powerful figure whereas the recipient is relegated to a position of low power. Helping allows the donor to demonstrate that he or she has useful abilities and resources and can influence the behavior of others."[49] This demonstration is intrinsically pleasing because it affirms one's power. Moreover, the affirmation is strengthened by giving within groups whose power and prestige reflect on its members.

Snobbery is another form of egotism in philanthropy. It has been defined as "arrogant pride in position, pretension to yet higher position, stiff hauteur to inferiors, supple abasement to superiors, obtuse fidelity to the vertical placings of the rank system."[50] Snobs reduce people's worth to their position on a scale of prestige based on authority, title, talent, beauty, social reputation, or any number of other things. Since money is the most common scale in contemporary American society, large giving becomes a forum for self-aggrandizement.

At their worst, snobs want others to be aware of their (alleged) superiority, frequently with the malicious motive to "make inequality hurt" by getting others to feel inferior.[51] Snobs are arrogant, whether in making unwarranted claims to superiority or in flaunting their genuine superiority in offensive ways, with disdain and condescension. Snobbish philanthropists view themselves as superior to their beneficiaries, to other philanthropists who give on a lesser scale, or to whomever they regard as their inferiors.

> I sit at my table *en grand seigneur,*
> And when I have done, throw a crust to the poor;
> Not only the pleasure itself of good living,
> But also the pleasure of now and then giving:
> > So pleasant it is to have money, heigh-ho!
> > So pleasant it is to have money.[52]

Enough said. I have pursued the case for cynicism because it contains some truth and because cynicism is more than an affliction of a few misanthropes; on occasion it is a temptation for most of us. Let us grant that vanity, ambition, power, self-aggrandizement, snobbery, and other selfish preoccupations are as common in philanthropy as anywhere else. Cynics, then, have some rationale for their attitudes, but it is not, on balance, an adequate rationale.

To begin with, cynics take an unduly pessimistic view of self-regarding motives for giving, let alone altruistic ones. Too quickly they move from identifying elements of self-interest to indicting for selfishness. Consider pride in giving. Certainly it can be an ugly self-elevation based on disdain for others, but more often it is admirable identification with family, community, or nation, as well as legitimate self-esteem for being able to help. We may not admire this identification and self-esteem, but nor should we object to them, especially when they come mixed with elements of altruism, as they usually do.

Again, philanthropists who seek power through giving are not necessarily selfish. Rather than manipulating people and violating rights, they may be seeking power in order to improve the world by exerting responsible influence based on others' voluntary consent. Power is morally neutral—everything depends on how and why it is used.

As one more illustration, consider the cynic's frequent dismissal of religious motives as mere selfishness. Of course, there is an element of self-interest in seeking rewards from God and desiring to avoid punishment. Yet many religious philanthropists are also inspired by other-centered religious motives: love for God, a desire to emulate God's goodness, obedience to moral authority, and the responsibilities commanded by God. Their faith reinforces altruism rather than replaces it with prudence.

Cynics' sweeping generalizations about motives are open to empirical challenge by studies that reveal mixed motives, rather than pure self-centeredness, as typical. The generalizations can also be challenged by commonsense observations which testify to human capacities for kindness and generosity. Cynics are aware of these challenges, but seem impermeable to them. They are predisposed to see selfishness, to attend selectively to the bad, to envision the worst possibilities.[53] Cynicism is a passion, rather than an opinion, whose causes and consequences need to be uncovered.[54] That is why cynicism is so difficult to overthrow by appealing to examples of decency and heroism.

Consider what Arland Williams did in January 1982. An Air Florida jet crashed, killing seventy-nine of the eighty-five people aboard, and throwing the few survivors into the freezing waters of the Potomac River. A rescue helicopter quickly arrived and lowered a rope to a group of survivors clinging to a fragment of the shattered aircraft. Arland Williams caught the rope and, rather than be pulled up, gave the rope to another person. He did so two more times, and possibly four times altogether (eye-witness accounts differ) before he sank into the icy waters.

Maybe Williams had a secret death wish; maybe he hated himself; maybe he sought the applause of witnesses; maybe he wanted posthumous glory, in heaven and on earth. A cynic will hypothesize a nasty underbelly to any behavior. But at some point thoroughgoing cynicism becomes preposterous, even pathological. From what we know of Williams, he acted from a concern to help others for their sake: "forty-six years old and a sedentary worker, [he] must have known that he was no better equipped than the others to endure the ordeal and that his chances of survival were slipping away fast. And he had a lot to live for; divorced some time earlier, he had recently fallen in love and become engaged."[55]

Cynicism can also become a convenient device for avoiding responsibility and excusing selfishness.[56] If everyone is essentially selfish, and philanthropy is just one more exercise in self-elevation, then why should I help others?

In *The Fall*, Albert Camus portrays an elaborate version of this excuse-making strategy. Jean-Baptiste Clamence, the protagonist, is disarmingly personable as he conducts his vocation of "judge-penitent." He unmasks his own sordid motives in order to hold a mirror up to others, prompting them to admit their failures. For example, he confesses to his companion that he was motivated by sheer vanity when, in his earlier career as a lawyer, he provided free services for the poor. At the time, he simply deceived himself into thinking he was noble and kind. This, and his other seemingly sincere confessions to his companion, serves as a ruse for "extending judgment to everybody in order to make it [his guilt] weigh less heavily on my own shoulders."[57] As a result, he escapes the serious self-criticism that could motivate greater moral responsibility: "I have accepted duplicity instead of being upset about it. On the contrary, I have settled into it and found there the comfort I was looking for throughout life."[58]

From a wider perspective, cynicism is only an extreme form of the refusal to acknowledge the goodness of other people. We hesitate to admit their goodness because it may imply admitting our failures. This insight was expressed by Harold M. Schulweis, who created a foundation to honor Christian rescuers of Jews during the Holocaust:

> Paradoxically, confronting goodness may be more painfully challenging than confronting evil. It is one thing to study and condemn the sadistic behavior of a Klaus Barbie but quite another to study and acknowledge . . . rescue behavior. . . . The latter presents us with a hard mirror. Would I rescue a pregnant woman, a hungry and homeless child, an aged, frightened couple—provide them with food and shelter, dispose of their refuse, and care for them in their sickness . . . ?[59]

Cynicism can also be tempting because of unrealistic expectations. Rather than acknowledge the presence of mixed motives in all caring relationships, we demand that philanthropy spring from unalloyed altruism, purified of all self-interest. Upon scenting the slightest whiff of self-interest, we debunk philanthropy as ignoble. Let us reflect further on this demand for pure altruism in philanthropy, a demand which is so easily transformed into disillusionment and cynicism.

Purity of Heart

Unlike cynics and psychological egoists, purists recognize that mixed motives are common in philanthropy, but they object to them. In their view, moral concern is tainted when it is mixed with self-seeking, such as seeking praise, reputation, power, economic benefits, or other external rewards. We should take pleasure in helping others, but the pleasure should be pure.

Occasionally, most of us have impulses to be purists, but I believe the impulses should be resisted.[60] Ideals of purity vary according to the criteria for appropriate motives, intentions, attitudes, and conduct. I will discuss three examples: Immanuel Kant's ideal conscientiousness, Søren Kierkegaard's ideal of devotion to goodness, and Jean-Paul Sartre's existentialist ideal of authenticity.

According to Kant's ideal of purity, a person with a "good will" chooses to act in accord with duty because it is duty, or more fully, because it constitutes respect for other rational beings. This good will has intrinsic moral worth, and all other motives are at most desirable as a means to dutiful conduct. In particular, acts of meeting the philanthropic duty of mutual aid have moral worth when they are met in a spirit of duty for duty's sake:

> To be kind where one can is duty, and there are, moreover, many persons so sympathetically constituted that without any motive of vanity or selfishness they find an inner satisfaction in spreading joy and rejoice in the contentment of others which they have made possible. But I say that however dutiful and amiable it may be, that kind of action has no true moral worth. It is on a level with [actions arising from] other inclinations, such as the inclination to honor, which, if fortunately directed to what in fact accords with duty and is generally useful and thus honorable, deserve praise and encouragement but no esteem.[61]

What a bizarre pronouncement! We can grant Kant's high estimation of conscientiousness in being motivated to do what is right because it is right, especially in the teeth of temptation. Yet surely we can also grant to altruism just as much "true moral worth."

Kathy Levin fits Kant's description of a person who finds "an inner satisfaction in spreading joy." She volunteers because she delights in helping. As a college student she felt the need to help the elderly, although she was unwilling to work the regimented hours required by hospitals: "The worst thing was that volunteers plug into institutions through this system, and volunteering should be a freedom, it should be a luxury. It should be a pleasure, and having to be joyful at the hour that they choose you should be joyful is a job."[62] Levin is motivated by benevolent inclinations, not by duty, and the inclinations are remarkable. They inspired her to find creative ways to serve the elderly in nursing homes without regimented hours and duties. She simply showed up during visiting hours to talk with patients. Quickly she became concerned about adults who failed to visit their parents in rest homes and who suffered guilt because of it. It occurred to her, "wouldn't it be fun to teach a group, a little group of kids, who could grow up to be fifty-year-olds who weren't so hung up."[63] She founded Magic Me, an organization which helps bring children and adolescents into caring relationships with senior citizens. The organization now has dozens of chapters throughout the United States and several other countries.

Interestingly, Levin expresses a Kantian yearning: "I'd like to be enriched by being able to be more dutiful. Because I have the freedom to go as I please, and to do what I please, I do! But there's a part of me that would like to be even more dutiful, community dutiful."[64] The yearning is understandable given the high risk of burnout in her form of volunteering. There are the demands of directing a major organization combined with the emotional demands of helping people in desperate need; people have died in her arms. We admire her precisely because of her spontaneous benevolence, and we understand her yearning for a stronger sense of duty as a further manifestation of that benevolence. Conscientiousness is admirable because it reveals respect for people; benevolence is another admirable virtue because it reveals direct caring for them.

If Kant's demand for purity unduly narrows the spectrum of admirable motives, so does the contrasting ideal of purity as benevolence or goodness, an ideal which often accompanies religious ideals. A strict dichotomy is established: serve God or mammon; you cannot do both.[65] Either "love the Lord your God with all your heart, and with all your soul, and with all your might" or corrupt that love with worldly cares.[66]

What does it mean to love God with all your heart? According to one interpretation, it means to forsake all other human aims in order to devote exclusive attention to God. That can be morally objectionable if it implies treating people as mere means to some further end (loving God), rather than caring about them for their sake. According to a more plausible interpretation, wholehearted love implies a paramount commitment to God, such that all other aims are subsumed and unified in that commitment. This interpretation captures the spirit of most world religions. It enjoins loving God by loving people for their sake.[67]

Kierkegaard's *Purity of Heart Is to Will One Thing* is a systematic presentation of this ideal. "For the Good without condition and without qualification, without preface and without compromise is, absolutely[,] the only thing that a man may and should will, and is only one thing."[68] By "the Good" Kierkegaard means God, including God's will, and by willing the Good he means unifying our lives through conforming to that benevolent will. Our long-term good is achieved through devotion to God, not through worldly goods.[69]

Kierkegaard's list of barriers to single-mindedness mostly derives from his other-worldliness.[70] One barrier is secular goods: the "press of busyness is like a charm" that continually deflects energies away from devotion to God and from helping others in a spirit of love, thereby fragmenting our lives.[71] Another barrier is fear of punishment: to "will the Good only out of fear of punishment" by God is to fail to take pleasure in doing what is right, and to will it out of fear of punishment through losing one's reputation enslaves one to the vagaries of human opinions.[72] Yet another barrier is the "reward-disease": "to will the Good for the sake of reward is double-mindedness. To will one thing is, therefore, to will the Good without considering the reward."[73] "The double-minded one stands at a parting of the ways. Two visions appear: the Good and the reward. It is not in his power to bring them into agreement, for they are fundamentally different from each other."[74]

On the contrary, fundamentally different motives can often be reconciled and coordinated. Life would be a nightmare if they could not. Except when rewards become a preoccupation that deflects moral attention, an interest in them is compatible with concern for goodness. In stating each of his barriers, Kierkegaard focuses on the extreme cases where the entire concern is for secular goods, avoiding punishment, or gaining rewards. Even if we grant what he says about those cases, it does not follow that these motives are suspect when they are mixed with moral concern.

Why is Kierkegaard so pessimistic about the possibility of reasonably balancing moral commitment with interests in secular goods, avoiding sanctions, or gaining rewards? On the one hand, he believes these other interests blur moral understanding: "It is as if a man, instead of naturally using both eyes to see one thing, should use one eye to see one side and the other eye to see the other side. This does not succeed. It only confuses sight."[75] In particular, seeking recognition can distort philanthropists' understanding of how and why they should help others. While this is true, it is only part of the truth. Recognition can also support moral effort, for example, especially when it comes from people we respect. To think one doesn't need support of this kind is itself a delusion, the delusion of imagining one is emotionally self-sufficient.

On the other hand, Kierkegaard believes that seeking rewards threatens self-knowledge, in particular, knowledge of one's motives: "Money [and other rewards] may have a great influence, one can easily be deceived, and it is very difficult to know oneself."[76] This, too, is only part of the truth. Granted, it is difficult to know precisely how deeply we care about the good of others when caring is mixed with desires for praise and honor. (We can give anonymously, but that is a fallible test for benevolence, given our capacity for self-deception; besides, conspicuous giving is desirable when it encourages others to make similar contributions.) Yet self-knowledge begins by honestly acknowledging that typically we do have mixed motives, in combinations we rarely understand perfectly. This acknowledgment alerts us to how easily self-interest distorts caring through self-righteousness, which is a further barrier to single-mindedness about which Kierkegaard makes some illuminating remarks.[77]

The most familiar form of self-righteousness is smug and unwarranted confidence in one's goodness. Kierkegaard is more interested in a subtler form, which is present in the man who "wills the Good simply in order that *he* may score the victory. . . . Actually he does not care to serve the Good, but to have the advantage of regarding it as a fruit of conquest."[78] Such a man aims to be a moral winner, acquiring the kudos of moral honor rather than caring about others for their sake. More commonly, a person has some genuine moral concern mixed with vanity: "He wills that the Good shall triumph through *him*, that he shall be the instrument, he the chosen one."[79]

One need not be a purist to be sensitive to the dangers of self-righteousness. Edmund L. Pincoffs alerts us to the narcissistic self-preener:

> Instead of thinking simply what is the honest or kind or just thing to do, he can think whether by doing the proposed act, he will embellish his character in this or that way. He is concerned to polish up his attainments of justice, honesty, or kindness so that he can be satisfied with the image of self that he then sees. He will *do* what is honest, and so forth, but his motives will be narcissistic ones.[80]

Self-righteousness is difficult to root out because it is generally camouflaged by self-deception. When it is present in ourselves, we eagerly misperceive it as legitimate self-respect and pride. Hence, there is something to be said for Kierkegaard's insistence on rooting out self-righteousness, but unfortunately that carries its own risks.

Ironically, ideals of single-mindedness can encourage the very self-righteousness they condemn. An obsessive search for perfect self-knowledge in an attempt to eliminate mixed motives leads to self-absorption, deflecting us from attention to others' needs. One upshot is moral complacency: "I may not contribute as much as I should, but at least I'm not a hypocrite." A worse possibility, as John Dewey cautioned us, is fanaticism in people who are "preoccupied with the state of their character, concerned for the purity of their motives and the goodness of their souls. The exaltation of conceit which sometimes accompanies this absorption can produce a corrosive inhumanity which exceeds the possibilities of any other known form of selfishness."[81] Convinced of their own goodness, fanatics embark on a crusade of self-aggrandizement glossed in the name of unmasking hypocrisy. As Judith Shklar observes, the purist's crusade for single-mindedness too often reveals a "passion for moral domination" and "a contest for moral supremacy."[82]

I see such a crusade in Sartre's ideal of purity as authenticity, which is a combination of honesty and courage. Authenticity implies acting without self-deception, in full awareness of our freedom to live as we choose, without objectively justified responsibilities binding us, including philanthropic ones. He dismisses people who refuse to endorse his existentialist perspective as cowards and scum.[83] This smacks of bigotry, the refusal to tolerate a range of alternative moral and intellectual perspectives when they are responsibly developed and defended. (Sartre is even harder on bigots, charging them with lacking any degree of humanity even in personal dealings with their families.)[84]

Whether or not their ideals lead to fanaticism, purists drastically constrict the vast plurality of values, often to just one. For Kant the value is conscientious devotion to duty; for Kierkegaard it is devotion to God; for Sartre it is avoiding self-deception about human freedom. I want to conclude by returning to the ideal of moral authenticity, now understood as an ideal of purity.

Moral authenticity means being motivated to pursue moral ideals because one values persons and in a manner that permeates a life so as to create moral integrity. One of its aspects is positive: the presence of a deep moral concern that is a substantial motive for responsible conduct, if not always a sufficient one. Another aspect is negative: the absence of motives that distort moral concern. The ideal is fully compatible with having mixed motives, so long as those motives do not erode desirable degrees of moral commitment.

Applied to philanthropy, the ideal of moral authenticity evokes altruism and condemns greed, cruelty, self-righteousness, and other forms of impurity that deflect attention from the needs of people we seek to help. At the same time, mixed motives for philanthropy are unobjectionable so long as the self-interested element does not subvert moral motivation and the moral motivation is present in a substantial degree. The philanthropy is especially admirable in the degree altruism is present.

Moral concern can be shown through benevolence, conscientiousness, honesty, courage, and many other moral virtues. According to the ideal of moral authenticity, it is desirable that moral concern be a sufficient or at least primary motive for philanthropic giving which is a moral responsibility. That is what it means to be morally authentic in responding to human suffering. By contrast, with regard to morally optional philanthropy, self-interest permissibly plays a larger role.

Moral authenticity, then, does not require jettisoning self-interest in philanthropy. The situation is comparable to helping professions, such as teaching and the ministry, in which authentic moral concern is compatible with earning a living. In fact, mixed motives are desirable in both situations insofar as they reinforce each other to strengthen commitment and yield energy for desirable conduct. Just as there is no general objection to professionals' pursuing both internal and external goods of practices, there is no general objection to philanthropists' simultaneously helping for the sake of people they help and finding additional satisfactions in helping.

To sum up, motives matter because altruism makes caring relationships possible. Results are vitally significant, but so are caring relationships defined by the presence of altruism. Mixed motives are typical in giving, and nothing is wrong with self-interested motives so long as they do not distort caring or entirely replace altruism. With these conclusions in mind, let us explore in a more positive way the connection between our good and promoting the good of others.

6

Paradoxes of Self-Fulfillment

The 'individual' apart from the community is an abstraction. It is not
anything real, and hence not anything that we can realize. . . . I am myself by
sharing with others, by including in my essence relations to them. . . .

—F. H. Bradley

The hand that gives, gathers.

—Proverb

IN GIVING WE receive. Self-sacrifice promotes self-development. To get happiness forget about it (and make others happy). Freedom is won by surrendering it (to worthy causes). We find ourselves by losing ourselves (in service
to others).

These are paradoxes: not contradictions, but seeming absurdities intended to convey hidden truths. They are superficially puzzling because they
combine opposite reference points for thinking about ourselves. Thus, the
ideas of self-fulfillment and self-development move the self to center stage,
whereas the notions of selflessness and self-sacrifice shift it to the backdrop.
More is at stake, however, than wordplay.

With different emphases, these conundrums challenge any one-sided emphasis on our good as separate from and in conflict with the good of others.
As paradoxes of egoism, they attack selfishness in its own terms, as self-defeating. As paradoxes of altruism, they remind us that short-term self-sacrifices can promote long-term benefits to givers and receivers alike. As
paradoxes of self-interest, they suggest that caring for others (for their sake)
promotes our freedom, happiness, and self-fulfillment. Whatever their names,
the paradoxes employ irony and enigma to remind us of connections between
the good of individuals and the good of communities.

The paradoxes are *dangerous*. They fail to mention the hazards of philanthropy and other forms of service. Indeed, they are ready-made tools for
exploiting people. In the hands of swindlers they are formulas for fleecing
the gullible; in the minds of masochists they function as recipes for self-ab-
negation; and in the mouths of tyrants they become a summons to an early
death for volunteers. Simone de Beauvoir warns that "if the individual is

taught to consent to his sacrifice, the latter is abolished as such, and the soldier who has renounced himself in favor of his cause will die joyfully; in fact, that is how the young Hitlerians died. We know how many edifying speeches this philosophy has inspired: it is by losing oneself that one finds oneself, by dying that one fulfills one's life, by accepting servitude that one realizes one's freedom; all leaders of men preach in this vein."[1]

Even without these abuses, the paradoxes as applied to philanthropy make one-sided assertions. They fail to note other areas of service, such as work, and they omit additional avenues for self-fulfillment which may conflict with voluntary service, including friendship, marriage, education, travel, and indeed solitude.[2] In addition, the paradoxes apply to morally concerned individuals who have some regard for the good of others, and certainly not to sociopaths who lack any sense of moral decency.

If the paradoxes are dangerous and one-sided, they nevertheless express significant truths. They gesture toward intriguing ways in which caring relationships contribute to self-fulfillment, several of which I will sort out and clarify as they pertain to philanthropy. Self-fulfillment, as I understand it, is an ongoing process of achieving our good, our well-being. More fully, it is (1) a process of self-development, (2) guided autonomously during adulthood, (3) which produces happiness and (4) which creates meaningful life. Each of these aspects of self-fulfillment generates paradox.

(i) Self-sacrifice promotes self-development: In giving we receive.

(ii) Self-surrender liberates: By surrendering freedom we win it.

(iii) Self-forgetfulness furthers happiness: Forgetting happiness leads to getting it.

(iv) Selflessness contributes to meaning: In losing ourselves we find ourselves.

A fifth paradox concerns faith and other positive attitudes such as hope and trust, which enable us to confront the ambiguities surrounding self-fulfillment. If faith is to avoid the charge of being irrational, there must be reasons for adapting it, but sometimes those reasons include the faith itself.

(v) Positive attitudes are often self-justifying: Faith is a reason for faith.

Self-Development and Self-Sacrifice

What kind of assertions do the paradoxes make? Are they empirical claims, stating tendencies which can be confirmed or denied through factual inquiry? Are they value claims which affirm that helping others makes us better people? Are they perhaps true by definition, asserting, for example, that altruism makes us better persons because "better" means altruistic? Depending on context, all these things can be meant.

Self-development is a pattern of growth in which desirable potentials unfold and undesirable potentials wither.[3] It is a normative process, with values defining its goals and progression. The relevant values may include all forms of goodness, not just moral but also intellectual, professional, aesthetic, and athletic. I will understand self-development as typically involving caring relationships, with the specific contribution of philanthropic caring as varying widely according to individuals and circumstances, and at most a matter of widespread tendencies.

Not all desirable potentials can be developed; most cannot. For example, each of us has the potential to work in a wide variety of different professions, but typically we must limit ourselves to one or a few during a lifetime in order to make a creative contribution. Again, we have possibilities for many different loves and friendships, but the very nature of those relationships limits their numbers. Self-development expresses both our human and individual natures.[4] Human nature is composed of general capacities and tendencies, such as perceiving, feeling, reasoning, eating, and social interaction. Individual nature consists of our particular talents, interests, and desires. The direction in which our nature unfolds is substantially a result of parents, society, and chance, but within limits we can shape our identity autonomously.

Everyday life is more a competition among goods than a battle between good and bad. Of necessity, to choose one good is to abandon others. This process of trade-offs constantly requires self-interested sacrifices: abandoning lesser goods in order to acquire something we desire more strongly. Let us set aside this sense of sacrifice in order to focus on altruistic self-sacrifices: voluntarily relinquishing something good for ourselves (in some respect) in order to promote the good of others. Forgoing a good may mean (a) self-restraint, in order not to waste resources, or (b) self-denial, in which we relinquish something we want or which could have been used to benefit us. In either case, the self-sacrificer may view the sacrifice as a form of self-expression and self-affirmation, rather than as a source of regret.[5]

Philanthropy, insofar as it involves altruistic sacrifices of money, time, or other resources, may contribute to the self-development of morally concerned individuals in a variety of ways. For example, philanthropy provides a way to put beliefs into action. Philanthropic giving transforms lip service into commitment by enabling us to put our money and time where our mouth is. That is essential for personal integrity in the sense of consistency between conviction and conduct. It is equally essential for moral integrity—the coherence of a life rooted in moral concern.

Philanthropy also provides a forum for developing talents and expanding personal interests. That is obvious in the case of self-help and mutual support organizations, such as science clubs, art groups, amateur athletics, churches and synagogues. It is equally true of service-oriented volunteering that develops skills and confidence in working with people.

In addition, volunteering is a way to experiment so as to gain knowledge of our strengths and limitations. Work does that too, but voluntary service has the advantage of carrying fewer risks by allowing the freedom to leave an unsatisfying organization or program without suffering economic penalties.

Most obvious, the caring relationships in philanthropy make possible a variety of satisfactions. Compassionate and kind people want to contribute to the well-being of others, and helping enriches meaning and self-respect by doing one's share to improve a troubled world. Beyond these moral satisfactions, there are the enjoyments of supporting organizations and causes we believe in. And joining with other volunteers and donors fosters the pleasures of friendship and collegiality.

All these contributions to self-development are illustrated in the life of Jane Addams. Addams yearned for "unity of spirit" with other people, especially those less privileged than herself.[6] She was raised to be socially concerned but denied opportunities outside the home to express that concern. Her description of the educated women of her generation applied to herself: "They feel a fatal want of harmony between their theory and their lives, a lack of coordination between thought and action."[7] Addams sought a way to translate her caring into action and in doing so to "try out" her convictions, to "learn of life from life itself."[8] It took eight years after graduating from college before she found that way. The catalyst was attending a bullfight while on vacation in Spain. She watched in fascination as five bulls and many more horses were killed. Later, confronted by her companions who were horrified by the spectacle, she was forcibly struck by the gap between her beliefs about cruelty and her capacity to enjoy it from a distance.

Within a year she and a friend established Hull-House, a settlement house (urban community center) in the midst of a Chicago slum. Together with the volunteers she recruited, Addams lived as a neighbor to immigrant families, responding to their needs as she learned them firsthand. At a time when government social services were virtually nonexistent, she offered family counseling, provided emergency aid, and assisted at funerals. One of her earliest projects was free kindergarten and childcare services for parents who worked twelve- to fourteen-hour days. She raised funds for an art museum, a theater, and a gymnasium, eventually expanding Hull-House to thirteen buildings. Even so, the immigrants' needs were overwhelming. She began to lobby for government assistance, including laws against child labor, legislation to improve working conditions, and minimum welfare rights.

As Addams learned, she wrote, and her publications earned her recognition as a pioneer in the emerging profession of social work. Yet she remained a full-time volunteer, acting on desires to help which she thought we all have: "It is natural to feed the hungry and care for the sick, it is certainly natural to give pleasure to the young, comfort to the aged, and to minister to the deep-seated craving for social intercourse that all men feel."[9] Voluntary service liberates these natural desires, which are dampened by separations among economic classes:

> Nothing so deadens the sympathies and shrivels the power of enjoyment as the persistent keeping away from the great opportunities for helpfulness and a continual ignoring of the starvation struggle which makes up the life of at least half of the race. To shut one's self away from that half of the race life is to shut one's self away from the most vital part of it; it is to live out but half the humanity to which we have been born heir and to use but half our faculties.[10]

Of course, even if there are natural impulses to help others, not everyone would find self-fulfillment in living as Addams did. Her individual nature suited her to that life. The history of philanthropy is vibrant with examples like Addams, but rarely does it mention individuals for whom voluntary service is not fulfilling. Kitty Scherbatsky, in Tolstoy's *Anna Karenina*, provides such an example.

Kitty falls in love with Count Vronsky but is jilted by him. In turn, she spurns Levin, who loves her (and whom she will later marry). Depressed and ill, she travels with her parents to Germany, where she meets Varenka, a volunteer nurse devoted to serving the sick and elderly. Kitty tries to emulate her: "Varenka made her realize that it was only necessary to forget oneself and love others in order to be at peace, happy and good."[11] Far from bringing happiness, however, Kitty's voluntary service leaves her miserable and at odds with her family and patients.

Eventually grasping the source of her difficulty, Kitty turns on herself: "It serves me right because it was all a sham, because it was all pretense, and did not come from my heart."[12] She had emulated Varenka largely from self-deceiving motives in order to believe herself virtuous, rather than from a moral devotion comparable to Varenka's. Acknowledging the truth brings a deepened authenticity: "Let me be bad, but at least not a liar, not a humbug!"[13] It also brings the self-knowledge that she was not naturally suited to that kind of volunteering: "She seemed to have recovered consciousness; she felt without hypocrisy or boastfulness the whole difficulty of remaining on the heights to which she had wished to rise. . . . "[14] Kitty illustrates the futility of trying to be selfless from entirely self-centered motives.[15]

Episodic self-sacrifice means occasionally giving up something that one values in order to help others. By contrast, Kitty aspired to a life of *wholesale* self-sacrifice: complete or constant self-denial for altruistic ends. Wholesale self-sacrifice is an ideal promulgated by some religious thinkers. Thus, according to Martin Luther, the true Christian "lives only for others and not for himself," seeking to "serve and benefit others in all that he does, considering nothing except the need and the advantage of his neighbor."[16] Freed by faith in God, the Christian "has such abundant riches in his faith that all his other works and his whole life are a surplus with which he can by voluntary benevolence serve and do good to his neighbor."[17]

Luther would have us go well beyond the Golden Rule of doing unto others as we would have them do unto us, a dictum which at most prescribes impartiality in valuing others as we value ourselves.[18] He recommends "other-biased altruism": systematic preference for the interests of others over our own (secular) interests.[19] That ideal suits the individual nature of relatively few individuals. Even Addams found her self-interest promoted, rather than sacrificed, through the kinds of service she engaged in. Too often, systematic self-sacrifice reveals a lack of respect for oneself as a person having equal moral worth with others.[20]

Lack of self-respect need not be involved, however, when emergencies force an episodic sacrifice to become the wholesale sacrifice of giving one's life for a cause: for example, fifty-nine American soldiers in the Vietnam War jumped on live grenades to save fellow soldiers;[21] in World War II kamikaze pilots killed themselves in the course of killing others;[22] Buddhist monks engaged in self-immolation to protest Thieu's dictatorship during the Vietnam War; and Bobby Sands starved himself to death in order to protest the British government's refusal to treat him and his fellow Irish Republican Army (IRA) provisionals as political prisoners.[23]

When self-sacrifice brings a premature end to a life rich in possibilities, it is difficult to understand how the sacrifice contributes to self-fulfillment, at least without assuming an afterlife. Much depends on the purpose served by the sacrifice, and self-fulfillment has further dimensions than self-development. If the cause is unjustified, we will probably view the sacrifice as a waste.[24] But sometimes a tragic death culminates a deeply fulfilling life grounded in devotion to valuable ideals. A life need not be long in order to be deeply meaningful, and even happy.

Freedom and Self-Surrender

Freedom is won by surrendering it, freely, on behalf of worthy causes. Freely means voluntarily, without external coercion or uncontrollable internal compulsions, but what does freedom mean, the freedom which is both surrendered and won? Few words are so richly ambiguous. According to one interpretive approach, the freedom paradox is a pun: Surrendering freedom in one sense yields more valuable freedom in another sense. According to a second approach, the paradox contrasts areas and degrees of freedom: Surrendering freedom in some areas of our lives yields greater freedom in other areas, in one sense of "freedom." I will illustrate both approaches but emphasize one version of the second interpretation as most relevant to philanthropy.

Without trying to list all meanings of freedom, here are several important ones.

(1) Liberty: the social-political freedom we have in the absence of coercive intrusions in our lives, such as laws or powerful authorities.

(2) Opportunity freedom: having a satisfying range of options, in terms of both quantity and quality.

(3) Psychological freedom: the absence of unwanted suffering, anxiety, and burdens.

(4) Autonomy: self-determination, which includes (a) moral rights to pursue our interests, (b) capacities for self-control, rationality, and moral reasonableness, and (c) competence in exercising those capacities in directing our lives.

To illustrate the first approach, which interprets the paradox as contrasting these (or other) senses, we might contrast senses (1) and (2): Greater opportunity freedom is won by voluntarily surrendering some liberty. If we construe liberty as negative, as not being interfered with, then liberty carries no assurance of having a satisfying range of options. Hence, we may choose to surrender some liberty in order to obtain more desirable opportunities. Employees, for example, routinely surrender large areas of liberty to corporations in return for the opportunities their work provides, and students submit to university regulations in order to gain an education. Similarly, volunteers agree to abide by the regulations of organizations they serve (hospitals, museums, the military) in order to gain opportunities to help others.

An another illustration, the paradox might juxtapose senses (3) and (4): Relinquishing autonomy produces psychological freedom. The apostle Paul reports being freed from the bondage of sin by surrendering to Jesus. In more general terms, William James regarded experiences of relinquishing control of one's life to a higher power as distinctively religious: "There is a state of mind, known to religious men, but to no others, in which the will to assert ourselves and hold our own has been displaced by a willingness to close our mouths and be as nothing in the floods and waterspouts of God."[25] As James described it:

> Give up the feeling of responsibility, let go your hold, resign the care of your destiny to higher powers, be genuinely indifferent as to what becomes of it all, and you will find not only that you gain a perfect inward relief, but often also, in addition, the particular goods you sincerely thought you were renouncing.[26]

Analogous experiences sometimes occur in voluntary service, whether or not they are grounded in religious faith, when individuals devote themselves in complete faith to a community endeavor or cause.

Shifting to the second approach, or set of approaches, the paradox might contrast different areas of freedom, using a specified sense of freedom. Four interpretations correspond to the four senses of "freedom."

(1) Relinquishing liberty in some areas of our lives expands it in others. For example, loyal citizens restrict their liberty in some areas and increase it in others when they willingly abide by the law. Voluntarily submitting to laws requires restricting conduct, but it also creates greater overall liberty than would occur without laws, under conditions of anarchy.

(2) Abandoning some opportunities, even highly desirable ones, may be a prerequisite for obtaining better ones. Sincere commitments imply a willingness to abandon pursuits incompatible with the commitments. Thus, traditional commitments of fidelity to spouses limit some options, but for many people the sacrifices are worth the gains. Similarly, commitments by volunteers restrict some options, namely, those precluded by being available when promised, but they open opportunities for self-development.

(3) Forgoing some kinds of psychological freedom may create other kinds. To enter voluntarily into caring relationships is to become emotionally interdependent in ways that are occasionally burdensome. ("Cares" become worries.) Caring relationships, however, may also liberate us from anxious self-preoccupation. By focusing attention away from ourselves, caring increases our sense of personal worth, emotional security, happiness, and meaning—a point I will return to in following sections.

(4) Forgoing autonomy in some respects promotes it in other respects. This is the most comprehensive version of the paradox as it applies to philanthropy in that it draws together the truths in the other interpretations. It is also the most intriguing version, given the enormous value we attach to autonomy. Autonomy is both inherently valuable and valuable as a means to promoting other goods. As an instrumental good, autonomy promotes meaningful and happy life. As an intrinsic good, autonomy functions as an ideal of rational self-guidance which is incompatible which slavish dependency, weakness of will, harmful forms of self-deception, and other forms of irrationality.[27] How, then, could giving up autonomy in some respects promote it in more desirable respects?

When we enter into interdependent caring relationships, we are substantially guided by the needs and decisions of other people, and to that extent we restrict independent choice. We waive our rights to guide our lives independently, or rather we pool our rights with those of others so as to make decisions collectively with others. In setting limits to self-determination, however, caring relationships enrich overall autonomy. As Harry G. Frankfurt remarks, "The suggestion that a person may be in some sense liberated through acceding to a power which is not subject to his immediate voluntary control is among the most ancient and persistent themes of our moral and religious tradition. It must surely reflect some quite fundamental structural feature of our lives."[28] "How [then]," he asks, "are we to understand the paradox that a person may be enhanced and liberated through being seized, made captive, and overcome?"[29]

Part of the answer concerns enhanced psychological and opportunity freedom, but part concerns autonomy as it interacts with caring, whether for people, practices, or ideals. Wholehearted caring combines elements of both involuntariness and control. On the one hand, caring implies the loss of some immediate voluntary control, as we surrender to the guidance by something outside ourselves. When the caring is most profound, as in genuine love, we feel unable to pull ourselves away. This "volitional necessity" means we lack the will to redirect devotion elsewhere, even though we may have the causal capacity to do so.[30]

On the other hand, the willing submission involved in caring remains voluntary. If we are unable to pull away from the object of our caring, it is because our own will prevents us from doing so. Our will is our caring about some things more deeply than others.[31] That explains why we feel most at one with ourselves in selflessly giving to what we care about deeply.

Frankfurt offers several illustrations of how caring is simultaneously involuntary and voluntary, in different respects. One example is rationality. Insofar as we are reasoning creatures, we voluntarily submit to the standards of reason, accepting them as guides to our beliefs and actions. By submitting ourselves to those standards, we are liberated in ways that bring greater self-determination and free us from ignorance, whim, and superstition. We are freed to become the rational creatures we "will" to be. A person who substantially rejected reason would have a chaotic identity, not an autonomous one.[32] Other examples of liberation through willing submission are love, rapt appreciation of beauty, losing ourselves in the thrill of the moment, and concentrated involvement in work. In each case, there is submission to something outside ourselves and simultaneously an enriched autonomy in exerting our own will.

Caring is a matter of degree, and the paradox of freedom primarily concerns *wholehearted* caring. What is that? It is to have and to act on desires that we affirm and fully identify with. Frankfurt understands it in terms of second-order desires—desires to have the desires. But perhaps it can be understood more directly in terms of having strong desires without accompanying feelings of shame, guilt, and alienation—feelings which typically accompany the desires of the compulsive overeater and the drug addict, for example. In addition, identification implies a stable conviction about the importance of the things desired. We feel most at one with ourselves when we have that stable conviction, and when we unify our will by decisively "making up our mind" about what we most care about. Conflicting desires may remain, but we refuse to identify with those which are incompatible with pursuing what we care about wholeheartedly.[33]

Wholehearted caring structures our lives.[34] It provides a core around which we set priorities, making some things central and others secondary or peripheral. It engenders a sense of purpose, a clear identity, and confidence that our lives are worthwhile. It also frees up energy and effort. In all these ways it enables us to guide our lives more effectively.

When we enter into caring relationships, in philanthropy and elsewhere, we willingly accept others' needs as a basis for responding with help and consideration.[35] With adults, that includes respecting their autonomy, and with children, that includes respecting their development toward autonomy. In doing so we surrender some options, if only the option to disregard their needs. Once within caring relationships, we are dependent on others, or rather interdependent, yet simultaneously autonomous in initiating our actions. During this process, individuality can be expanded rather than compromised. Caring is not slavish dependency or unthinking conformity. Individual initiative and assertion are "fulfilled *in* community rather than against it."[36]

The life of Clara Barton illustrates how community involvement can express individuality and strengthen autonomy by enriching personal identity, structuring endeavors, and freeing powers to act. Barton had a "passion for service."[37] In her ten-year career as a schoolteacher, she founded a school for the 125 children working in the factories owned by her parents, and later the first free public school in New Jersey. Later, during the Civil War, she served without pay as a one-person trauma center. She developed an uncanny knack for being first to arrive after a battle, bringing wagonloads of medical supplies which she had solicited from donors and dispensing them as a nurse. Following the war, she continued her volunteer work by helping families locate information about missing or dead soldiers. After spending five years lobbying for support to create the American Red Cross, she served as its president for over two decades.

Barton devoted her life to helping people in desperate need, willingly accepting the plight of others as the basis for her actions. As one historian wrote, "surely her singular and endearing characteristic was lack of interest in reforming anything or anybody. She did not launch crusades to end wars, famine, plagues, fires, or floods; she simply met emergencies as they arose and to the best of her abilities."[38] In doing so she developed a remarkably rich character, pursued a life structured around caring relationships, and found her abilities and energies expanded.

Clara Barton is a special case, of course, in terms of the scale of her voluntary service. But the paradox of freedom applies to all wholehearted caring within desirable relationships. The ways in which personal identity is expanded, lives are structured, and energy liberated are as varied as the forms of caring relationships.

Happiness and Self-Forgetfulness

According to the paradox of happiness, "the way to get happiness is to forget it."[39] Seeking happiness directly, with a steady eye on the prize, is self-defeating. Instead, we should immerse ourselves in activities and relationships without being preoccupied with our happiness. Then, with any luck, happiness will come indirectly, unbidden as it were.

The paradox has a strong and a weak version. The strong version says that promoting the happiness or well-being of others for their sake, especially through philanthropy, is the primary or sole way to find our happiness. The weaker and more plausible version says that promoting others' happiness is a significant avenue to happiness, though there are others. John Stuart Mill, who will guide my discussion, stated the paradox in the weaker form:

> Those only are happy . . . who have their minds fixed on some object other than their own happiness; on the happiness of others, on the improvement of mankind, even on some art or pursuit, followed not as a means, but as itself an ideal end. Aiming thus at something else, they find happiness by the way.[40]

What is happiness, in the sense in which we speak of happy lives and parts or aspects of lives? Let us set aside the sense in which "happy" is a synonym for "pleasurable." In that sense we speak of feeling happy (cheerful) at a luncheon, having a happy (enjoyable) party, and being happy about (pleased by) an award. Pleasures are short-lived states of consciousness desired for themselves, and enjoyments are activities desired for themselves. By contrast, when we are happy for years, we do not continuously feel pleasure, if only because we are asleep much of the time.

Perhaps because of these varied usages, Mill sometimes confused happiness with pleasure. In his more careful moments, however, he tacitly distinguished them by defining happiness in terms of patterns of pleasures and pains: Happiness is "an existence exempt as far as possible from pain, and as rich as possible in enjoyments, both in point of quantity and quality."[41]

Quality, for Mill, meant the "higher pleasures" embedded in intellectual activity, virtue, responses to beauty, and personal relationships.[42] These are inherently better than physical pleasures, he argued, because most people who have experienced both prefer the higher ones. However, that conclusion follows only if Victorian-era judges are used. Today's judges might give equal or greater status to physical pleasures, especially those of sex and sports. Perhaps Mill's "higher pleasures" are better praised in terms of lasting longer and leading to a greater variety of further pleasures,[43] but physical pleasures should not be downgraded in quality or in their contribution to happiness. Some people, in fact, find happiness through a preponderance of physical over intellectual and social pleasures, while others experience the so-called higher pleasures without being happy. So much depends upon personal interests and attitudes, making it difficult to generalize about how patterns of pleasures generate happiness.

As Mill noted, the ingredients of happiness include many and varied enjoyments, or rather the activities, achievements, and relationships which produce those enjoyments. Yet happiness is more than a life of satisfactions; it is a satisfying life.[44] It is a life (or aspect of a life) which the happy person is pleased with and can honestly affirm overall. The affirmation is usually tacit, but it can be explicitly formulated in conscious judgments such as "This is the life I want."

Finally, we can be mistaken about when and how much we are happy, whether owing to self-deception or a lack of perspective. In that respect, judgments about happiness are objective. In addition, there is the honorific sense of "true happiness" used to make appraisals of others' happiness in terms of what we believe is the most worthwhile life. Nevertheless, happiness is essentially a subjective matter, certainly in terms of the pleasures which enter into it for a given individual, but also in terms of the standards which enable a person to affirm a life overall. Usually we are happy when we are in the process of satisfying our important needs and desires—important in terms of our values. Those desires are for future achievements, but also for current activities and relationships. Notoriously, we may be happier while struggling toward goals than in reaching them.[45]

Using this concept of happiness, what is being asserted in the happiness paradox? For one thing, the paradox reminds us that we must pursue and satisfy desires other than only the desire for happiness per se. Happiness has two aspects: (1) a primary content, comprising activities, relationships, interests, commitments, and accomplishments, and their accompanying pleasures and pains, and (2) a second-order affirmative attitude toward the primary content. Without the primary content, happiness would be impossible—there would be no life toward which we could have a positive attitude. We seek a will-o'-the-wisp when we say, "All I want in life is to be happy," and then begin searching for happiness as if it were an abstraction independent of activities and relationships.

This logical or definitional truth allows that the primary content of happiness may be largely shaped in self-centered ways. The paradox also conveys, however, several psychological generalizations about the dangers of excessive self-centeredness.

Thus, the paradox reminds us that activities, relationships, achievements, and other ingredients of happiness require desires for things beyond ourselves. Pleasures come from satisfying desires: no desires, no pleasures. Moreover, the desires must be for activities and relationships themselves, rather than solely for pleasures or for secondary rewards such as prestige, fame, and money.[46] Obsession with our pleasures and with secondary rewards is a form of egotism that deflects us from pleasurable immersion in activities and relationships. Self-absorption tends to be a recipe for boredom by drastically narrowing and diminishing our range of interests. Joseph Butler expressed the idea this way:

> [A] person may have so steady and fixed an eye upon his own interest, whatever he places it in, as may hinder him from attending to many gratifications within his reach, which others have their minds free and open to. . . . Immoderate self-love does very ill consult its own interest; and how much soever a paradox it may appear, it is certainly true, that, even from self-love, we should endeavour to get over all inordinate regard to and consideration of, ourselves.[47]

The paradox of happiness also reminds us that preoccupation with ourselves—with our pleasures, problems, appearance, accomplishments, or character—often makes us "self-conscious," that is, anxious about how other people view us and excessively worried about our well-being. As Mill suggests, the ability to disregard our happiness lifts us above this anxiety:

> [P]aradoxical as the assertion may be, the conscious ability to do without happiness gives the best prospect of realizing such happiness as is attainable. For nothing except that consciousness can raise a person above the chances of life by making him feel that, let fate and fortune do their worst, they have not power to subdue him.[48]

Furthermore, self-preoccupation leads us to expect too much. Instead of accepting simple delights for what they are, we ruin them by holding them up against unrealistic standards: "The enjoyments of life . . . are sufficient to make it a pleasant thing, when they are taken *en passant*, without being made the principal object. Once make them so, and they are immediately felt to be insufficient."[49] That does not mean we should avoid all reflection about enjoyments.[50] The danger lies in obsessive, calculating, solicitous preoccupation with maximizing our pleasures, but other kinds of self-reflection are beneficial: periodic reflection on the kinds of enjoyments worth seeking and general reflection on how specific relationships and activities contribute to our happiness.[51]

These rough generalizations are conveyed in the weaker version of the happiness paradox. The stronger version of the paradox says our happiness comes primarily through promoting others' happiness and especially through voluntary service. That is false as a general claim, but it is true for some individuals. Eleanor Roosevelt was one. Immediately after completing school in 1902 she began extensive volunteering in service organizations. She taught at a New York settlement house. Later she joined the Consumers League, a political activist group which tried to end child labor, twelve-hour working days, and inequality in pay. During the early years of her marriage to Franklin D. Roosevelt and while raising five children, she served on many charitable boards, and during World War I, she was a Red Cross volunteer. Following F. D. R.'s election as president during the 1930s depression, she planned employment projects for writers and artists, became a civil rights leader, and sought legislation for fair employment practices. After F. D. R.'s death, she served as the U.S. delegate to the United Nations, chaired the U.N. commission which wrote the 1948 Universal Declaration of Human Rights, and was active in world peace organizations. In one of her speeches, Roosevelt expressed the happiness paradox, in her own homespun style:

> It is a wonderful thing to keep your mind always full of something that is worth while doing. If you can get hold of something that you feel is going to help the people around you, you'll find that you're so busy trying to add one more thing to it that you won't have time to be sorry for yourself or to wonder what you're going to do with your spare time. . . . [52]

Voluntary service does not always promote happiness in the way it did for Eleanor Roosevelt. Sometimes it causes grief, especially if one learns that one's money was misused rather than helped intended beneficiaries,[53] and as Simone de Beauvoir reminded us, the history of philanthropy is replete with instances where the call to self-forgetfulness was exploitive.[54] At most we can say that voluntary service promotes happiness when it matches an individual's natural inclinations, as with Eleanor Roosevelt, Jane Addams, and Clara Barton.

Once again we can learn from Mill, this time from a severe and suicidal depression he suffered during his twentieth year. His father had given him an extraordinary education: Greek at age three, Latin at eight, and by fourteen a study of most Greek and Latin classics, much history, and substantial amounts of logic and mathematics. No doubt the intensity of the education contributed to his breakdown, but Mill identified another cause. From an early age, Mill was committed to help reform the world in accord with the principle of utilitarianism, to promote the greatest overall happiness, taking everyone into account equally. Thus, he had embraced a philanthropic ideal: "I had what might truly be called an object in life; to be a reformer of the world. My conception of my own happiness was entirely identified with this object."[55] This philanthropic ideal, however, did not bring happiness, contrary to what is claimed in the stronger version of the paradox. On the brink of depression,

> it occurred to me to put the question directly to myself: "Suppose that all your objects in life were realized; that all the changes in institutions and opinions which you are looking forward to, could be completely effected at this very instant: would this be a great joy and happiness to you?" And an irrepressible self-consciousness distinctly answered, "No!" At this my heart sank within me. . . . [56]

His commitment to the philanthropic ideal was too intellectual, too independent of emotions and attitudes that would bring immediate delight as he pursued it. Rather than withdraw the commitment, he gradually widened his interests. He came to appreciate the importance of "the internal culture of the individual" that brings "a due balance among the faculties."[57] In part this meant developing interests beyond those of morality and adjusting his philanthropic endeavors accordingly, and in part it meant linking his emotions more intimately to his moral ideals.

Happiness is highly personal. Because the individual remains the final judge of the kind of life that is most satisfying overall, the paradox of happiness can plausibly assert only rough generalizations, though ones that apply to a great many people. The next paradox, which concerns meaningful life, more directly involves objective values, but I will continue in an ecumenical spirit which affirms many ways for lives to be worthwhile.

Meaning and Selflessness

We find ourselves by losing ourselves in selfless service. The "finding" is both a discovery and a becoming, a transformation into a more meaningful life and identity. Selflessness, as I will understand it, is service motivated primarily by caring for others for their sake, which allows for compatible admixtures of self-interest. But what does it mean to say that lives have meaning, not as having inherent moral value, which all human lives have to the same extent, but in the gradation sense in which lives can take on greater meaning?

To begin with, meaning is not the same as happiness. A life can be happy but not deeply meaningful; witness the happy-go-lucky gangster or mass murderer. Conversely, meaningful lives may not be exceptionally happy, if only because tragedy can undermine happiness without erasing meaning. Recall Candy Lightner, the founder of Mothers Against Drunk Driving. Whether or not voluntary service made her happy, undoubtedly it added some meaning lost when her daughter was killed by a drunk driver. Creating the organization helped make sense of an otherwise senseless death: "when my daughter was killed, and when I finally sobered up and realized what had occurred—'cause I did get drunk after she was killed, I just didn't want to deal with the pain—my first thought was, you know, something good has got to come out of this."[58]

Lives are meaningful or significant in two senses: they are intelligible, and they are valuable. To be intelligible is to make sense in terms of patterns of activities and relationships which cohere, or "hang together." To be valuable is to be worthwhile, rather than utterly futile or degrading. These two senses are closely connected: a human life is intelligible primarily in terms of the values that guide it.

Value, hence meaning, can be assessed subjectively, interpersonally, or objectively.[59] Subjective meaning is a sense of one's worth and the importance of one's life. Interpersonal meaning is one's significance to other people, whether appraised according to criteria of social usefulness, as when a society prizes its scientists or leaders, or in being valued by friends and lovers who bestow special worth on us.[60] Objective meaning is living according to justified values, whether the values pertain to morality, rationality, science, religion, law, aesthetic goodness, or physical excellence. *Fully* meaningful lives, I will say, are meaningful in all three ways. They are guided by justified values, infused with a sense of meaning that evokes interests and energies in a sustained way, and valued by other people as well.

How does selflessness promote fully meaningful lives and higher selves? One way is epistemological: we learn about our identity and value (in part) by entering into caring relationships. Ironically, we learn about ourselves by looking away from ourselves in order to understand our relationships with other people and practices, how we affect them and they affect us: "Self-knowledge does not mean preoccupation with one's own thoughts; rather it means concern about the effects one creates. . . . The right sort of self-examination . . . consists not in idle brooding over oneself but in examining the effects one produces."[61] Self-knowledge has a temporal aspect: who we are now is grasped in light of the past, especially in light of relationships emerging from the past. Josiah Royce called this "the deepest paradox of the inner life": "We get self-possession, self-apprehension, self-knowledge, only through endlessly fleeing from ourselves, and then turning back to look at what we were."[62] Like self-development, which it guides, self-knowledge is the ongoing achievement of awareness of needs, relationships, and possibilities in light of both the past and the projected future.[63]

Selflessness promotes meaning in additional ways that correspond to the different assessments of meaning. Subjective meaning is increased insofar as altruistic service increases the sense that our lives are worthwhile. Clara Barton, Jane Addams, Albert Schweitzer, Eleanor Roosevelt, Martin Luther King, Jr., and innumerable other philanthropists have said that their lives increased in meaning for them as they devoted themselves to helping others, and there is no reason to challenge the authenticity of their testimony. Interpersonal meaning is increased when helping others prompts them (and observers) to appreciate our lives, to see our lives as valuable. And objective meaning increases because virtuous giving tends to create caring relationships that enrich givers, as well as receivers. Our higher (true, morally better) identity consists in being related in caring ways to other people, including through philanthropy. In this sense, "I am myself by sharing with others, by including in my essence relations to them."[64] In part this is a tautology: the morally valuable self is the person as related in morally desirable ways to others. In part it is a moral faith—a faith in the validity of moral values.

The selflessness paradoxes are prominent in religious traditions that link finding oneself to salvation: "For whosoever will save his life shall lose it; but whosoever will lose his life for my sake, the same shall save it."[65] Trying to "save" one's life through self-seeking means losing salvation, which comes by transcending self-preoccupation through selfless devotion to God and one's neighbor. The paradox is also expressed in the language of two selves. In the language of the "born-again Christian," one self is destroyed in order to give birth to another. In the contrasting language of Meister Eckhart, "the more ourselves we are, the less self is in us."[66] That is, the closer we come to self-fulfillment as a higher self, the less narrowly self-centered we are. Literally there is only one person who progresses from one identity (self) to another, with identities defined by basic convictions and value commitments.

The religious paradoxes can be unfolded with an other-worldly emphasis, whereby the higher self is fulfilled through rewards in an afterlife for having led a selfless life. This emphasis makes self-fulfillment an external reward tacked on to altruistic service, rather than an internal good embedded in service itself. By contrast, and of greater interest here, the paradoxes can be understood with a humanistic emphasis, with God's gifts coming in this life (at least in part) as internal rewards from helping others: service brings delight, joy, and a sense of meaning from helping, as well as peace in being freed from undue anxiety and lack of moral focus.

The second, humanistic interpretation stresses the moral aspects of self-transformation through service. It is illustrated in the life and writing of Dag Hammarskjöld, who served as secretary-general of the United Nations for nine years before he was killed in an airplane crash in 1961. World-renowned, he had ample occasion for self-glorification and anxious self-preoccupation, but he avoided those dangers. In his journal he wrote of "the freedom of the continual farewell [to self-preoccupation], the hourly self-surrender, [which] gives to your experience of reality the purity and clarity which signify—self-realization."[67] He also wrote, "the explanation of how man should live a life of active social service in full harmony with himself as a member of the community of the spirit, I found in the writings of those great medieval mystics for whom 'self-surrender' had been the way to self-realization. . . ."[68]

Whether these effects are traceable to God's grace or, within a secular perspective, to psychological (placebo) effects of faith,[69] we can acknowledge an element of mystery in fundamental transformations through selfless giving. Graham Greene conveys this element of mystery in his allegorical novel, *A Burnt-Out Case*. The title has several connotations. Querry, a world-renowned architect, is psychologically burned out. Cynically despising himself for a career in which he exploited others and cared little for anything besides fame, he abandons his profession and wanders until he happens upon a Catholic mission in Africa. Bored, he begins doing errands for Dr. Colin, who treats victims of leprosy. As Colin explains, severe leprosy is like an unstoppable fire which must burn itself out, removing fingers and limbs as in the case of Deo Gratias, the housekeeper assigned to Querry. By the end of the novel, Querry has undergone an analogous spiritual burning out of his guilt and selfishness.

One night Deo Gratias disappears into the jungle. Irritated by the natives' refusal to enter the jungle at night, Querry spontaneously sets out to find him. His act is surprising, given his indifference to Deo Gratias, and even Querry finds himself baffled about his motives. After locating Deo Gratias, who is too seriously injured to move, Querry attempts to leave to get help, but Deo Gratias cries out in fear. Querry stays with him throughout the night because, as he later told Dr. Colin, he had "an odd feeling that he needed me," odd, no doubt, in light of Querry's previous inability to care for people.[70]

The missionaries understand the event as God's grace, an interpretation invited by the portrayal of Querry ("the seeker") calling out for Deo Gratias ("thanks be to God") at night (the "Dark Night of the Soul"). By contrast, Dr. Colin understands the event in terms of how caring relationships help (or heal) giver and receiver alike. For his part, Querry remains perplexed, especially as the aftermath of the event is a sense of peace and a desire to build a new hospital for Dr. Colin. However it is understood, the event retains an element of mystery—which is not to say mystification.

Earlier I said that faith underlies the moral claim expressed in the selflessness paradox, whether or not that faith has a religious dimension. I meant faith in moral values—faith that they are worthy of our commitment, without standing in need of a further defense in terms of self-interest. This bears emphasis. In noting the contributions of altruism to self-fulfillment, I am not attempting to justify moral values by appeals to self-interest.

The history of philosophy is replete with such attempts, beginning with Plato. Plato recounts a myth about a shepherd named Gyges who found a magical ring which enabled him to become invisible at will.[71] Using his new-found power, he entered the palace, seduced the queen, murdered the king, seized the throne, and was honored for his power. The challenge is to prove that there are good reasons for being moral even if we, like Gyges, could get away with immorality in ways we find pleasurable. In response, Plato sets out to prove that a morally good person who, like Socrates, has unfairly acquired a reputation for immorality will be happier than Gyges, who is utterly immoral and yet has a good reputation. (By happier he meant something closer to self-fulfillment than to happiness.) Specifically, he argues that a moral person will have a well-ordered life, with reason governing the appetites so as to produce mental and physical well-being.

Plato's argument identifies the contribution of the virtues to human flourishing, though it overlooks the possibility of disciplining a life according to immoral ideals. The main difficulty is that it implies that morality must be justifiable in terms of self-interest. There are self-interested reasons for entering into caring relationships, as I have emphasized, but moral reasons stand on their own as valid reasons for conduct and character development. Affirming the validity of moral values is a type of faith, a faith especially dependent on having been given a decent upbringing.

Ultimately, the selflessness paradox is an expression of moral faith. It affirms that the most valuable identities are those achieved through caring relationships and the communities defined by those relationships. Philanthropy is a primary forum, albeit not the only one, for linking our lives in caring ways with the lives of others. When we give with care, we identify ourselves with valuable causes that add meaning to our lives by promoting better communities, both substantively by helping and symbolically as expressions of hope for better communities.

In addition to this general faith in the cogency of moral ideals, moral faith affirms the prospects for realizing those ideals in caring relationships. This brings us to the last paradox, and to the role of faith in dealing with risks.

Ambiguity and Faith in a Life of Service

Philanthropy is risky because of several ambiguities: uncertainty about the future; unclarity concerning moral ideals; vagueness surrounding the moral implications of giving; and unstable mixtures of good and bad. Ambiguities, hence doubt, uncertainty, and ambivalence, surround all aspects of philanthropy explored in this book, including the implications of ideals of virtue, the extent of responsibilities to help, how to avoid undesirable side effects, how to show respect for autonomy, which mixed motives are unacceptable, and when service contributes to self-fulfillment.

In response to these ambiguities, caring implies caution, but also faith. Only faith, along with other positive attitudes such as hope, trust, and other risk-taking virtues, enables us to act with optimism in the prospects of making a difference for the better. Faith operates at several levels within philanthropy. Some is problem-targeted: our voluntary service can and will make a difference in solving a given problem. Some is outcome-targeted: this contribution will succeed in helping in a specific way. And some is global: a life of service is the most meaningful life. Each implies faith in the mutual good will of morally concerned individuals, as well as a general faith in moral values.

Faith is paradoxical in that it needs to be grounded in evidence or else becomes wishful thinking, yet in some situations it is self-verifying, hence a reason for itself. It is self-verifying when its content, that is, what we believe, turns out to be true or false depending on whether we adopt the faith. William James explored this self-confirming aspect of faith in "The Will to Believe," an essay whose focus is religious faith, but which also applies to faith in philanthropy.[72]

James did not defend all faith. As a distinguished scientist, he condemned "vile" faith based on prejudice, sentimentality, dogmatism, and egotism.[73] The faith he defended is grounded in a spirit of truth-seeking and goodness-promoting, and it comes as a response to ambiguous "genuine options." Options are sets of alternative beliefs, and ambiguous options are those which cannot be resolved by available evidence.[74] A genuine option is "forced, living, and momentous": forced, in that we must make a decision on the issue, since suspending judgment counts as a decision; living, in that each alternative appeals to us as a real possibility; and momentous, in that something important is at stake.

Beliefs about whether to engage in voluntary service often confront us as ambiguous genuine options. They are forced because postponing them amounts to a decision that has practical implications. They are living because we appreciate the real possibility of helping and also of using our resources for other desired purposes. They are momentous because something important is at stake in humanitarian acts and community service. Finally, they are ambiguous: the prospects for success are inconclusive, especially where groups of givers, receivers, and intermediary organizations are involved. Further investigation may reduce ambiguities about organizations or causes, but usually there will remain areas of uncertainty about whether to get involved. If we wait for conclusive evidence, we may never act, at least not in time to do any good.

Evidence shapes our beliefs, but so does our "willing nature"—values, passions, desires, emotions, attitudes, and mental temperament. Our willing nature plays three inescapable roles: (1) It determines which alternatives we regard as live and momentous. (2) It resolves ambiguous genuine options where the evidence is too inconclusive for our intellect alone to decide, "for to say, under such circumstances, 'Do not decide, but leave the question open,' is itself a passional decision,—just like deciding yes or no,—and is attended with the same risk of losing the truth."[75] (3) Most important, our willing nature comprises our attitudes about our responsibilities in forming beliefs. The "skeptical attitude" is to shun error at all cost, even if it means going without important truths. By contrast, the "believing attitude" is to seek the truth, willing on occasion to adopt faith in order to pursue a good, accepting the risk of error. The believing attitude is the more reasonable in response to ambiguous genuine options. Insofar as it is self-verifying, it makes possible the gaining of truths and the creation of goods that would otherwise be lost.

Self-verifying in what way? The idea is puzzling if we focus on beliefs justified solely by evidence independent of the beliefs themselves. Whether it will rain tomorrow is decided by facts about the world, not by faith. Yet there are many situations, including philanthropy, in which we are participants rather than mere observers. Our beliefs shape how we act, and our actions make a difference in the outcomes that confirm or refute the beliefs. As James says elsewhere, "For again and again success depends on energy of act; energy again depends on faith that we shall not fail; and that faith in turn on the faith that we are right,—which faith thus verifies itself."[76] Faith, along with hope and courage, increases our willingness to take risks and make sacrifices on behalf of desirable causes. It also opens us to the possibilities of caring relationships which churlish or cynical attitudes would foreclose.

As James argues, faith makes possible caring relationships within communities:

> A social organism of any sort whatever, large or small, is what it is because each member proceeds to his own duty with a trust that the other members will simultaneously do theirs. Wherever a desired result is achieved by the co-operation of many independent persons, its existence as a fact is a pure consequence of the precursive faith in one another of those immediately concerned.[77]

"Precursive faith" within groups leads to initiatives based on trust, and those initiatives often make the faith self-fulfilling. In addition to generating personal effort, faith inspires others to join with us in creating common goods that otherwise would not exist.

Naive faith is dangerous, but so are cynicism and despair. James offers the parable of a trainload of people subdued by a few highwaymen. It would be foolish to resist by oneself; one simply gets shot. But a group whose members had faith in one another could overcome the robbers and deter future thefts. The analogue is that the self-verifying faith is shared faith in the prospects for collective action in philanthropy. Philanthropy, when it involves giving with care, is a forum that develops that faith *and* provides reasons for having it. Philanthropy is possible because of self-confirming faith—faith in our ability to help and faith in the prospects for caring relationships.

If it is reasonable to adopt the believing attitude in response to ambiguous genuine options when doing so may produce self-verifying faiths that yield vital goods, how do we decide when that is? Don't we need evidence, at a new level, for the prospects that faith can produce the good effects in our circumstances?

Yes and no. We do need evidence that philanthropic endeavors have worthy goals and reasonable prospects of success. With respect to specific philanthropic options, that implies making inquiries. The willingness to trust an organization, to *entrust* our money or time in it, is reasonable only when there are reasons for believing the organization is committed to good ends and is directed by competent and committed people.[78] With respect to the general disposition to become involved in philanthropy we can reflect on the innumerable examples of successful helping. We can also examine historical evidence about the overall prospects for improving societies.[79] And we can reflect on the near certainty of things getting worse if no one is willing to act on faith.

Nevertheless, ambiguity will recur: there will usually be some uncertainty about whether the faith will be self-verifying in the situation at hand. The response to that ambiguity is itself faith, attuned to the possible goods as well as to the risks. In this respect, faith is "self-covering": moral faith implies faith in itself.

I began with Simone de Beauvoir's caution about voluntary service. I conclude with her reminder that ambiguity is not absurdity: "To declare that existence is absurd is to deny that it can ever be given a meaning; to say that it is ambiguous is to assert that its meaning is never fixed, that it must be constantly won."[80] With all its ambiguities and perils, philanthropy provides a forum for moral creativity, for putting our vision of a good society into practice, and for fostering caring relationships that enrich individuals and communities alike. Faith in communities, evidenced in philanthropic giving, is faith in ourselves.

Notes

Preface

1. William K. Frankena discusses the central virtue of "responsible benevolence" in connection with philanthropy, although in a narrower sense of "philanthropy" than I use; see "Beneficence/Benevolence," in Ellen Frankel Paul, Fred D. Miller, Jr., Jeffrey Paul, and John Ahrens (eds.), *Beneficence, Philanthropy and the Public Good* (New York: Basil Blackwell, 1987), pp. 1–20.

2. Alfie Kohn provides an insightful discussion of why in general we tend to emphasize the negative side of human nature; see *The Brighter Side of Human Nature* (New York: Basic Books, 1990).

1. Giving with Care

1. The definition of philanthropy as private giving for public purposes was used by Robert L. Payton in "American Values and Private Philanthropy," although he uses honorific definitions in "Philanthropic Values" (and other writings); see both essays in Kenneth W. Thompson (ed.), *Philanthropy: Private Means, Public Ends* (Lanham, MD: University Press of America, 1987), pp. 3–47. In other writing Payton has used "philanthropy" more widely to refer to voluntary giving, nonprofit organizations, and voluntary associations.

2. Cf. Richard Cornuelle, *Reclaiming the American Dream* (New York: Random House, 1965). For a provocative case study, see Kathleen M. Blee, *Women of the Klan: Racism and Gender in the 1920s* (Berkeley: University of California Press, 1991).

3. The essays were published in a special edition of *Social Philosophy and Policy* 4, no. 2 (Spring 1987), and also as a book: Ellen Frankel Paul, Fred D. Miller, Jr., Jeffrey Paul, and John Ahrens (eds.), *Beneficence, Philanthropy and the Public Good* (New York: Basil Blackwell, 1987). Most of them were presented earlier at an Exxon Education Foundation Conference.

4. Mary Midgley explores the divorce of philosophy from the public in *Wisdom, Information, and Wonder* (New York: Routledge, 1989). As she notes with encouragement, things have begun to improve during the past two decades with the growth of applied ethics.

5. Molière, *The Critique of the School for Wives*, trans. Donald M. Frame, in *Tartuffe and Other Plays by Molière* (New York: New American Library, 1967), p. 197.

6. I present this approach to ethical theories more fully in *Everyday Morality: An Introduction to Applied Ethics* (Belmont, CA: Wadsworth, 1989).

7. In speaking of virtue-oriented ethics, then, I intend no presuppositions about character issues being more important, logically basic, or morally fundamental than issues about right and wrong conduct. Some other definitions of virtue ethics do. See, for example, Joel Kupperman, "Character and Ethical Theory," *Midwest Studies in Philosophy* 13 (1988): 115–125.

8. Ludwig Wittgenstein, *Culture and Value*, trans. Peter Winch (Chicago: University of Chicago Press, 1980), p. 16.

9. Such a book would be akin to James Douglas's *Why Charity? The Case for a Third Sector* (Beverly Hills: Sage Publications, 1983).

10. Cf. Alan Gewirth, "Private Philanthropy and Positive Rights," in Paul et al. (eds.), *Beneficence, Philanthropy and the Public Good*, p. 70.

11. Martin Luther King, Jr., *Strength to Love* (Philadelphia: Fortress Press, 1963), p. 30. See also Herta Loeser, *Women, Work, and Volunteering* (Boston: Beacon Press, 1974), p. 31. Loeser's comment on Richard Nixon's attitudes toward philanthropy is applicable to Ronald Reagan's administration as well: "Voluntary action is never an alternative to government funding and responsibility; the trumpet call for volunteers must not drown out the clamor for massive financial support from the government for domestic needs, including health, education, and welfare, as well as for cultural institutions and programs."

12. Robert L. Payton refers to philanthropy as a moral sector in *Philanthropy: Voluntary Action for the Public Good* (New York: Macmillan, 1988), p. 121. Aside from such overgenerous moments, Payton avoids giving blanket praise to philanthropy and warns us of its occasional harm.

13. Robert Nozick, *The Examined Life* (New York: Simon and Schuster, 1989), p. 287. Here Nozick rejects the libertarian (minimum government) philosophy he had defended vigorously in *Anarchy, State, and Utopia* (New York: Basic Books, 1974).

14. See Jane S. Smith, *Patenting the Sun: Polio and the Salk Vaccine.* (New York: William Morrow, 1990).

15. Ludwig Wittgenstein called these similarities "family resemblances"; *Philosophical Investigations*, trans. G. E. M. Anscombe (New York: Macmillan, 1953), remarks 65–69. He also argued that precise necessary and sufficient conditions cannot be specified for most concepts used in ordinary language. The looseness of nontechnical language (and some technical languages), which is essential for both economy of discourse and creative extension of terms to new situations, means that uncertain and borderline applications of terms will always arise.

16. Paul Dean, "Ollie's New War," *Los Angeles Times*, (September 17, 1989), part IV, p. 10.

17. Peter Dobkin Hall, "A Historical Overview of the Private Nonprofit Sector," in Walter W. Powell (ed.), *The Nonprofit Sector: A Research Handbook* (New Haven: Yale University Press, 1987), p. 21.

18. The legend has a rich and varied history. See J. C. Holt, *Robin Hood* (New York: Thames and Hudson, 1982).

19. Aristotle defended private property by appealing to the need for people to own things in order to be able to give them away philanthropically, which he saw as inherently valuable when done in accord with virtue. T. H. Irwin shows that his argument fails. Socialist governments which abolish private property could "loan" some goods to individuals and allow them discretion in deciding whether to keep them for themselves or give them away. See T. H. Irwin, "Generosity and Property in Aristotle's Politics," in Paul et al. (eds.), *Beneficence, Philanthropy and the Public Good*, pp. 37–54.

20. Cf. Joseph R. Des Jardins and Ronald Duska, "Drug Testing in Employment," in W. Michael Hoffman and Jennifer Mills Moore (eds.), *Business Ethics*, 2d ed. (New York: McGraw-Hill, 1990), p. 303.

21. Bill Berkowitz, *Local Heroes* (Lexington, MA: D. C. Heath, 1987), pp. 198–207.

22. Charles L. Stevenson, "Persuasive Definitions," *Mind* 47 (1938): 331–350.

23. William K. Frankena, "Beneficence/Benevolence," in Paul et al. (eds.), *Beneficence, Philanthropy and the Public Good*, p. 20.

24. Brian O'Connell, "What Colleges Ought to Do to Instill a Voluntary Spirit in Young Adults," *Chronicle of Higher Education*, (April 15, 1987): 104.

25. John O'Connor, "Philanthropy and Selfishness," in Paul et al. (eds.), *Beneficence, Philanthropy and the Public Good*, p. 113.

26. Payton, "Philanthropic Values," pp. 22–23.

27. Barry D. Karl and Stanley N. Katz, "Foundations and Ruling Class Elites," *Daedalus* 116 (Winter 1987): 5–6.

28. Recent writers differ in their preferred generic term. For example, Robert H. Bremner uses "philanthropy" as generic and includes volunteering (giving of one's time and talents) as a special case: *American Philanthropy*, 2d ed. (Chicago: University of Chicago Press, 1988); Susan J. Ellis and Katherine H. Noyes do the opposite, picking "volunteerism" as generic and treating philanthropy (giving of monetary form) as a special case: *By the People: A History of Americans as Volunteers*, rev. ed. (San Francisco: Jossey-Bass, 1990); Jon Van Til prefers "voluntarism" as generic: *Mapping the Third Sector: Voluntarism in a Changing Social Economy* (New York: Foundation Center, 1988); and James Douglas prefers the legal sense of the word "charity" as generic: *Why Charity?*

29. For example, the Association of American Colleges, in its Program on Studying Philanthropy, used the word in this sense: "The Association uses the term 'philanthropy' to include all forms of charitable giving and voluntary service, voluntary association and not-for-profit initiative" (from "Request for Proposals," brochure for the program).

30. In addition to this activity sense, "philanthropy" sometimes refers to the content of what is given, that is, the gift itself.

31. The main thrust of Alasdair MacIntyre's *After Virtue*, 2d ed. (Notre Dame: University of Notre Dame Press, 1984) is to argue that contemporary moral discourse is in grave and disastrous disorder. I do not share his skepticism. I am more in sympathy with Jeffrey Stout's assessment of the moral scene in *Ethics after Babel: The Languages of Morals and Their Discontents* (Boston: Beacon Press, 1988), pp. 200–242, 266–272. Like Stout, I see the main value in MacIntyre's book in the groundwork it lays for "a detailed investigation of our actual social practices" (ibid., p. 267). MacIntyre, I should note, does not apply his conception of practices to philanthropy.

32. MacIntyre, *After Virtue*, p. 187.

33. For an especially illuminating discussion, see Susan A. Ostrander and Paul G. Schervish, "Giving and Getting: Philanthropy as a Social Relation," in Jon Van Til (ed.), *Critical Issues in American Philanthropy* (San Francisco: Jossey-Bass, 1990), pp. 67–98.

34. MacIntyre says that internal goods "can only be identified and recognized by the experience of participating in the practice in question" (*After Virtue*, pp. 188–189). That seems too strong. "Health" can be understood, at least to a significant extent, by people who do not participate in the practice of medicine.

35. Ibid., p. 194.

36. For a quick overview of innovation in American philanthropy, see Bremner, *American Philanthropy*.

37. MacIntyre, *After Virtue*, p. 191 (italics deleted).

38. Ibid., p. 219.

39. Ibid., pp. 223, 273.

40. Edmund L. Pincoffs, *Quandaries and Virtues* (Lawrence: University Press of Kansas, 1986), p. 79.

41. Pincoffs says that "only one of the virtue considerations is clearly applicable" to institutions: "namely, justice. It would be more than odd to speak of the honesty or loyalty of an institution" (ibid., p. 110). On the contrary, it is not odd to speak of honest and dishonest institutions, or of institutions that are loyal or disloyal to their members, or

responsible or irresponsible toward society. Cf. Michael D. Smith, "The Virtuous Organization," in Albert Flores (ed.), *Professional Ideals* (Belmont, CA: Wadsworth, 1988), pp. 172–175.

42. Pincoffs, *Quandaries and Virtues*, pp. 89–93. Many of the virtues which Pincoffs considers nonmoral are in my view moral ones, including nobility, dignity, courage, and tolerance (ibid., p. 85). Amélie Rorty insightfully discusses the difficulties in characterizing which personality traits are virtues in "Virtues and Their Vicissitudes," in *Mind in Action* (Boston: Beacon Press, 1988), pp. 314–329.

43. Philip Hallie, *Lest Innocent Blood Be Shed* (New York: Harper and Row, 1985), p. 104.

44. Ibid., pp. 20–21. For a comprehensive study of the motives of rescuers during the Holocaust, see Samuel P. Oliner and Pearl M. Oliner, *The Altruistic Personality* (New York: Free Press, 1988).

45. Hallie, *Lest Innocent Blood Be Shed*, p. 72.

46. For insightful discussions of caring, see Milton Mayeroff, *On Caring* (New York: Harper and Row, 1971); and Nel Noddings, *Caring: A Feminine Approach to Ethics and Moral Education* (Berkeley: University of California Press, 1984).

47. Frankena discusses this distinction in connection with philanthropy in "Beneficence/Benevolence," in Paul et al. (eds.), *Beneficence, Philanthropy and the Public Good*, pp. 1–20.

48. Richard M. Titmuss provides the classic discussion in *The Gift Relationship: From Human Blood to Social Policy* (New York: Vintage Books, 1971).

49. S. I. Benn insightfully discusses the distinction, although he goes too far in separating the two; see "Individuality, Autonomy and Community," in Eugene Kamenka (ed.), *Community as a Social Ideal* (New York: St. Martin's Press, 1983), pp. 43–62.

50. The expression "mediating structures" is used by Peter L. Berger and Richard John Neuhaus in *To Empower People: The Role of Mediating Structures in Public Policy* (Washington, DC: American Enterprise Institute, 1977).

51. For an illuminating discussion, see David B. Wong, "On Flourishing and Finding One's Identity in Community," *Midwest Studies in Philosophy* 13 (1988): 324–341.

52. The third, fourth, and sixth of these features roughly parallel the three "modes of community" (affective, productive, and rational) distinguished by Robert Paul Wolff in *The Poverty of Liberalism* (Boston: Beacon Press, 1968), pp. 185–193.

53. Virginia Held, "The Grounds for Social Trust," in *Rights and Goods* (Chicago: University of Chicago Press, 1984), pp. 62–85.

54. Robert L. Payton, "Morality, Polity, and Voluntary Initiative," paper read at the International Conference on "Voluntarism, Non-Governmental Organizations and Public Policy," Jerusalem (May 1989).

55. Robert N. Bellah et al., *Habits of the Heart: Individualism and Commitment in American Life* (Berkeley: University of California Press, 1985), p. 285. I share the reservations concerning Bellah's methodology and conclusions voiced by Jeffrey Stout, *Ethics after Babel: The Languages of Morals and Their Discontents* (Boston: Beacon Press, 1988), pp. 191–219.

56. Ibid., p. 290.

2. Virtues in Giving

1. Aristotle, *Nicomachean Ethics*, trans. Terence Irwin (Indianapolis: Hackett, 1985), p. 87. I also used this translation in the epigraph, although I substituted the more customary word "noble" where Irwin uses "fine."

2. Aristotle's *eleutheriotes* also differs from our word "generosity" in that it also referred to appropriate degrees of acquiring wealth, as well as to giving it.

3. For stylistic reasons I sometimes refer to the virtues with adjectives rather than nouns (e.g., compassionate rather than compassion).

4. See Lawrence A. Blum, "Compassion," in Amélie Rorty (ed.), *Explaining Emotions* (Berkeley: University of California Press, 1980); Joseph Butler, "Upon Compassion," sermons 5 and 6 in *Fifteen Sermons Preached at the Rolls Chapel* (London: G. Bell and Sons, 1964); and Robert Wuthnow, *Acts of Compassion* (Princeton: Princeton University Press, 1991).

5. Mother Teresa of Calcutta, *My Life for the Poor*, ed. Jose Luis Gonzalez-Balado and Janet N. Playfoot (New York: Ballantine Books, 1985), p. 10. See also Malcolm Muggeridge, *Something Beautiful for God: Mother Teresa of Calcutta* (New York: Harper and Row, 1971).

6. Occasionally "pity" and "compassion" are used as synonyms. For example, Nietzsche did not distinguish them when he (insightfully) criticized pity as an ignoble way to bolster one's self-esteem by looking down on others, and when he (mistakenly) attacked compassion as wallowing in others' suffering; see *Thus Spoke Zarathustra*, trans. Walter Kaufmann (New York: Penguin, 1978).

7. Blum, "Compassion," p. 232.

8. James D. Wallace, *Virtues and Vices* (Ithaca: Cornell University Press, 1978), pp. 143–144. See also John McDowell, "Virtue and Reason," in Stanley G. Clarke and Evan Simpson (eds.), *Anti-Theory in Ethics and Moral Conservatism* (Albany: State University of New York Press, 1989), pp. 87–109.

9. Eudora Welty, *The Ponder Heart* (New York: Harcourt Brace Jovanovich, 1953).

10. Mark 12, *The New Testament*, trans. J. B. Phillips (New York: Macmillan, 1965). See Elizabeth Cady Stanton's comment on this scripture in *The Woman's Bible* (Seattle: Coalition Task Force on Women and Religion, 1974), p. 131.

11. For the most part, Kant overlooked supererogatory acts, collapsing them into the category of moral permissibility; see *The Doctrine of Virtue*, trans. Mary J. Gregor (Philadelphia: University of Pennsylvania Press, 1964), pp. 21–22. J. O. Urmson drew attention to supererogatory deeds in "Saints and Heroes," in A. I. Melden (ed.), *Essays in Moral Philosophy* (Seattle: University of Washington Press, 1958), pp. 198–216. For two book-length studies, see David Heyd, *Supererogation* (Cambridge: Cambridge University Press, 1982); and Gregory Mellema, *Beyond the Call of Duty: Supererogation, Obligation, and Offence* (Albany: State University of New York Press, 1991).

12. Wallace distinguished between the first two types of generosity in *Virtues and Vices*, pp. 131–152. For another insightful discussion, see Lester H. Hunt, "Generosity and the Diversity of the Virtues," in Robert B. Kruschwitz and Robert C. Roberts (eds.), *The Virtues* (Belmont, CA: Wadsworth, 1987), pp. 216–228.

13. Immanuel Kant, *Foundations of the Metaphysics of Morals*, trans. Lewis White Beck, in A. I. Melden (ed.), *Ethical Theories* (Englewood Cliffs, NJ: Prentice Hall, 1967), pp. 317–366. Even romantic love involves a mixture of involuntary events and voluntary actions, with the latter making it possible for love to be guided by the virtues, indeed to embody the virtues. See Mike W. Martin, "Love's Constancy," *Philosophy* 68 (1993): 63–77.

14. Moral equals, that is, when they have the capacity or potential (as with children) to respect our rights in return. I find it problematic whether sociopathic murderers (who lack any sense of right and wrong) deserve full moral respect.

15. On support for just institutions, see John Rawls, *A Theory of Justice* (Cambridge: Harvard University Press, 1971).

16. A. I. Melden, *Rights and Persons* (Berkeley: University of California Press, 1977), esp. ch. 5.

17. Robert C. Solomon, *A Passion for Justice* (New York: Addison-Wesley, 1990), esp. ch. 6.

18. Alasdair MacIntyre, *Whose Justice? Which Rationality?* (Notre Dame: University of Notre Dame Press, 1988).

19. Jonathan Kozol, *Rachel and Her Children: Homeless Families in America* (New York: Crown, 1988).

20. Melden, *Rights and Persons*, pp. 32–56.

21. Kurt Vonnegut, *God Bless You, Mr. Rosewater* (New York: Dell, 1965).

22. See Lawrence C. Becker, *Reciprocity* (New York: Routledge and Kegan Paul, 1986).

23. See Fred R. Berger, "Gratitude," *Ethics* 85 (1975): 298–309. See also Paul F. Camenisch, "Gift and Gratitude in Ethics," *Journal of Religious Ethics* 9 (1981): 1–34; and Gilbert C. Meilaender, "The Virtue of Gratitude," in *The Theory and Practice of Virtue* (Notre Dame: University of Notre Dame Press, 1984), pp. 152–175.

24. Camenisch, "Gift and Gratitude in Ethics," p. 23. See also Paul Tournier, *The Meaning of Gifts*, trans. John S. Gilmour (Richmond, VA: John Knox Press, 1963).

25. Harry S. Broudy, *Enlightened Cherishing* (Urbana: University of Illinois Press, 1972), p. 6.

26. Robert H. Bremner, *American Philanthropy*, 2d ed. (Chicago: University of Chicago Press, 1988), pp. 14–18.

27. The concepts are borrowed from Becker, *Reciprocity*, pp. 155–157. But I use "cooperative" for his "sociality," and "congenial" for his "sociability." In a related religious context, see Daniel Day Williams' postulate of a "will to communion" in *The Spirit and the Forms of Love* (Lanham, MD: University Press of America, 1981), pp. 136, 205.

28. Benjamin Franklin, *Autobiography* (New York: W. W. Norton, 1986), p. 74.

29. Josiah Royce, *The Philosophy of Loyalty* (New York: Macmillan, 1916), pp. 16–17 (italics deleted). Royce calls this a preliminary definition; his fuller definition makes "loyalty" a religious concept: "Loyalty is the Will to Believe in something eternal, and to express that belief in the practical life of a human being" (p. 357; italics deleted). For more cautious and secular discussions of loyalty, see Robert Paul Wolff, "Loyalty," in *The Poverty of Liberalism* (Boston: Beacon Press, 1968), pp. 51–83; Andrew Oldenquist, "Loyalties," *Journal of Philosophy* 79 (1982): 173–193; and Andrew Oldenquist, *The Non-Suicidal Society* (Bloomington: Indiana University Press, 1986).

30. Royce, *The Philosophy of Loyalty*, p. 22.

31. Cf. John Ladd, "Loyalty," in Paul Edwards (ed.), *The Encyclopedia of Philosophy*, vol. 5 (New York: Macmillan, 1967), pp. 97–98.

32. See Jean-Paul Sartre, *Anti-Semite and Jew*, trans. George J. Becker (New York: Schocken Books, 1965).

33. Royce, *The Philosophy of Loyalty*, p. 377 (italics deleted).

34. Jane S. Smith, *Patenting the Sun: Polio and the Salk Vaccine* (New York: William Morrow, 1990), p. 85.

35. See Annette Baier, "Secular Faith," in *Postures of the Mind* (Minneapolis: University of Minnesota Press, 1985), pp. 292–308. For a stimulating book on religious hope, see James L. Muyskens, *The Sufficiency of Hope* (Philadelphia: Temple University Press, 1979).

36. Harry C. Boyte, *Community Is Possible* (New York: Harper and Row, 1984), pp. 125–159.

37. Hebrews 11:1. At the end of this book I develop the theme of self-fulfilling faith.

38. John Dewey, *A Common Faith* (New Haven: Yale University Press, 1934).

39. As illustrative approaches to interpreting the sacred in secular terms, see Dewey, ibid.; Julian Huxley, *Religion without Revelation* (New York: New American Library, 1957); and Herbert Fingarette, *Confucius: The Secular as Sacred* (New York: Harper and Row, 1972).

40. I wish to rule out intolerant church dogmas such as belief in an angry and jealous God who damns people who do not believe in His existence.

41. For a discussion of the Islamic concept, which is less familiar in the West than Jewish and Christian concepts, see Al-Ghazzali, *The Mysteries of Almsgiving*, trans. Nabih Amin Faris (Kashmiri Bazar-Lahore, 1974).

42. Robert Adams approaches faithlessness as a sin of theists; "The Virtue of Faith," in *The Virtue of Faith* (New York: Oxford University Press, 1987), pp. 9–24.

43. Dorothy Day, *The Long Loneliness* (New York: Harper and Row, 1952); Dorothy Day, *Loaves and Fishes* (New York: Harper and Row, 1963). See also Robert Coles, *Dorothy Day* (Reading, MA: Addison-Wesley, 1987).

44. Teresa Odendahl, *Charity Begins at Home: Generosity and Self-Interest among the Philanthropic Elite* (New York: Basic Books, 1990), pp. 204–207.

45. John Muir, *To Yosemite and Beyond*, ed. R. Engberg and Donald Wesling (Madison: University of Wisconsin Press, 1980), p. 113.

46. Anne L. Bailey, "Arnold Beckman: Making Plans to Give Away a Fortune," *Chronicle of Philanthropy* 2 (May 15, 1990): 4–5, 8.

47. Jose Ortega y Gasset, *The Revolt of the Masses* (New York: W. W. Norton, 1932), p. 65.

48. Quoted by Lerone Bennett, Jr., in *Before the Mayflower* (New York: Penguin, 1964), p. 149 (italics deleted); cf. Melden, *Rights and Persons*, p. 23.

49. Richard Taylor discusses pride and its contrasts in *Ethics, Faith, and Reason* (Englewood Cliffs, NJ: Prentice Hall, 1985), pp. 98–106.

50. "My work in the [service] club made me feel important; it made me feel like I really had something to contribute to the community," says Elvia Alvarado in a moving account of authentic pride that has nothing to do with conceit; Elvia Alvarado, *Don't Be Afraid, Gringo: A Honduran Woman Speaks from the Heart*, trans. Medea Benjamin (New York: Harper and Row, 1987), p. 12.

51. Cf. Nelson W. Aldrich, Jr., *Old Money* (New York: Vintage Books, 1989), chs. 2 and 3.

52. Cf. Henry Fairlie, *The Seven Deadly Sins Today* (Notre Dame: University of Notre Dame Press, 1979), pp. 39–58.

53. Andrew Carnegie, *The Gospel of Wealth and Other Timely Essays* (New York, 1900).

54. Joseph Frazier Wall, *Andrew Carnegie* (Pittsburgh: University of Pittsburgh Press, 1989), p. 820.

55. Wallace, *Virtues and Vices*, pp. 107–110. Cf. Mike W. Martin, "Honesty with Oneself," in Mary I. Bockover (ed.), *Rules, Rituals, and Responsibility: Essays Dedicated to Herbert Fingarette* (La Salle, IL: Open Court, 1991), pp. 115–136.

56. Charles E. Shepard, *Forgiven: The Rise and Fall of Jim Bakker and the PTL Ministry* (New York: Atlantic Monthly Press, 1989).

57. William Loren Katz, *The Invisible Empire: The Ku Klux Klan Impact on History* (Washington, DC: Open Hand, 1986); Wyn Wade, *The Fiery Cross: The Ku Klux Klan in America* (New York: Simon and Schuster, 1987).

58. Sarah Orne Jewett, "The Town Poor," in Sandra M. Gilbert and Susan Gubar (eds.), *The Norton Anthology of Literature by Women* (New York: W. W. Norton, 1985), p. 988.

59. The expression "virtues of self-direction" is borrowed from John Kekes, *The Examined Life* (Lewisburg: Bucknell University Press, 1988), p. 95.

60. Lawrence Becker defines wisdom as solely an instrumental virtue, but he adds that it entails knowing what is "best all-things-considered," suggesting that it includes knowledge of ends; Becker, *Reciprocity*, p. 162. My discussion of wisdom is most influenced

by Robert Nozick, *The Examined Life* (New York: Simon and Schuster, 1989), pp. 267–278. See also Kekes' insightful discussion in *The Examined Life*, pp. 145–160; Mary Midgley, *Wisdom, Information, and Wonder* (New York: Routledge, 1989); and Stanley Godlovitch's somewhat Platonic, other-worldly conception in "On Wisdom," in Sommers and Sommers (eds.), *Vice and Virtue in Everyday Life*, pp. 263–283.

61. Charles Dickens, *Bleak House* (New York: Bantam, 1983), ch. 4.

62. Ibid., p. 42.

63. Cf. Wallace, *Virtues and Vices*, p. 157. Mrs. Jellyby and her friends have ominous plans to resettle some of England's "superabundant" population in Africa, suggesting bigotry and paternalism as well as the absence of benevolence.

64. Cf. John Kekes, *Moral Tradition and Individuality* (Princeton: Princton University Press, 1989).

65. Immanuel Kant never wrote a more misleading passage than the following: "I do not, therefore, need any penetrating acuteness in order to discern what I have to do in order that my volition may be morally good. Inexperienced in the course of the world, incapable of being prepared for all its contingencies, I only ask myself: Can I will that my maxim become a universal law?" *Foundations of the Metaphysics of Morals*, trans. Lewis White Beck, in A. I. Melden (ed.), *Ethical Theories* (Englewood Cliffs: Prentice Hall, 1967), p. 328.

66. Cf. Martin Benjamin, *Splitting the Difference* (Lawrence: University Press of Kansas, 1990), ch. 5. James D. Wallace provides an illuminating discussion of moral vagueness and conflict in *Moral Relevance and Moral Conflict* (Ithaca: Cornell University Press, 1988).

67. Margaret Drabble, *The Needle's Eye* (New York: Ballantine Books, 1989), p. 73.

68. Jerold Panas, *Megagifts: Who Gives Them, Who Gets Them* (New York: Pluribus Press, 1984), pp. 123–124.

69. Anthony Trollope, *The Warden* (Oxford: Oxford University Press, 1980).

70. Cf. Thomas E. Hill, Jr., *Autonomy and Self-Respect* (Cambridge: Cambridge University Press, 1991), p. 112.

71. Franklin, *Autobiography*, pp. 75–76.

72. Cf. Hill, Jr., *Autonomy and Self-Respect*. Consider also Henry David Thoreau's explanation of why he gave up hunting: "No humane being, past the thoughtless age of boyhood, will wantonly murder any creature, which holds its life by the same tenure that he does"; "Higher Laws," in *Walden and Civil Disobedience* (New York: Penguin, 1983), p. 260.

73. Bremner, *American Philanthropy*, pp. 63ff.

74. John Griggs (ed.), *Simple Acts of Kindness: Volunteering in the Age of AIDS* (New York: United Hospital Fund of New York, 1989).

75. Wallace, *Virtues and Vices*, p. 77.

76. Douglas N. Walton, *Courage* (Berkeley: University of California Press, 1986), p. 189.

77. Ibid., pp. 124–125.

78. Bill Berkowitz, *Local Heroes* (Lexington, MA: Lexington Books, 1987), pp. 149–166; Charles C. Moskos, *A Call to Civic Service* (New York: Free Press, 1988), pp. 79–82.

79. Myron Peretz Glazer and Penina Migdal Glazer, *The Whistleblowers* (New York: Basic Books, 1989).

80. Peter Maas, *Serpico* (New York: Bantam, 1974).

81. Cf. Stuart Hampshire, "Sincerity and Single-Mindedness," in *Freedom of Mind and Other Essays* (Princeton: Princeton University Press, 1971), pp. 232–256.

82. Mary E. Wilkins Freeman, "A Mistaken Charity," in *The Revolt of Mother and Other Stories* (Old Westbury, NY: Feminist Press, 1974), p. 10.

83. Ibid., p. 12.

84. Barbara Kellerman, "Leadership as a Political Act," in Barbara Kellerman (ed.), *Leadership* (Englewood Cliffs, NJ: Prentice Hall, 1984), p. 70.

85. Edmund L. Pincoffs, *Quandaries and Virtues* (Lawrence: University Press of Kansas, 1986), p. 68. Mary Midgley prefers "moral originality" to "moral creativity" in "Creation and Originality," in *Heart and Mind* (New York: St. Martin's Press, 1981), pp. 43–58. See also A. S. Cua, *Dimensions of Moral Creativity* (University Park: Pennsylvania State University Press, 1978).

86. Charles Handy, "The Language of Leadership," in William E. Rosenbach and Robert L. Taylor (eds.), *Contemporary Issues in Leadership*, 2d ed. (Boulder: Westview Press, 1989), p. 238.

87. Odendahl, *Charity Begins at Home*, pp. 138–140.

88. Anne Witte Garland (ed.), *Women Activists* (New York: Feminist Press at CUNY, 1988), pp. 120–131.

89. Dennis R. Young, "Executive Leadership in Nonprofit Organizations," in Walter W. Powell (ed.), *The Nonprofit Sector: A Research Handbook* (New Haven: Yale University Press, 1987), pp. 167–179.

90. Brian O'Connell, *Philanthropy in Action* (New York: Foundation Center, 1987), p. 3.

91. Sanford D. Horwitt, *Let Them Call Me Rebel: Saul Alinsky, His Life and Legacy* (New York: Alfred A. Knopf, 1989).

92. Charles R. Holloman, "Leadership and Headship: There Is a Difference," in William E. Rosenbach and Robert L. Taylor (ed.), *Contemporary Issues in Leadership*, 2d ed. (Boulder: Westview Press, 1989), p. 109.

93. Karen Eppler, "Transforming Power in the Labor Movement—Cesar Chavez," in Robert L. Holmes (ed.), *Nonviolence In Theory and Practice* (Belmont, CA: Wadsworth, 1990), pp. 191–193.

94. Gray Cox, *The Ways of Peace* (New York: Paulist Press, 1986), p. 129.

95. Roger Fisher and William Ury, *Getting to Yes* (New York: Penguin, 1983). Cox discusses these three approaches to peace in *The Ways of Peace*, ch. 16.

96. Raghavan Iyer (ed.), *The Moral and Political Writings of Mahatma Gandhi*, vols. 1–3 (New York: Oxford University Press, 1986). While Gandhi was the primary influence on King, civil disobedience has a much longer history. See Hugo Adam Bedau (ed.), *Civil Disobedience* (Indianapolis: Bobbs-Merrill, 1969).

97. Cf. Robert Merrihew Adams, "The Problem of Total Devotion," in Robert Audi and William J. Wainwright (eds.), *Rationality, Religious Belief, and Moral Commitment* (Ithaca: Cornell University Press, 1986), esp. pp. 189–193; and Holloman, "Leadership and Headship," p. 111.

98. King was not, however, a saint in his personal life. See David J. Garrow, *Bearing the Cross: Martin Luther King, Jr., and the Southern Leadership Conference* (New York: Vintage Books, 1988), pp. 374, 617. More recently it was discovered that King engaged in plagiarism as a college student. Gandhi had similar flaws in his relationship with his family. In general, saints and moral heroes can have great influence without being moral models in all areas of their lives. See John Stratton Hawley (ed.), *Saints and Virtues* (Berkeley: University of California Press, 1987); and Owen Flanagan, *Varieties of Moral Personality* (Cambridge: Harvard University Press, 1991), pp. 1–12.

99. Garrow, *Bearing the Cross*, pp. 283–284.

100. King's philosophy of nonviolent resistance was formulated during the first month of the Montgomery Bus Boycott. See Garrow, ibid., p. 32. See also Taylor Branch, *Parting the Waters* (New York: Simon and Schuster, 1988).

101. Garrow, *Bearing the Cross*, p. 550.

3. Responsibilities to Help

1. The expression "mandatory virtue" is used by Edmund L. Pincoffs in *Quandaries and Virtues* (Lawrence: University Press of Kansas, 1986), p. 85. Lawrence C. Becker develops an argument to show that the virtues of reciprocity place obligations on us; see his *Reciprocity* (New York: Routledge and Kegan Paul, 1986), chs. 2 and 3. For a related discussion of justice, see Robert C. Solomon, *A Passion for Justice* (New York: Addison-Wesley, 1990).

2. Cf. J. Roland Pennock, "The Problem of Responsibility," in Carl J. Friedrich (ed.), *Responsibility* (New York: Liberal Arts Press, 1960), pp. 9, 13.

3. Cf. T. M. Scanlon, "Preference and Urgency," *Journal of Philosophy* 72 (1975), pp. 659–660; and Thomas Nagel, *The View from Nowhere* (New York: Oxford University Press, 1986), p. 167.

4. Cf. David Braybrooke, *Meeting Needs* (Princeton: Princeton University Press, 1987); and Michael Ignatieff, *The Needs of Strangers* (New York: Penguin, 1986).

5. Martin Gansberg, "38 Who Saw Murder Didn't Call Police," in Christina Sommers and Fred Sommers (eds.), *Vice and Virtue in Everyday Life*, 2d ed. (San Diego: Harcourt Brace Jovanovich, 1989), pp. 51–54. See also A. M. Rosenthal, *Thirty-Eight Witnesses* (New York: McGraw-Hill, 1964); and Bibb Latane and John M. Darley, *The Unresponsive Bystander* (New York: Appleton-Century-Crofts, 1970).

6. Andrew Young, as quoted in the *Cleveland Plain Dealer* (Dec. 15, 1978), p. 6-C; and see Frances Moore Lappé and Joseph Collins, *World Hunger* (New York: Grove Press, 1986), p. 2.

7. Peter Singer, "Famine, Affluence, and Morality," in William Aiken and Hugh La Follette (eds.), *World Hunger and Moral Obligation* (Englewood Cliffs, NJ: Prentice Hall, 1977), p. 24. That volume contains several helpful critiques of Singer, esp. John Arthur's "Rights and the Duty to Bring Aid," pp. 37–48.

8. Singer, ibid., p. 32.

9. Peter Singer, *Practical Ethics* (Cambridge: Cambridge University Press, 1979), pp. 158–181.

10. See Bernard Williams, "A Critique of Utilitarianism," in J. J. C. Smart and B. Williams, *Utilitarianism: For and Against* (Cambridge: Cambridge University Press, 1973); Bernard Williams, "Persons, Character, and Morality," in *Moral Luck* (Cambridge: Cambridge University Press, 1981); James S. Fishkin, *The Limits of Obligation* (New Haven: Yale University Press, 1982), pp. 153–171; James S. Fishkin, *Tyranny and Legitimacy* (Baltimore: Johns Hopkins University Press, 1979), ch. 9; David Heyd, *Supererogation* (Cambridge: Cambridge University Press, 1982), esp. pp. 172–183; and Nagel, *The View from Nowhere*, ch. 9. Shelly Kagan responds to this literature, though in my view inconclusively, in *The Limits of Morality* (Oxford: Clarendon Press, 1989), esp. pp. 357–369.

11. Cf. Nagel, *The View from Nowhere*, pp. 202–203; Owen Flanagan, *Varieties of Moral Personality* (Cambridge: Harvard University Press, 1991), pp. 6–7, 33–34.

12. Richard B. Brandt, *Ethical Theory* (Englewood Cliffs, NJ: Prentice Hall, 1959).

13. For a view along these lines, emphasizing negative rules of conduct, see Bernard Gert, *Morality* (New York: Oxford University Press, 1988).

14. John Rawls, *A Theory of Justice* (Cambridge: Harvard University Press, 1971), pp. 114, 338ff. Also see David A. J. Richards, *A Theory of Reasons for Action* (New York: Oxford University Press, 1971), pp. 185–189. Both books are inspired by Immanuel Kant, who formulated a version of the duty of mutual aid in *Foundation of the Metaphysics of Morals*, trans. Lewis White Beck, in *Ethical Theories*, edited by A. I. Melden (Englewood Cliffs, NJ: Prentice Hall, 1967), pp. 317–366.

15. Immanuel Kant, *The Doctrine of Virtue*, trans. Mary J. Gregor (Philadelphia: University of Pennsylvania Press, 1964), p. 112. Kant writes: "A wide [i.e., imperfect] duty is not to be taken as a permission to make exceptions to the maxim of actions, but only as a permission to limit one maxim of duty by another (e.g., love of one's neighbour in general by love of one's parents)"; *The Doctrine of Virtue*, p. 49. In this work Kant also discusses duties to oneself, though he does not explicitly apply them as limits on obligations to others. Patricia M. McGoldrick does, in "Saints and Heroes: A Plea for the Supererogatory," *Philosophy* 59 (1984): 523–528. For an interpretation of Kant, see Roger J. Sullivan, *Immanuel Kant's Moral Theory* (Cambridge: Cambridge University Press, 1989), pp. 50–54. See also John Stuart Mill, *Utilitarianism* (Indianapolis: Hackett, 1979), ch. 5. In *Rights in Moral Lives* (Berkeley: University of California Press, 1988) A. I. Melden points out that even perfect duties leave considerable room for discretion in meeting them. For example, parents have wide latitude in exercising judgment as how best to meet obligations to their children, and even the obligation to keep promises leaves some room for discretion. We can add that imperfect duties sometimes specify whom we must help, as in the Kitty Genovese case. Melden urges abandoning the distinction, but I think it can be salvaged by making it a matter of degree: thus, in general the imperfect duty of beneficence still allows *much more* room for discretion in deciding how to meet it, especially in deciding whom to help.

16. Kant, *The Doctrine of Virtue*, p. 120.

17. Robert Nozick, *Anarchy, State, and Utopia* (New York: Basic Books, 1974). Nozick does, however, approve of nonobligatory giving; see esp. pp. 265–268. Nozick has since rejected his strong libertarian views; see Robert Nozick, *The Examined Life* (New York: Simon and Schuster, 1989), p. 287.

18. A. I. Melden, *Rights and Persons* (Berkeley: University of California Press, 1977), p. 109. See also Henry Shue, *Basic Rights* (Princeton: Princeton University Press, 1980); Alan Gewirth, "Private Philanthropy and Positive Rights," in Ellen Frankel Paul et al. (eds.), *Beneficence, Philanthropy and the Public Good* (New York: Basil Blackwell, 1987), pp. 55–78; and William Aiken, "The Right to Be Saved from Starvation," in Aiken and La Follette (eds.), *World Hunger and Moral Obligation*, pp. 85–102. For the most part, Aiken argues as a rights ethicist, even though at one point he hints that rights are justified by appeal to utility (p. 89).

19. For brevity I will sometimes use "reciprocity" to refer to a virtue and sometimes to a principle of conduct, relying on context to mark the difference.

20. Alvin Gouldner, "The Norm of Reciprocity," *American Sociological Review* 25 (1960): 161–178; Marcel Mauss, *The Gift* (New York: W. W. Norton, 1967); Marshall Sahlins, *Stone Age Economics* (New York: Aldine, 1972).

21. Becker, *Reciprocity*, pp. 80–84, 89–94, 130–133. Becker's insightful book shapes most of what I say in this section, although he says little about philanthropy per se. I should note that Becker broadens the notion of reciprocity to include such principles as "Evil received should not be returned with evil" and "Evil received should be resisted"—principles that are better treated as aspects of nonmaleficence and self-respect.

22. Ibid., p. 74.

23. Ibid., pp. 125–126.

24. Fred R. Berger, "Gratitude," *Ethics* 85 (1975): 298–309.

25. John A. Simmons, *Moral Principles and Political Obligations* (Princeton: Princeton University Press, 1979), p. 166.

26. A. D. M. Walker, "Political Obligation and the Argument from Gratitude," *Philosophy and Public Affairs* 17 (1988): 195–199.

27. This is a loose paraphrase of a principle formulated by Richard J. Arneson in "The Principle of Fairness and Free-Rider Problems," *Ethics* 92 (1982): 623. Arneson develops the principle as a refinement of John Rawls's principle of fairness in John Rawls, *A Theory of Justice* (Cambridge: Harvard University Press, 1971), pp. 111–114, 342–350; and of H. L. A. Hart's principle of mutual restriction in H. L. A. Hart, "Are There Any Natural Rights?" *Philosophical Review* 64 (1955): 175–191.

28. Brian Barry, "Justice as Reciprocity," in Eugene Kamenka and Alice Erh-Soon Tay (eds.), *Justice* (New York: St. Martin's Press, 1980), p. 56.

29. Receiving some public goods, such as police protection and military defense, is backed by legally enforced taxation as a form of reciprocation, and hence has nothing to do with philanthropy.

30. Annette Baier, "The Rights of Past and Future Persons," in Ernest Partridge (ed.), *Responsibilities to Future Generations* (Buffalo: Prometheus Books, 1981), pp. 171–183; Becker, *Reciprocity*, ch. 7. Becker points out that this argument bypasses standard objections to talk about obligations to future (nonexistent) people.

31. I believe my use of "supererogatory" conforms with ordinary usage, but it differs from David Heyd's definition, which stipulates that the supererogatory is beyond moral obligation; see Heyd, *Supererogation*, p. 120.

32. Albert Schweitzer, *Memoirs of Childhood and Youth*, trans. C. T. Campion (New York: Macmillan, 1961), p. 61.

33. Albert Schweitzer, *Out of My Life and Thought: An Autobiography*, trans. C. T. Campion (New York: A Mentor Book, 1949), p. 75.

34. A. I. Melden, "Saints and Supererogation," in Ilham Dilman (ed.), *Philosophy and Life: Essays on John Wisdom* (The Hague: Martinus Nijhoff, 1984), p. 75. The criticism I raise against Melden, as I discovered later, is also made by Owen Flanagan, *Varieties of Moral Personality* (Cambridge: Harvard University Press, 1991), pp. 5–6.

35. Bob Geldof, *Is That It?* (New York: Ballantine Books, 1986), p. 246.

36. Quoted in Earl Babbie, *You Can Make a Difference* (New York: St. Martin's Press, 1985), pp. 33–34. Cf. Bill Berkowitz, *Local Heroes* (Lexington, MA: D. C. Heath, 1987), pp. 125–135.

37. J. O. Urmson, "Saints and Heroes," in A. I. Melden (ed.), *Essays in Moral Philosophy* (Seattle: University of Washington Press, 1958), p. 203. In a related vein, R. M. Hare suggested that the only "ought" involved in such cases derives from what Kant called hypothetical imperatives: If one wants to act beyond the universal requirements of duty, then one ought to pursue a certain course of action. This is a pure means-end "ought," not Kant's "categorical imperative" of morality which is not conditional on a prior desire. See R. M. Hare, *Freedom and Reason* (New York: Oxford University Press, 1963), ch. 9. For a critique of Hare, based on a position close to mine, see Michael S. Pritchard, *On Becoming Responsible* (Lawrence: University Press of Kansas, 1991), pp. 160–180.

38. Harry G. Frankfurt, *The Importance of What We Care About* (Cambridge: Cambridge University Press, 1988), 85–94.

39. Melden, "Saints and Supererogation," p. 64. Melden argues against calling saints' obligations supererogatory, but only because he defines the supererogatory as "beyond an individual's obligation or duty," rather than (as I do) "beyond those minimal obligations incumbent on everyone in similar circumstances."

40. Ibid., p. 79. Owen Flanagan also challenges Melden's oversharp dichotomy between saints and ordinary mortals; see Flanagan, *Varieties of Moral Personality*, p. 5.

41. Nicholas Rescher, *Ethical Idealism* (Berkeley: University of California Press, 1987), p. 132.

42. George H. Mead, "Philanthropy from the Point of View of Ethics," in Ellsworth Faris, Ferris Laune, and Arthur J. Todd (eds), *Intelligent Philanthropy* (Montclair, NJ: Patterson Smith, 1969), p. 133. Pincoffs also comes close to capturing the idea of supererogatory responsibilities, without calling them such, in Pincoffs, *Quandaries and Virtues*, pp. 115–129.

43. Mead, "Philanthropy from the Point of View of Ethics," p. 148.

44. Ibid., p. 145.

45. Russell Grice, *The Grounds of Moral Judgement* (Cambridge: Cambridge University Press, 1967), p. 160.

46. Ibid., p. 166.

47. Kenneth Kipnis, "Professional Responsibility and the Distribution of Legal Services," in Kenneth Kipnis and Diana T. Meyers (eds.), *Economic Justice* (Totowa, NJ: Rowman and Allanheld, 1985), pp. 130–142.

48. Steven B. Rosenfeld, "Mandatory *Pro Bono*: Historical and Constitutional Perspectives," *Cardozo Law Review* 2 (1981): 255–297.

49. Barlow F. Christensen, "The Lawyer's *Pro Bono Publico* Responsibility," *American Bar Foundation Research Journal* (1981): 1–19; Chesterfield H. Smith, "A Mandatory *Pro Bono* Service Standard—Its Time Has Come," *University of Miami Law Review* 35 (1981): 727–737.

50. Michael D. Bayles, *Professional Ethics*, 2d ed. (Belmont, CA: Wadsworth, 1989), pp. 53–55.

51. David L. Shapiro, "The Enigma of the Lawyer's Duty to Serve," *New York University Law Review* 55 (1980): 735–792.

52. American Bar Association, *Model Rules of Professional Conduct*, reprinted in Peter Y. Windt et al. (eds.), *Ethical Issues in the Professions* (Englewood Cliffs, NJ: Prentice Hall, 1989), pp. 565–566.

53. Berkowitz, *Local Heroes*, pp. 61–77.

54. American Medical Association, *Principles of Medical Ethics*, reprinted in Windt et al. (eds.), *Ethical Issues in the Professions*, pp. 566–567. For a discussion of supererogatory commitments in medicine, see John P. Reeder, "Beneficence, Supererogation, and Role Duty," in Earl E. Shelp (ed.), *Beneficence and Health Care* (Boston: D. Reidel, 1982), pp. 83–108.

55. Robert J. Baum, "Access to Engineering Services: Rights and Responsibilities of Professionals and the Public," *Business and Professional Ethics Journal* 4 (1985): 117–135.

56. Michael Useem, "Corporate Philanthropy," in Walter W. Powell (ed.), *The Nonprofit Sector: A Research Handbook* (New Haven: Yale University Press, 1987), pp. 340–359.

57. Robert N. Bellah et al., *Habits of the Heart: Individualism and Commitment in American Life* (Berkeley: University of California Press, 1985), pp. 8–13.

58. Jay Mathews, *Escalante* (New York: Henry Holt, 1988). *Stand and Deliver* is a movie about Jaime Escalante. For a study of a comparably supererogatory effort by a fifth grade teacher, see Tracy Kidder, *Among Schoolchildren* (Boston: Houghton Mifflin, 1989).

59. John Kultgen, *Ethics and Professionalism* (Philadelphia: University of Pennsylvania Press, 1988), p. 349.

60. Aristotle, *Nicomachean Ethics*, trans. Terence Irwin (Indianapolis: Hackett, 1985), p. 3.

61. For a related list, see F. Emerson Andrews, *Philanthropic Giving* (New York: Russell Sage Foundation, 1950), pp. 23–24.

62. Just as it would be a mistake to say that philanthropy is the sole way to meet the responsibilities of mutual aid and reciprocity, so it would be a mistake to say that service careers are the sole way. Norman Care often seems to be saying this in "Career Choice," in *On Sharing Fate* (Philadelphia: Temple University Press, 1987), pp. 26–48. Given the extent of worldwide destitution, he argues that we all ought to adopt a "service career" rather than a self-fulfilling one, and he fails to seriously consider the option of picking a satisfying career and then engaging in philanthropy. In other passages, however, his language is more flexible so as to allow the latter option: "In today's world morality requires that service to others be put before self-realization in the matter of career choice" (p. 29). Either way, his extreme demands are open to the same objections raised against Peter Singer.

63. Jane S. Smith, *Patenting the Sun: Polio and the Salk Vaccine* (New York: William Morrow, 1990).

64. Cf. Andrew Oldenquist, *The Non-Suicidal Society* (Bloomington: Indiana University Press, 1986), pp. 127ff.

65. Cf. Becker, *Reciprocity*, pp. 218ff.

66. Are the interests of members of future generations worthy of equal consideration with those of people alive today? I do not think so: even though future generations are morally significant, we have special responsibilities toward people alive today. For an opposing view, however, see Gregory Kavka's fine discussion, "The Futurity Problem," in Partridge (ed.), *Responsibilities to Future Generations*, pp. 109–122.

67. John Kekes, "Benevolence: A Minor Virtue," in Paul et al. (eds.), *Beneficence, Philanthropy and the Public Good*, pp. 21–36.

68. Jean-Paul Sartre, "Existentialism Is a Humanism," in Walter Kaufmann (ed.), *Existentialism from Dostoevsky to Sartre*, rev. ed. (New York: New American Library, 1975), p. 354.

69. Ibid., p. 356.

70. Recent defenders of moral pluralism who, unlike Sartre, maintain a belief in the objectivity of moral reasons are Bernard Williams, *Ethics and the Limits of Philosophy* (Cambridge: Harvard University Press, 1985); Stuart Hampshire, *Morality and Conflict* (Cambridge: Harvard University Press, 1983); Thomas Nagel, *The View from Nowhere* (New York: Oxford University Press, 1986); and John Kekes, *Moral Tradition and Individuality* (Princeton: Princeton University Press, 1989).

71. W. D. Ross, *The Right and the Good* (New York: Oxford University Press, 1930), p. 19. For alternative approaches, see Christopher W. Gowans (ed.), *Moral Dilemmas* (New York: Oxford University Press, 1987).

72. James D. Wallace, *Moral Relevance and Moral Conflict* (Ithaca: Cornell University Press, 1988), p. 20.

73. Frankfurt, *The Importance of What We Care About*, p. 85.

74. Cf. Mike W. Martin, *Everyday Morality: An Introduction to Applied Ethics* (Belmont, CA: Wadsworth, 1989), ch. 1; and John Kekes, *The Examined Life* (Lewisburg: Bucknell University Press, 1988), ch. 8.

75. Wallace, *Moral Relevance and Moral Conflict*, ch. 3.

4. Respect for Autonomy

1. Here, as elsewhere in this section, I am guided by David Sidorsky, "Moral Pluralism and Philanthropy," in Ellen Frankel Paul et al. (eds.), *Beneficence, Philanthropy and the Public Good* (New York: Basil Blackwell, 1987), pp. 93–112.

2. John Stuart Mill, *On Liberty* (Indianapolis: Hackett, 1978), ch. 2.

3. Moses Maimonides, excerpts from Jacob S. Minkin (ed.), *The World of Moses Maimonides* (New York: Thomas Yoseloff Press, 1957), pp. 45–49; excerpts republished in Brian O'Connell (ed.), *America's Voluntary Spirit* (New York: Foundation Center, 1983), p. 2.

4. Jennifer Moore, "A Different Kind of Aid for the World's Poor," *Chronicle of Philanthropy* (October 16, 1990), pp. 6–7, 14–15.

5. Bill Berkowitz, *Local Heroes* (Lexington, MA: Lexington Books, 1987), pp. 95–107.

6. F. Emerson Andrews, *Philanthropic Giving* (New York: Russell Sage Foundation, 1950) p. 246.

7. Edward Alsworth Ross, "Philanthropy from the Viewpoint of the Sociologist," in Ellsworth Faris, Ferris Laune, and Arthur J. Todd (eds.), *Intelligent Philanthropy* (Montclair, NJ: Patterson Smith, 1969), pp. 227–229; James O. S. Huntington, "Philanthropy—Its Success and Failure," in Jane Addams et al., *Philanthropy and Social Progress* (Montclair, NJ: Patterson Smith, 1970), pp. 98–156; Willard Gaylin, Ira Glasser, Steven Marcus, and David J. Rothman, *Doing Good: The Limits of Benevolence* (New York: Pantheon Books, 1981).

8. Ernesto J. Cortes, Jr., quoted in Bill Moyers, "Interview with Ernesto J. Cortes, Jr.," in *A World of Ideas*, vol. 2 (New York: Doubleday, 1990), p. 147.

9. Cf. Stephen Worchel, "The Darker Side of Helping," in Ervin Staub et al. (eds.), *Development and Maintenance of Prosocial Behavior* (New York: Plenum Press, 1984), pp. 379–395.

10. Jimmy Carter and Rosalynn Carter, *Everything to Gain*, (New York: Ballantine Books, 1987), pp. 100–105.

11. Susan A. Ostrander, *Women of the Upper Class* (Philadelphia: Temple University Press, 1984), p. 5.

12. Ibid., pp. 112–113.

13. Ibid., p. 137.

14. Immanuel Kant, *The Doctrine of Virtue*, trans. Mary J. Gregor (Philadelphia: University of Pennsylvania Press, 1964), pp. 115–116.

15. Ronald M. Green, "Altruism in Health Care," in Earl E. Shelp (ed.), *Beneficence and Health Care* (Dordrecht, Holland: D. Reidel, 1982), p. 242; R. C. Fox and J. P. Swazey, *The Courage to Fail*, 2d ed. (Chicago: University of Chicago Press, 1978), p. 383. Fox and Swazey use the expression "tyranny of the gift."

16. Kenneth J. Gergen and Mary M. Gergen, "Foreign Aid that Works," *Psychology Today* (June 1974): 53–58; Kenneth J. Gergen and Mary M. Gergen, "International Assistance from a Psychological Perspective," *Yearbook of World Affairs* 25 (London: Institute of World Affairs, 1971). See also Robert F. Arnove (ed.), *Philanthropy and Cultural Imperialism* (Bloomington: Indiana University Press, 1982).

17. Worchel, "The Darker Side of Helping," pp. 388–393.

18. Martin Benjamin and Joy Curtis, *Ethics in Nursing*, 2d ed. (New York: Oxford University Press, 1986), p. 57.

19. C. Dyke, "The Vices of Altruism," *Ethics* 81 (1970–71): 249.

20. Teresa Odendahl, *Charity Begins at Home: Generosity and Self-Interest among the Philanthropic Elite* (New York: Basic Books, 1990), pp. 163–186.

21. Ibid., pp. 163–4.

22. Ibid., p. 185.

23. Cf. Daniel Lyons, "Welcome Threats and Coercive Offers," *Philosophy* 50 (1975): 427, 431.

24. Norman Lewis, *The Missionaries: God against the Indians* (New York: Penguin, 1990), pp. 1–8. Moral issues about autonomy and contemporary missionary activities are explored by Margaret P. Battin in *Ethics in the Sanctuary* (New Haven: Yale University Press, 1990).

25. Anne Lowrey Bailey, "Philanthropy Research's Built-In Conflict: Grant Makers Are Often Subjects of Studies," *Chronicle of Higher Education* (September 21, 1988): A, 34, 36.

26. As Alan Wertheimer notes, this was a theme on the television show "The Millionaire"; Alan Wertheimer, *Coercion* (Princeton: Princeton University Press, 1987), p. 223.

27. Ibid., pp. 222–225.

28. Jerold Panas, *Mega Gifts: Who Gives Them, Who Gets Them* (Chicago: Pluribus Press, 1984), p. 30.

29. Wertheimer, *Coercion*, pp. 204–221.

30. E. Richard Brown, *Rockefeller Medicine Men* (Berkeley: University of California Press, 1980); Steven C. Wheatley, *The Politics of Philanthropy* (Madison: University of Wisconsin Press, 1988). See also Barry D. Karl and Stanley N. Katz, "Foundations and Ruling Class Elites," *Daedalus*, Special Issue on *Philanthropy, Patronage, Politics* 116 (Winter 1987): 1–40; and Arnove (ed.), *Philanthropy and Cultural Imperialism*.

31. Sasha R. Weitman, "Prosocial Behavior and Its Discontents," in Lauren Wispé (ed.), *Altruism, Sympathy, and Helping: Psychological and Sociological Principles* (New York: Academic Press, 1978).

32. See Sissela Bok, *Lying* (New York: Vintage Books, 1979).

33. Andrews, *Philanthropic Giving*, p. 160.

34. Scott M. Cutlip, "The Cheats in Fund Raising," in *Fund Raising in the United States* (New Brunswick: Rutgers University Press, 1965), pp. 441–473; Harvey Katz, "Charity Gone Sour," in *Give! Who Gets Your Charity Dollar?* (Garden City, NY: Anchor, 1974), pp. 117–135.

35. As reported on the television news show "20–20" (September 9, 1988).

36. In extortion the threatened act must be illegal, whereas in bribery it need not be; Wertheimer, *Coercion*, pp. 90–91.

37. Paul H. Schneiter, *The Art of Asking: A Handbook for Successful Fund Raising* (New York: Walker and Company, 1978), pp. 30–31.

38. Vince Stehle, "Prospect Reseachers, Who Collect Confidential Information about Donors, Are Divided over Ethical Questions," *Chronicle of Philanthropy* (September 5, 1989): 5, 11.

39. The tragedy generated many books, including Ethan Feinsod, *Awake in a Nightmare: Jonestown, the Only Eyewitness Account* (New York: W. W. Norton, 1981); and Tim Reiterman, *Raven* (New York: E. P. Dutton, 1982).

40. Joel Feinberg, "The Child's Right to an Open Future," in William Aiken and Hugh LaFollette (eds.), *Whose Child?* (Totowa, NJ: Littlefield, Adams, 1980), pp. 129–130.

41. Ibid., pp. 124–153.

42. Paul Ramsey, *The Patient as Person* (New Haven: Yale University Press, 1970).

43. "Sibling 'Consents' to Bone Marrow Transplant," in Aiken and LaFollette (eds.), *Whose Child?* pp. 24–25.

44. Anastasia Toufexis, "Creating a Child to Save Another," *Time* (March 5, 1990): 56; Irene Chang, "Baby Provides Bone Marrow for Her Sister," *Los Angeles Times* (June 5, 1991): A-1, 16.

45. J. Roland Pennock, "Coercion: An Overview," in J. Roland Pennock and John W. Chapman (eds.), *Coercion* (New York: Atherton, 1972), pp. 3–4.

46. Joel Feinberg, "Noncoercive Exploitation," in Rolf Sartorius (ed.), *Paternalism* (Minneapolis: University of Minnesota Press, 1983), pp. 201–235.

47. Pat McCormick, "NOW Task Force on Volunteerism" (November 1973), reprinted in *Ms.* 3, part 2 (1975): 73.

48. Susan J. Ellis and Katherine H. Noyes, *By the People: A History of Americans as Volunteers*, rev. ed. (San Francisco: Jossey-Bass, 1990), pp. 265–266.

49. Wendy Kaminer, *Women Volunteering* (Garden City, NY: Anchor, 1984), p. 6.

50. Ibid., p. 217.

51. Herta Loeser, *Women, Work, and Volunteering* (Boston: Beacan Press, 1974), pp. 26–33.

52. Ibid., p. 29.

53. Doris B. Gold, "Women and Voluntarism," in Vivian Gornick and Barbara K. Moran (eds.), *Woman in Sexist Society* (New York: New American Library, 1972), pp. 545–546. Cf. Kerstin Eriksson-Joslyn, "A Nation of Volunteers: Participatory Democracy or Administrative Manipulation?" *Berkeley Journal of Sociology* 17 (1973–74): 159–181.

54. Gold, "Women and Voluntarism," p. 534.

55. G. Petrovic, "Alienation," in Paul Edwards (ed.), *The Encyclopedia of Philosophy*, vol. 1 (New York: Macmillan, 1967), pp. 76–81; Richard Schacht, *Alienation* (New York: Anchor, 1971), ch. 7.

56. F. K. Prochaska, *Women and Philanthropy in Nineteenth-Century England* (Oxford: Clarendon Press, 1980), p. 3.

57. Judith Farr Tormey, "Exploitation, Oppression and Self-Sacrifice," in Carol C. Gould and Marx W. Wartofsky (eds.), *Women and Philosophy* (New York: G. P. Putnam's Sons, 1976), p. 221. Cf. Larry Blum et al., "Altruism and Women's Oppression," in Gould and Wartofsky (eds.), *Women and Philosophy*, pp. 222–247.

58. Cf. Mary Daly, *Beyond God the Father: Toward a Philosophy of Women's Liberation* (Boston: Beacon Press, 1973); and for a rejoinder, see Jean Grimshaw, "Women and Autonomy," in *Philosophy and Feminist Thinking* (Minneapolis: University of Minnesota Press, 1986), pp. 139–161.

59. Margaret Adams, "The Compassion Trap," in Gornick and Moran (eds.), *Woman in Sexist Society*, pp. 555–575. See also esp. Carol Gilligan, *In a Different Voice* (Cambridge: Harvard University Press, 1982).

60. Elizabeth Cady Stanton and the Revision Committee, *The Woman's Bible* (Seattle: Coalition on Women and Religion, 1974), p. 131.

61. Simone de Beauvoir, *The Second Sex*, trans. H. M. Parshley (New York: Vintage Books, 1953), p. 288.

62. My conception of autonomy is most influenced by Lawrence Haworth, *Autonomy* (New Haven: Yale University Press, 1986); and Diana T. Meyers, *Self, Society, and Personal Choice* (New York: Columbia University Press, 1989).

63. Kaminer, *Women Volunteering*, p. 160.

64. Ibid.

65. Arlene Kaplan Daniels, *Invisible Careers: Women Civic Leaders from the Volunteer World* (Chicago: University of Chicago Press, 1988).

66. Ibid.

67. Ibid., pp. 17–19. Daniels points out that *"noblesse oblige"* also carries a pejorative connotation of felt superiority and inequality.

68. Richard M. Titmuss, *The Gift Relationship: From Human Blood to Social Policy* (New York: Vintage Books, 1971), p. 245.

69. Ibid., p. 243.

70. Ibid., p. 239.

71. Compare the common corporation practice of putting a dollar figure on human life, based on estimated lifetime income and other factors, in making cost-benefit analyses for how many safety features to build into cars.

72. Marx Wartofsky, "On Doing It for Money," in Thomas A. Mappes and Jane S. Zembaty (eds.), *Biomedical Ethics* (New York: McGraw-Hill, 1981), p. 193. For a helpful discussion of the issue, see Lisa Newton, "Inducement, Due and Otherwise," *IRB: A Review of Human Subjects Research* 4 (March 1982): 4–6.

73. To minimize the exploitative aspect of relying on the poor as volunteers, Wartofsky endorses Hans Jonas' suggestion to rely on health professionals and others who closely identify with medicine; see Hans Jonas, "Philosophical Reflections on Experimenting with Human Subjects," in Paul A. Freund (ed.), *Experimentation with Human Subjects* (New York: George Braziller, 1970).

74. For opposing views on commercial surrogacy, see Carmel Shalev, *Birth Power: The Case for Surrogacy* (New Haven: Yale University Press, 1989); and A. M. Capron and M. J. Radin, "Choosing Family Law over Contract Law as a Paradigm for Surrogate Motherhood," *Law, Medicine, and Health Care* 16, no. 1–2 (Spring 1988): 34–43.

75. Cf. Carl Cohen, "Medical Experimentation on Prisoners," *Perspectives in Biology and Medicine* 21 (1978): 357–372.

76. Charles C. Moskos, *A Call to Civic Service* (New York: Free Press, 1988). Moskos' book helped shape the Nunn-McCurdy bill.

77. William F. Buckley, Jr., *Gratitude: Reflections on What We Owe to Our Country* (New York: Random House, 1990), p. 117.

78. William James, "The Moral Equivalent of War," in Ralph Barton Perry (ed.), *Essays on Faith and Morals* (New York: Meridian Books, 1962), p. 325.

79. Joseph J. Ellis, "Higher-Education Leaders Should Keep an Open Mind about Proposals to Link Student Aid to National Service," *Chronicle of Higher Education* (April 5, 1989): B, 1–2.

80. Buckley, Jr., *Gratitude*, p. 144.

81. William D. Ford, "Bill in Congress on Public Service for Young People Shows Confusion about Student Aid and Patriotism," *Chronicle of Higher Education* (March 15, 1989), A, 40. For further discussion, see Williamson M. Evers (ed.), *National Service: Pro and Con* (Stanford: Hoover Institution Press, 1990).

5. Mixed Motives

1. Gordon Manser and Rosemary Higgins Cass, *Voluntarism at the Crossroads* (New York: Family Service of America, 1976), p. 17 (italics deleted). Technically, Manser and Cass almost make this claim true by definition, offering a persuasive definition of voluntarism as "those activities of individuals and agencies arising out of a spontaneous, private (as contrasted with governmental) effort to promote or advance some aspect of the common good, as this good is perceived by the persons participating in it" (p. 14; italics deleted).

2. Ibid., p. 35.

3. Cf. David Horton Smith, "Altruism, Volunteers and Volunteerism," in John D. Harman (ed.), *Volunteerism in the Eighties* (Lanham, MD: University Press of America), p. 28.

4. Jon Van Til, *Mapping the Third Sector: Volunteerism in a Changing Social Economy* (New York: Foundation Center, 1988), p. 25. The *Journal of Voluntary Action Research*, in which the studies were published, is now called *Nonprofit and Voluntary Sector Quarterly*.

I agree with Nancy Eisenberg in allowing that several sources of motivation may properly be called altruistic and caring, including emotions such as sympathy and compassion, perceptions of others' needs, principles about what we owe to others, self-evaluative emotions and the desire to avoid guilt and shame, and a sense of how one's own worth is connected with the well-being of others. See Nancy Eisenberg, *Altruistic Emotion, Cognition, and Behavior* (Hillsdale, NY: Lawrence Erlbaum Associates, 1986).

A familiar pattern of explanation in the social sciences is to begin by defining altruism as other-regarding behavior, then offering as causes purely self-regarding motives, and concluding with the explicit or tacit reduction of other-regarding to self-regarding behavior. For examples, see many of the essays in J. Macaulay and L. Berkowitz (eds.), *Altruism and Helping Behavior: Social Psychological Studies of Some Antecedents and Consequences* (New York: Academic Press, 1970); and Lauren Wispé (ed.), *Altruism, Sympathy, and Helping: Psychological and Sociological Principles* (New York: Academic Press, 1978).

5. Laurie Davidson Cummings, "Voluntary Strategies in the Environmental Movement: Recycling as Cooptation," *Journal of Voluntary Action Research* 6 (July-December 1977): 154.

6. Benjamin Gidron, "Sources of Job Satisfaction among Service Volunteers," *Journal of Voluntary Action Research* 12, no. 1 (1983): 32.

7. Jessica Reynolds Jenner, "Participation, Leadership, and the Role of Volunteerism among Selected Women Volunteers," *Journal of Voluntary Action Research* 11, no. 4 (October-December, 1982): 35.

8. John C. Anderson and Larry F. Moore, "The Motivation to Volunteer," *Journal of Voluntary Action Research* 7, nos. 3 and 4 (1978): 123.

9. Ibid.

10. Smith, "Altruism, Volunteers and Volunteerism," p. 26.

11. Mary Midgley, *Beast and Man: The Roots of Human Nature* (New York: New American Library, 1980), p. 331.

12. Bill Berkowitz, *Local Heroes* (Lexington, MA: Lexington Books, 1987), p. 15.

13. Ibid.

14. Ibid., p. 23.

15. Cf. Stuart Hampshire, "Sincerity and Single-Mindedness," in *Freedom of Mind and Other Essays* (Princeton: Princeton University Press, 1971), p. 235.

16. Cf. James Griffin, *Well-Being* (Oxford: Clarendon Press, 1986), p. 158.

17. Armand Hammer, *Hammer* (New York: G. T. Putnam's Sons, 1987), p. 14.

18. Mona Gable, "The Bitter Legacy of Armand Hammer," *California* 16 (April 1991): 50.

19. Lawrence A. Blum, *Friendship, Altruism and Morality* (London: Routledge and Kegan Paul, 1980), pp. 144–145.

20. Ibid., p. 76.

21. For some of these distinctions, see Laurence Thomas, *Living Morally: A Psychology of Moral Character* (Philadelphia: Temple University Press, 1989), p. 214.

22. Ibid., p. 215.

23. For a helpful orientation to the recent literature on this topic, see Samuel Scheffler (ed.), *Consequentialism and Its Critics* (New York: Oxford University Press, 1988).

24. The literature on psychological egoism is enormous. For a sampling, see the essays in Ronald D. Milo (ed.), *Egoism and Altruism* (Belmont, CA: Wadsworth, 1973). My discussion in this section is most influenced by Gregory S. Kavka, *Hobbesian Moral and Political Theory* (Princeton: Princeton University Press, 1986), pp. 35–82; Joel Feinberg, "Psychological Egoism," in Joel Feinberg (ed.), *Reason and Responsibility*, 7th ed. (Belmont, CA: Wadsworth, 1989); and James Rachels, "Egoism and Moral Skepticism," in Christina Hoff Sommers and Fred Sommers (eds.), *Vice and Virtue in Everyday Life*, 2d. ed. (New York: Harcourt Brace Jovanovich, 1989): 398–411.

25. Thomas Hobbes, *Leviathan* (London: Molesworth, 1841), ch. 14. In ch. 15 Hobbes adds: "For no man giveth, but with intention of good to himself; because gift is voluntary and of all voluntary acts, the object is to every man his own good." Hobbes is not altogether consistent, and there are disputes over interpretation; see Kavka, *Hobbesian Moral and Political Theory*, pp. 44–51.

26. Kavka, *Hobbesian Moral and Political Theory*, p. 42, following the lead of C. D.

Broad, "Egoism as a Theory of Human Motives," in Milo (ed.), *Egoism and Altruism*, pp. 88–100.

27. Joseph Butler, *Fifteen Sermons Preached at the Rolls Chapel* (London: G. Bell and Sons, 1964), p. 24.

28. Cf. Joseph Butler: "The thing to be lamented is, not that men have so great regard to their own good or interest in the present world, for they have not enough; but that they have so little to the good of others"; ibid., p. 24.

29. Ayn Rand, the novelist-philosopher, defended psychological egoism with sufficient brashness to entitle one of her books *The Virtue of Selfishness* (New York: New American Library, 1964). But Rand confuses self-interest with selfishness, mistakenly claiming that "the exact meaning and dictionary definition of the word 'selfishness' is: *concern with one's own interests*" (p. vii).

30. II Corinthians 9:7.

31. Of course, there are other types (categories) of objects of desires, including things harmful to oneself, things harmful to others, worthwhile things, etc.

32. See Mary Midgley's incisive critique of sociobiologists' abuse of language in Midgley, *Beast and Man*; and Mary Midgley, *Evolution as a Religion* (New York: Methuen, 1985).

33. Edward O. Wilson, *On Human Nature* (New York: Bantam, 1979), p. 162.

34. Ibid., p. 170.

35. Ibid., p. 162.

36. Kavka, *Hobbesian Moral and Political Theory*, p. 62.

37. Ibid., pp. 64–67.

38. Hugh LaFollette develops this point in "The Truth in Psychological Egoism," in Joel Feinberg (ed.), *Reason and Responsibility*, 7th ed. (Belmont, CA: Wadsworth, 1989), pp. 500–507. This connects with the law of reinforcement, the most fundamental principle of learning theory, which says that people (and other animals) learn to act in ways that bring rewards and avoid unpleasantness.

39. François duc de la Rochefoucauld, *Maxims*, trans. Leonard Tancock (New York: Penguin, 1986), p. 72, remark 263.

40. Ibid., p. 70, remark 246.

41. Henry David Thoreau, *Walden and Civil Disobedience* (New York: Penguin, 1983), p. 119.

42. Ibid., p. 120.

43. Ibid., p. 122. Thoreau was not a cynic in general, and he allowed that some philanthropy is admirable.

44. Nathaniel Hawthorne, *The House of the Seven Gables*, in Norman Holmes Pearson (ed.), *The Complete Novels and Selected Tales of Nathaniel Hawthorne* (New York: Modern Library, 1937), p. 382.

45. Ibid., p. 380.

46. For analyses of hypocrisy and self-deception, see Herbert Fingarette, *Self-Deception* (Atlantic Highlands, NJ: Humanities Press, 1969); Béla Szabados, "Hypocrisy," *Canadian Journal of Philosophy* 9, no. 2 (1979): 195–210; Eva Feder Kittay, "On Hypocrisy," *Metaphilosophy* 13, nos. 3 and 4 (1982): 277–289; and Mike W. Martin, *Self-Deception and Morality* (Lawrence: University Press of Kansas, 1986), ch. 3.

47. Nathaniel Hawthorne, *The Blithedale Romance*, ed. Seymour Gross and Rosalie Murphy (New York: W. W. Norton, 1978), p. 66.

48. Thomas Hobbes, *On Human Nature*, in W. Molesworth (ed.), *The English Works of Thomas Hobbes* (London: John Bohn, 1945), ch. 9, parts 9 and 17. Ironically, Hobbes was a compassionate and charitable man. Once he was observed giving alms to an infirm

old man. When questioned he explained that he was thinking of himself: "I was in paine to consider the miserable condition of the old man; and now my almes, giving him some reliefe, doth also ease me"; Oliver Lawson Dick (ed.) *Aubrey's Brief Lives* (Ann Arbor: University of Michigan Press, 1957), p. 157, cited by Alasdair MacIntyre, "Egoism and Altruism," in Paul Edwards (ed.), *The Encyclopedia of Philosophy*, vol. 2 (New York: Macmillan, 1967), p. 463.

49. Stephen Worchel, "The Darker Side of Helping," in Ervin Staub et al. (eds.), *Development and Maintenance of Prosocial Behavior* (New York: Plenum Press, 1984), p. 381.

50. John Sutherland, introduction to William Makepeace Thackeray, *The Book of Snobs* (New York: St. Martin's Press, 1978), p. 3.

51. Judith N. Shklar, "What Is Wrong with Snobbery?" in *Ordinary Vices* (Cambridge: Harvard University Press, 1984), p. 87.

52. Arthur Hugh Clough, "Spectator ab Extra," in F. L. Mulhauser (ed.), *The Poems of Arthur Hugh Clough*, 2d ed. (Oxford: Clarendon Press, 1974), quoted in Terence Penelhum, "Human Nature and External Desires," *Monist* 62 (1979): 309.

53. Cf. Alfie Kohn, *The Brighter Side of Human Nature* (New York: Basic Books, 1990), pp. 37–45.

54. Cf. Jean-Paul Sartre's portrayal of the anti-Semite in Jean-Paul Sartre, *Anti-Semite and Jew*, trans. George J. Becker (New York: Schocken Books, 1965).

55. Morton Hunt, *The Compassionate Beast* (New York: William Morrow and Company, 1990), pp. 11–12 (italics deleted).

56. This is a special case of the general technique of portraying one's conduct as on a par with everyone else's—what is called the "consensus-raising strategy" by C. R. Snyder, Raymond L. Higgins, and Rita J. Stucky, *Excuses* (New York: John Wiley and Sons, 1983), pp. 49–50.

57. Albert Camus, *The Fall*, trans. Justin O'Brien (New York: Vintage Books, 1956), p. 137.

58. Ibid., p. 141.

59. Harold M. Schulweis, foreword to Samuel P. Oliner and Pearl M. Oliner, *The Altruistic Personality* (New York: Free Press, 1988), p. xi.

60. In doing so I am influenced by John Kekes, "Constancy and Purity," *Mind* 92 (1983): 499–518. See also John Kekes, *Moral Tradition and Individuality* (Princeton: Princeton University Press, 1989), pp. 219–235.

61. Immanuel Kant, *Foundations of the Metaphysics of Morals*, trans. Lewis White Beck, reprinted in *Foundations of the Metaphysics of Morals*, ed. Robert Paul Wolff (Indianapolis: Bobbs-Merrill, 1969), p. 17.

62. Berkowitz, *Local Heroes*, p. 273.

63. Ibid., p. 277.

64. Ibid., p. 291.

65. Matthew 6:24. Thomas Jeavons discusses this issue in connection with religious philanthropy in "Giving, Getting, Grace, and Greed: An Historical and Moral Analysis of Fund Raising," paper read at the 1990 Symposium of the Indiana University Center on Philanthropy, Indianapolis June 6–8, 1990.

66. Deuteronomy 6:4.

67. For an especially illuminating discussion, see Robert Merrihew Adams, "The Problem of Total Devotion," in Robert Audi and William J. Wainwright (eds.), *Rationality, Religious Belief, and Moral Commitment* (Ithaca: Cornell University Press, 1986), pp. 169–194. An opposing criticism of traditional Christian commandments is given in Irving Singer, *The Nature of Love*, vol. 1, 2d ed. (Chicago: University of Chicago Press, 1984), pp. 343–355.

68. Søren Kierkegaard, *Purity of Heart Is to Will One Thing*, trans. Douglas V. Steere (New York: Harper and Row, 1956), p. 54.

69. Ibid., pp. 70, 74.

70. The following four threats or barriers, are discussed in ibid., chs. 7, 5, 4, 6.

71. Ibid., p. 107.

72. Ibid., p. 88.

73. Ibid., p. 72.

74. Ibid., p. 74.

75. Ibid., p. 69.

76. Ibid., p. 71.

77. Cf. Richard Norman, *The Moral Philosophers* (Oxford: Clarendon Press, 1983), p. 61.

78. Kierkegaard, *Purity of Heart Is to Will One Thing*, p. 99.

79. Ibid., p. 100.

80. Edmund L. Pincoffs, *Quandaries and Virtues* (Lawrence: University Press of Kansas, 1986), pp. 113–114.

81. John Dewey, *Human Nature and Conduct* (New York: Modern Library, 1957), pp. 8–9. Dewey used the expression "spiritual egoism" rather than "moral egoism."

82. Judith N. Shklar, "Let Us Not Be Hypocritical," *Daedalus* 108 (Summer 1979): 9, 11.

83. Jean-Paul Sartre, "Existentialism Is a Humanism," in Walter Kaufmann (ed.), *Existentialism from Dostoevsky to Sartre*, rev. ed. (New York: New American Library, 1975), p. 366.

84. Sartre, *Anti-Semite and Jew*, pp. 21–22.

6. Paradoxes of Self-Fulfillment

1. Simone de Beauvoir, *The Ethics of Ambiguity*, trans. Bernard Frechtman (Secaucus, NJ: Citadel Press, 1948), p. 104. Cf. Virginia Woolf, *Three Guineas* (New York: Harcourt Brace Jovanovich, 1938), pp. 78, 80, on the importance of freeing ourselves from "unreal [unjustified] loyalties."

2. See Anthony Storr, *Solitude: A Return to the Self* (New York: Free Press, 1988).

3. Israel Scheffler insightfully discusses several myths concerning human potential in *Of Human Potential: An Essay in the Philosophy of Education* (Boston: Routledge and Kegan Paul, 1985), pp. 10–16.

4. Joel Feinberg, "Absurd Self-Fulfillment," in Peter van Inwagen (ed.), *Time and Cause* (Dordrecht, Holland: D. Reidel, 1980), pp.266–271.

5. Cf. Richard Norman, *The Moral Philosophers* (Oxford: Clarendon Press, 1983), pp. 221, 249. See also Mark Carl Overvold, "Self-Interest and the Concept of Self-Sacrifice," *Canadian Journal of Philosophy* 10 (1980): 105–118.

6. Jane Addams, *Twenty Years at Hull-House* (New York: New American Library, 1960).

7. Ibid., p. 91.

8. Ibid., p. 72.

9. Ibid., p. 88.

10. Ibid., p. 92.

11. Leo Tolstoy, *Anna Karenina*, trans. David Magarshack (New York: New American Library, 1961), pp. 233–234.

12. Ibid., p. 244.

13. Ibid., p. 244.

14. Ibid., p. 245.

15. Ilham Dilman, "Self Deception," in Ilham Dilman and D. Z. Phillips, *Sense and Delusion* (New York: Humanities Press, 1971), p. 73. Dilman gives an illuminating discussion of Kitty Scherbatsky.

16. Martin Luther, *The Freedom of a Christian*, in John Dillenberger (ed.), *Martin Luther: Selections from His Writings* (Garden City, NY: Anchor, 1961), pp. 73–74. Compare Philippians 2:3, cited by Luther: "Let nothing be done through strife or vainglory; but in lowliness of mind let each esteem other better than themselves."

17. Ibid.

18. For an insightful discussion, see Alan Gewirth, "The Golden Rule Rationalized," *Midwest Studies in Philosophy* 3 (1978): 133–147.

19. The expression "other-biased altruism" is borrowed from David Pugmire, who also criticizes Luther in "Altruism and Ethics," *American Philosophical Quarterly* 15, no. 1 (1978): 75. Cf. Garth L. Hallett, who speaks of "other-preference" in *Christian Moral Reasoning: An Analytic Guide* (Notre Dame: University of Notre Dame Press, 1983), p. 149.

20. C. Gene Outka, *Agape: An Ethical Analysis* (New Haven: Yale University Press, 1972), pp. 21–22; and Daniel Day Williams, *The Spirit and the Forms of Love* (Lanham, MD: University Press of America, 1981), pp. 192–213.

21. Morton Hunt, *The Compassionate Beast* (New York: William Morrow, 1990), p. 26.

22. See Joseph Fletcher, "Attitudes toward Suicide," in John Donnelly (ed), *Suicide*. (Buffalo: Prometheus Press, 1990), p. 64.

23. Cf. Suzanne Stern-Gillet, "The Rhetoric of Suicide," in John Donnelly (ed.), *Suicide*, pp. 97–99

24. E. M. Forster wrote, "I hate the idea of causes, and if I had to choose between betraying my country and betraying my friend, I hope I should have the guts to betray my country"; E. M. Forster, *Two Cheers for Democracy* (London: Edward Arnold, 1951), p. 78. For an illuminating response to Forster, see A. I. Melden, *Rights in Moral Lives* (Berkeley: University of California Press, 1988), pp. 123–137.

25. William James, *The Varieties of Religious Experience* (New York: Modern Library, 1902), p. 47.

26. Ibid., p. 108.

27. See esp. Robert Young, *Personal Autonomy* (London: Croom Helm, 1986); Gerald Dworkin, *The Theory and Practice of Autonomy* (Cambridge: Cambridge University Press, 1988); Lawrence Haworth, *Autonomy* (New Haven: Yale University Press, 1986); and Harry G. Frankfurt, "Freedom of the Will and the Concept of a Person," in *The Importance of What We Care About* (Cambridge: Cambridge University Press, 1988): 11–25.

28. Frankfurt, *The Importance of What We Care About*, p. 89.

29. Ibid.

30. Ibid., p. 86.

31. Ibid., p. 91.

32. Fyodor Dostoevsky portrays such a person in *Notes from Underground*, in Walter Kaufmann (ed.), *Existentialism from Dostoevsky to Sartre*, rev. ed. (New York: New American Library, 1975), pp. 80–82, 66. Frithjof Bergmann gives an illuminating discussion of the character in *On Being Free* (Notre Dame: University of Notre Dame Press, 1977), ch. 2.

33. Frankfurt, *The Importance of What We Care About*, p. 172.

34. Cf. Milton Mayeroff, *On Caring* (New York: Harper and Row, 1971), pp. 51–52.

35. Ibid., p. 29.

36. Robert N. Bellah et al., *Habits of the Heart: Individualism and Commitment in American Life* (Berkeley: University of California Press, 1985), p. 162.

37. Ishbel Ross, *Angel of the Battlefield: The Life of Clara Barton* (New York: Harper and Brothers, 1956), p. 5.

38. Robert H. Bremner, *American Philanthropy*, 2d ed. (Chicago: University of Chicago Press, 1988), p. 90.

39. Joel Feinberg, "Psychological Egoism," in Joel Feinberg (ed.), *Reason and Responsibility*, 7th ed. (Belmont, CA: Wadsworth, 1989), p. 493 (italics deleted).

40. John Stuart Mill, *The Autobiography of John Stuart Mill* (Garden City, NY: Doubleday), p. 110.

41. John Stuart Mill, *Utilitarianism* (Indianapolis: Hackett, 1979), p. 11. In another passage Mill defined happiness as "not a life of rapture, but moments of such, in an existence made up of few and transitory pains, many and various pleasures, with a decided predominance of the active over the passive, and having as the foundation of the whole not to expect more from life than it is capable of bestowing"; Mill, *Utilitarianism*, p. 13. This definition emphasizes the pleasurable contents of a happy life, and only hints at the importance of attitudes toward one's life in the last clause.

42. When Mill applies his test he gets confused and compares, not pleasures, but "manners of existence," that is, ways of life: those containing pleasures of the mind and of relationships, and those pig-like lives containing only physical pleasures.

43. Cf. J. J. C. Smart, "Utilitarianism," in J. J. C. Smart and Bernard Williams (eds.), *Utilitarianism: For and Against* (Cambridge: Cambridge University Press, 1973).

44. Cf. John Kekes, "Happiness," *Mind* 91 (1982): 358; and Elizabeth Telfer, *Happiness* (New York: St. Martin's Press, 1980), p. 8.

45. For an overview of analyses of happiness, see Douglas Den Uyl and Tibor R. Machan, "Recent Work on the Concept of Happiness," *American Philosophical Quarterly* 20 (April 1983), pp. 115–134. The main alternative analyses derive from Aristotle's definition of the happy life as one lived in accord with virtue combined with some good luck. Essentially Aristotle equated happiness with self-fulfillment (or complete well-being). I prefer to stay closer to ordinary language, which allows that a person could be moral but not happy, or happy but not moral, and which treats happiness as only one aspect of self-development.

46. Cf. Bertrand Russell, *The Conquest of Happiness* (New York: Liveright, 1971), pp. 17–18.

47. Joseph Butler, *Fifteen Sermons Preached at Rolls Chapel*, ed. W. R. Matthews (London: G. Bell and Sons, 1964), p. 171.

48. Mill, *Autobiography*, p. 16.

49. Ibid., p. 110.

50. In a related context, Richard Norman distinguishes the first and third levels of reflection and reasoning in Richard Norman, *The Moral Philosophers* (Oxford: Clarendon Press, 1983), p. 62.

51. Cf. Telfer, *Happiness*, p. 33.

52. Joseph P. Lash, *Eleanor and Franklin* (New York: Signet, 1973), p. 554.

53. Larry Martz et al., "God and Money," *Newsweek* (April 6, 1987): 16–22.

54. Harvey Katz, *Give! Who Gets Your Charity Dollar?* (Garden City, NY: Anchor, 1974).

55. Mill, *Autobiography*, p. 102.

56. Ibid., p. 104.

57. Ibid., p. 111.

58. Bill Berkowitz, *Local Heroes* (Lexington, MA: Lexington Books, 1987), p. 127.

59. Several useful collections of essays explore the meaning of "the meaning of life": E. D. Klemke (ed.), *The Meaning of Life* (New York: Oxford University Press, 1981); Steven

Sanders and David R. Cheney (eds.), *The Meaning of Life* (Englewood Cliffs, NJ: Prentice Hall, 1980); Oswald Hanfling (ed.), *Life and Meaning* (New York: Basil Blackwell, 1987).

60. Irving Singer distinguishes between appraisal (evaluation) and bestowal of value in Irving Singer, *The Nature of Love*, vol. 1, 2d ed. (Chicago: University of Chicago Press, 1984).

61. Richard Wilhelm and Cary F. Baynes (eds. and trans.), *The I Ching* (Princeton: Princeton University Press, 1967), p. 85.

62. Josiah Royce, *The Spirit of Modern Philosophy* (New York: W. W. Norton, 1967), p. 206.

63. Alasdair MacIntyre, *After Virtue*, 2d ed. (Notre Dame: University of Notre Dame Press, 1984), pp. 218–219.

64. F. H. Bradley, *Ethical Studies*, 2d ed. (New York: Oxford University Press, 1962), p. 173. For a critique of Bradley, see Hastings Rashdall, "Self-Realization and Self-Sacrifice," in *The Theory of Good and Evil*, vol. 2 (Oxford: Clarendon Press, 1907), ch. 3.

65. Luke 9:24.

66. Raymond B. Blakney (ed.), *Meister Eckhart* (New York: Harper and Brothers, 1941), p. 17. In an insightful discussion of mystic selflessness, Herbert Fingarette shows that selflessness does not imply lack of a sense of oneself and (tacitly) of one's worth; see Herbert Fingarette, *The Self in Transformation* (New York: Basic Books, 1963), ch. 7.

67. Dag Hammarskjöld, *Markings*, trans. Leif Sjoberg and W. H. Auden (New York: Alfred A. Knopf, 1965), p. 130.

68. Ibid., p. viii.

69. Cf. Norman Cousins, *Anatomy of an Illness as Perceived by the Patient* (New York: W. W. Norton, 1979), ch. 2. Conceivably, of course, the psychological rewards of religious belief could be both placebo effects and divine rewards, with God exerting His grace via the placebo effect.

70. Graham Greene, *A Burnt-Out Case* (New York: Penguin, 1977), p. 57.

71. Plato, *The Republic*, book 2. Some of these themes are reworked in David Gauthier, *Morals by Agreement* (Oxford: Clarendon Press, 1986), a book whose outlook is otherwise sharply dissimilar to Plato's.

72. William James, *Essays on Faith and Morals*, ed. Ralph Barton Perry (New York: Meridian Books, 1962), pp. 32–33. Ironically, James' defense of religious faith is the least compelling part of his argument. He argues that religious faith may provide evidence for itself by generating experiences that support God's existence, whereas skeptical attitudes foreclose experiences of God. But first, what counts as evidence for religious claims depends on how experiences are interpreted, and since religious faith shapes interpretations it cannot provide independent evidence. Second, why would a morally perfect being restrict evidence to humans who take a faith initiative? Surely God, unlike reticent humans, might generously provide evidence to morally concerned people who are honestly skeptical about the supernatural.

My interpretation of James is most influenced by Robert J. O'Connell, *William James on the Courage to Believe* (New York: Fordham University Press, 1984). See also Ellen Kappy Suckiel, *The Pragmatic Philosophy of William James* (Notre Dame: University of Notre Dame Press, 1982); James C. S. Wernham, *James's Will-to-Believe Doctrine* (Kingston: McGill-Queen's University Press, 1987); Gail Kennedy, "Pragmatism, Pragmaticism, and the Will to Believe—A Reconsideration," *Journal of Philosophy* 55 (1958): 578–588; and Peter Kauber and Peter H. Hare, "The Right and Duty to Will to Believe," *Canadian Journal of Philosophy* 4 (1974): 327–343.

73. James wrote "The Will to Believe" as a talk to college students predisposed to

skepticism. Elsewhere he insisted that "what *should* be preached is courage weighted with responsibility" and that "what mankind at large most lacks is criticism and caution, not faith"; James, *Essays on Faith and Morals*, p. 332.

74. James sometimes used "ambiguous" in this sense, though not in "The Will to Believe." See Stephen T. Davis, "Wishful Thinking and 'The Will to Believe,'" *Transactions of the Charles S. Peirce Society* 8 (1974): 231–245.

75. James, *Essays on Faith and Morals*, p. 42 (italics deleted).

76. Ibid., p. 100.

77. Ibid., p. 55.

78. Annette Baier discusses the importance of grounds for trust in Annette Baier, "Trust and Antitrust," *Ethics* 96 (1986): 231–260. She discusses the importance of moral faith in Annette Baier, "Secular Faith," in *Postures of the Mind* (Minneapolis: University of Minnesota Press, 1985), p. 295.

79. Cf. Melvin Rader, *The Right to Hope* (Seattle: University of Washington Press, 1981), pp. 15–16.

80. Simone de Beauvoir, *The Ethics of Ambiguity*, p. 129.

Bibliography

Adams, Margaret. "The Compassion Trap." Pp. 555–575 in *Woman in Sexist Society*, edited by Vivian Gornick and Barbara K. Moran. New York: New American Library, 1972.

Adams, Robert Merrihew. "The Problem of Total Devotion." Pp. 169–194 in *Rationality, Religious Belief, and Moral Commitment*, edited by Robert Audi and William J. Wainwright. Ithaca: Cornell University Press, 1986.

———— "Pure Love" and "The Virtue of Faith." Pp. 174–192 and pp. 9–24 in *The Virtue of Faith*. New York: Oxford University Press, 1987.

Addams, Jane, et al. *Philanthropy and Social Progress*. Montclair, NJ: Patterson Smith, 1970. First published 1893.

———— *The Social Thought of Jane Addams*. Edited by Christopher Lasch. New York: Irvington Publishers, 1982.

———— *Twenty Years at Hull-House*. New York: New American Library, 1960.

Aiken, William. "The Right to Be Saved from Starvation." Pp. 85–102 in *World Hunger and Moral Obligation*, edited by William Aiken and Hugh La Follette. Englewood Cliffs, NJ: Prentice Hall, 1977.

Aldrich, Nelson W., Jr. *Old Money*. New York: Vintage Books, 1989.

Al-Ghazzali. *The Mysteries of Almsgiving*. Translated by Nabih Akin Faris. Kashmiri Bazar-Lahore, 1974.

Alvarado, Elvia. *Don' t Be Afraid, Gringo: A Honduran Woman Speaks from the Heart*. Translated by Medea Benjamin. New York: Harper and Row, 1987.

American Bar Association. *Model Rules of Professional Conduct*. Pp. 565–566 in *Ethical Issues in the Professions*, edited by Peter Y. Windt et al. Englewood Cliffs, NJ: Prentice Hall, 1989.

American Medical Association. *Principles of Medical Ethics*. Pp. 566–567 in *Ethical Issues in the Professions*, edited by Peter Y. Windt et al. Englewood Cliffs, NJ: Prentice Hall, 1989.

Anderson, John C., and Larry F. Moore. "The Motivation to Volunteer." *Journal of Voluntary Action Research* 7, nos. 3 and 4 (1978): 120–125.

Andrews, F. Emerson. *Philanthropic Giving*. New York: Russell Sage Foundation, 1950.

Aquinas, St. Thomas. "Gratitude" and "Ingratitude." Pp. 83–113 in *Summa Theologica*. Vol. 41. New York: McGraw-Hill, 1964.

Aristotle. *Nicomachean Ethics*. Translated by Terence Irwin. Indianapolis: Hackett, 1985.

Arneson, Richard J. "The Principle of Fairness and Free-Rider Problems." *Ethics* 92 (1982): 616–633.

Arnove, Robert. F., ed. *Philanthropy and Cultural Imperialism*. Bloomington: Indiana University Press, 1982.

Arrow, Kenneth J. "Gifts and Exchanges." *Philosophy and Public Affairs* 1 (1971–72): 344–362.

Arthur, John. "Rights and the Duty to Bring Aid." Pp. 37–48 in *World Hunger and*

Moral Obligation, edited by William Aiken and Hugh La Follette. Englewood Cliffs, NJ: Prentice Hall, 1977.

Axelrod, Robert. *The Evolution of Cooperation*. New York: Basic Books, 1984.

Babbie, Earl. *You Can Make a Difference* New York: St. Martin's Press, 1985.

Baier, Annette. "The Rights of Past and Future Persons." Pp. 171–183 in *Responsibilities to Future Generations*, edited by Ernest Partridge. Buffalo: Prometheus Books, 1981.

——— "Secular Faith." Pp. 292–308 in *Postures of the Mind*. Minneapolis: University of Minnesota Press, 1985.

——— "Trust and Antitrust." *Ethics* 96 (1986): 231–260.

Bailey, Anne L. "Arnold Beckman: Making Plans to Give Away a Fortune." *Chronicle of Philanthropy* 2 (May 15, 1990): 4–5, 8.

——— "Philanthropy Research's Built-In Conflict: Grant Makers Are Often Subjects of Studies." *Chronicle of Higher Education* (September 21, 1988): A, 34, 36.

Barry, Brian. "Justice as Reciprocity." Pp. 50–78 in *Justice*, edited by Eugene Kamenka and Alice Erh-Soon Tay. New York: St. Martin's Press, 1980.

Battin, Margaret P. *Ethics in the Sanctuary*. New Haven: Yale University Press, 1990.

Baum, Robert J. "Access to Engineering Services: Rights and Responsibilities of Professionals and the Public." *Business and Professional Ethics Journal* 4 (1985): 117–135.

Bayles, Michael D. *Professional Ethics*. 2d ed. Belmont, CA: Wadsworth, 1989.

Beauvoir, Simone de. *The Ethics of Ambiguity*. Translated by Bernard Frechtman. Secaucus, NJ: Citadel Press, 1948.

——— *The Second Sex*. Translated by H. M. Parshley. New York: Vintage Books, 1953.

Becker, Lawrence C. *Reciprocity*. New York: Routledge and Kegan Paul, 1986.

Bedau, Hugo Adam, ed. *Civil Disobedience*. Indianapolis: Bobbs-Merrill, 1969.

Bellah, Robert N., Richard Madsen, William M. Sullivan, Ann Swidler, and Steven M. Tipton. *Habits of the Heart: Individualism and Commitment in American Life*. Berkeley: University of California Press, 1985.

——— *Individualism and Commitment in American Life: Readings on the Themes of Habits of the Heart*. New York: Harper and Row, 1987.

Benjamin, Martin. *Splitting the Difference*. Lawrence: University Press of Kansas, 1990.

Benjamin, Martin, and Joy Curtis. *Ethics in Nursing*. 2d ed. New York: Oxford University Press, 1986.

Benn, S. I. "Individuality, Autonomy and Community." Pp. 43–62 in *Community as a Social Ideal*, edited by Eugene Kamenka. New York: St. Martin's Press, 1983.

Bennett, Lerone, Jr. *Before the Mayflower*. New York: Penguin, 1964.

Berger, Fred R. "Gratitude." *Ethics* 85 (1975): 298–309.

Berger, Peter L., and Richard John Neuhaus. *To Empower People: The Role of Mediating Structures in Public Policy*. Washington, DC: American Enterprise Institute, 1977.

Bergmann, Frithjof. *On Being Free*. Notre Dame: University of Notre Dame Press, 1977.

Berkowitz, Bill. *Local Heroes*. Lexington, MA: Lexington Books, 1987.

Berman, Edgar. *In Africa With Schweitzer*. New York: Harper and Row, 1986.

Blakney, Raymond B., ed. *Meister Eckhart*. New York: Harper and Brothers, 1941.

Blee, Kathleen M. *Women of the Klan: Racism and Gender in the 1920s*. Berkeley: University of California Press, 1991.

Blum, Lawrence A. "Compassion." Pp. 507–517 in *Explaining Emotions*, edited by Amelie Rorty. Berkeley: University of California Press, 1980.

——— *Friendship, Altruism and Morality*. London: Routledge and Kegan Paul, 1980.

Blum, Lawrence, Marcia Homiak, Judy Housman, and Naomi Scheman. "Altruism and Women's Oppression." Pp. 222–247 in *Women and Philosophy*, edited by Carol C. Gould and Marx W. Wartofsky. New York: G. P. Putnam's Sons, 1976.

Bok, Sissela. *Lying*. New York: Vintage Books, 1979.

Boyte, Harry C. *Community Is Possible*. New York: Harper and Row, 1984.

Bradley, F. H. *Ethical Studies*. 2d ed. New York: Oxford University Press, 1962

Branch, Taylor. *Parting the Waters*. New York: Simon and Schuster, 1988.

Brandt, Richard B. *Ethical Theory*. Englewood Cliffs, NJ: Prentice Hall, 1959.

——— "The Psychology of Benevolence and Its Implications for Philosophy." *Journal of Philosophy* 73 (1976): 429–453.

Braybrooke, David. *Meeting Needs*. Princeton: Princeton University Press, 1987.

Bremner, Robert H. *American Philanthropy*. 2d ed. Chicago: University of Chicago Press, 1988.

Brilliant, Eleanor L. *The United Way: Dilemmas of Organized Charity*. New York: Columbia University Press, 1990.

Broad, C. D. "Egoism as a Theory of Human Motives." *Hibbert Journal* 48 (1950): 105–114. Reprinted pp. 88–100 in *Egoism and Altruism*, edited by Ronald D. Milo. Belmont, CA: Wadsworth, 1973.

Brody, Baruch. "The Role of Private Philanthropy in a Free and Democratic State." Pp. 79–92 in *Beneficence, Philanthropy and the Public Good*, edited by Ellen Frankel Paul et al. New York: Basil Blackwell, 1987.

Broudy, Harry S. *Enlightened Cherishing*. Urbana: University of Illinois Press, 1972.

Brown, E. Richard. *Rockefeller Medicine Men*. Berkeley: University of California Press, 1980.

Buchanan, Allen. "Justice as Reciprocity versus Subject-Centered Justice." *Philosophy and Public Affairs* 19 (1990): 227–252.

Buckley, William F., Jr. *Gratitude: Reflections on What We Owe to Our Country*. New York: Random House, 1990.

Butler, Joseph. *Fifteen Sermons Preached at the Rolls Chapel*. London: G. Bell and Sons, 1964.

Camenisch, Paul F. "Gift and Gratitude in Ethics." *Journal of Religious Ethics* 9 (1981): 1–34.

Camus, Albert. *The Fall*. Translated by Justin O'Brien. New York: Vintage Books, 1956.

Capron, A. M., and M. J. Radin. "Choosing Family Law over Contract Law as a Paradigm for Surrogate Motherhood." *Law, Medicine, and Health Care* 16, no. 1–2 (Spring 1988): 34–43.

Card, Claudia, ed. *Feminist Ethics*. Lawrence: University Press of Kansas, 1991.

——— "Gratitude and Obligation." *American Philosophical Quarterly* 25 (1988): 115–127.

Care, Norman. *On Sharing Fate*. Philadelphia: Temple University Press, 1987.

Carnegie, Andrew. *The Autobiography of Andrew Carnegie*. Boston: Northeastern University Press, 1986.

——— *The Gospel of Wealth and Other Timely Essays*. New York, 1900.

Carter, Jimmy, and Rosalynn Carter. *Everything to Gain*. New York: Ballantine Books, 1987.

Chang, Irene. "Baby Provides Bone Marrow for Her Sister." *Los Angeles Times* (June 5, 1991): A, 1, 16.

Christensen, Barlow F. "The Lawyer's *Pro Bono Publico* Responsibility." *American Bar Foundation Research Journal* (1981): 1–19.

Cohen, Carl. "Medical Experimentation on Prisoners." *Perspectives in Biology and Medicine* 21 (1978): 357–372.

Coles, Robert. *Dorothy Day*. Reading, MA: Addison-Wesley, 1987.

Cornuelle, Richard. *Reclaiming the American Dream*. New York: Random House, 1965.

Cousins, Norman. *Anatomy of an Illness as Perceived by the Patient*. New York: W. W. Norton, 1979.

Cox, Gray. *The Ways of Peace*. New York: Paulist Press, 1986.

Cua, A. S. *Dimensions of Moral Creativity*. University Park: Pennsylvania State University Press, 1978.

Cummings, Laurie Davidson. "Voluntary Strategies in the Environmental Movement: Recycling as Cooptation." *Journal of Voluntary Action Research* 6 (July-December 1977): 153–160.

Cutlip, Scott M. *Fund Raising in the United States*. New Brunswick: Rutgers University Press, 1965.

Daly, Mary. *Beyond God the Father: Toward a Philosophy of Women's Liberation*. Boston: Beacon Press, 1973.

Dancy, Jonathan. "Supererogation and Moral Realism." Pp. 170–188 in *Human Nature: Language, Duty and Value: Philosophical Essays in Honor of J. O. Urmson*, edited by Jonathan Dancy, J. M. E. Moravcsik, and C. C. W. Taylor. Stanford: Stanford University Press, 1988.

Daniels, Arlene Kaplan. *Invisible Careers: Women Civic Leaders from the Volunteer World*. Chicago: University of Chicago Press, 1988.

Davis, Stephen T. "Wishful Thinking and 'The Will to Believe.'" *Transactions of the Charles S. Peirce Society* 8 (1974): 231–245.

Day, Dorothy. *Loaves and Fishes*. New York: Harper and Row, 1963.

——— *The Long Loneliness*. New York: Harper and Row, 1952.

Dean, Paul. "Ollie's New War." *Los Angeles Times* (September 17, 1989), part IV, p. 10.

Derlega, Valerian J., and Janusz Grzelak, eds. *Cooperation and Helping Behavior*. New York: Academic Press, 1982.

Des Jardins, Joseph R., and Ronald Duska. "Drug Testing in Employment." Pp. 301–309 in *Business Ethics*, 2d ed., edited by W. Michael Hoffman and Jennifer Mills Moore. New York: McGraw-Hill, 1990.

Dewey, John. *A Common Faith*. New Haven: Yale University Press, 1934.

——— *Human Nature and Conduct*. New York: Modern Library, 1957.

Dick, Oliver Lawson, ed. *Aubrey's Brief Lives*. Ann Arbor: University of Michigan Press, 1957.

Dickens, Charles. "Telescopic Philanthropy." Pp. 32–43 in *Bleak House*. New York: Bantam, 1983.

Dilman, Ilham. "Self Deception." Pp. 62–92 in Ilham Dilman and D. Z. Phillips, *Sense and Delusion*. New York: Humanities Press, 1971.

——— *Philosophy and Life: Essays on John Wisdom*. The Hague: Martinus Nijhoff, 1984.

Dostoevsky, Fyodor. *Notes from Underground.* Pp. 53–82 in *Existentialism from Dostoevsky to Sartre,* rev. ed., edited by Walter Kaufmann. New York: New American Library, 1975.

Douglas, James. *Why Charity? The Case for a Third Sector.* Beverly Hills: Sage Publications, 1983.

Drabble, Margaret. *The Needle's Eye.* New York: Ballantine Books, 1989.

Dreiser, Theodore. "Charity and Wealth in America." Pp. 277–296 in *Tragic America.* New York: Liveright, 1931.

Dworkin, Gerald. *The Theory and Practice of Autonomy.* Cambridge: Cambridge University Press, 1988.

Dyke, C. "The Vices of Altruism." *Ethics* 81 (1970–71): 241–252.

Egan, Eileen. *Such a Vision of the Street: Mother Teresa—The Spirit and the Work.* New York: Image Books, 1986.

Eisenberg, Nancy. *Altruistic Emotion, Cognition, and Behavior.* Hillsdale, NY: Lawrence Erlbaum Associates, 1986.

Ellis, Joseph J. "Higher-Education Leaders Should Keep an Open Mind about Proposals to Link Student Aid to National Service." *Chronicle of Higher Education* (April 5, 1989): B, 1–2.

Ellis, Susan J., and Katherine H. Noyes. *By the People: A History of Americans as Volunteers.* Rev. ed. San Francisco: Jossey-Bass, 1990.

Elster, Jon. "Selfishness and Altruism." Pp. 44–52 in *Beyond Self-Interest,* edited by Jane J. Mansbridge. Chicago: University of Chicago Press, 1990.

Eppler, Karen. "Transforming Power in the Labor Movement—Cesar Chavez." Pp. 191–193 in *Nonviolence in Theory and Practice,* edited by Robert L. Holmes. Belmont, CA: Wadsworth, 1990.

Eriksson-Joslyn, Kerstin. "A Nation of Volunteers: Participatory Democracy or Administrative Manipulation?" *Berkeley Journal of Sociology* 17 (1973–74): 159–181.

Evans, Sara M., and Harry C. Boyte. *Free Spaces: The Sources of Democratic Change in America.* New York: Harper and Row, 1986.

Evers, Williamson M., ed. *National Service: Pro and Con.* Stanford: Hoover Institution Press, 1990.

Fairlie, Henry. *The Seven Deadly Sins Today.* Notre Dame: University of Notre Dame Press, 1979.

Falk, W. D. "Morality, Self, and Others." Pp. 25–67 in *Morality and Language of Conduct,* edited by Hector-Neri Castañeda and George Nakhnikian. Detroit: Wayne State University Press, 1965.

Faris, Ellsworth, Ferris Laune, and Arthur J. Todd, eds. *Intelligent Philanthropy.* Montclair, NJ: Patterson Smith, 1969. First published 1930.

Feinberg, Joel. "Absurd Self-Fulfillment." Pp. 266–271 in *Time and Cause,* edited by Peter van Inwagen. Dordrecht, Holland: D. Reidel, 1980.

——— "The Child's Right to an Open Future." Pp. 124–153 in *Whose Child?* Totowa, NJ: Littlefield, Adams, 1980.

——— "Noncoercive Exploitation." Pp. 201–235 in *Paternalism,* edited by Rolf Sartorius. Minneapolis: University of Minnesota Press, 1983.

——— "Psychological Egoism." Pp. 489–500 in *Reason and Responsibility,* 7th ed., edited by Joel Feinberg. Belmont, CA: Wadsworth, 1989.

Feinsod, Ethan. *Awake in a Nightmare: Jonestown, the Only Eyewitness Account.* New York: W. W. Norton, 1981.

Fingarette, Herbert. *Confucius: The Secular as Sacred*. New York: Harper and Row, 1972.
——— *On Responsibility*. New York: Basic Books, 1967.
——— *The Self in Transformation*. New York: Basic Books, 1963.
——— *Self-Deception*. Atlantic Highlands, NJ: Humanities Press, 1969.
Fisher, Roger, and William Ury. *Getting to Yes*. New York: Penguin, 1983.
Fishkin, James S. *The Limits of Obligation*. New Haven: Yale University Press, 1982.
——— *Tyranny and Legitimacy*. Baltimore: Johns Hopkins University Press, 1979.
Flanagan, Owen. *Varieties of Moral Personality*. Cambridge: Harvard University Press, 1991.
Fletcher, Joseph. "Attitudes toward Suicide." Pp. 61–73 in *Suicide*, edited by John Donnelly. Buffalo: Prometheus Press, 1990.
Ford, William D. "Bill in Congress on Public Service for Young People Shows Confusion about Student Aid and Patriotism." *Chronicle of Higher Education* (March 1989): A, 40.
Forster, E. M. *Two Cheers for Democracy*. London: Edward Arnold, 1951.
Fox, R. C., and J. P. Swazey. *The Courage to Fail*. 2d ed. Chicago: University of Chicago Press, 1978.
Frank, Robert H. *Passions within Reason: The Strategic Role of the Emotions*. New York: W. W. Norton, 1988.
Frankena, William K. "Beneficence/Benevolence." Pp. 1–20 in *Beneficence, Philanthropy and the Public Good*, edited by Ellen Frankel Paul et al. New York: Basil Blackwell, 1987.
Frankfurt, Harry G. *The Importance of What We Care About*. Cambridge: Cambridge University Press, 1988.
Franklin, Benjamin. *Autobiography*. New York: W. W. Norton, 1986.
Frayn, Michael. *Benefactors: A Play in Two Acts*. New York: Methuen, 1984.
Freeman, Mary E. Wilkins. "A Mistaken Charity." Pp. 1–18 in *The Revolt of Mother and Other Stories*. Old Westbury, NY: Feminist Press, 1974.
French, Peter A., Theodore E. Uehling, Jr., and Howard K. Wettstein, eds. *Ethical Theory: Character and Virtue*. Vol. 13 of *Midwest Studies in Philosophy*. Notre Dame: University of Notre Dame Press, 1988.
Gable, Mona. "The Bitter Legacy of Armand Hammer." *California* 16 (April 1991): 50–55, 91–92, 120.
Gamwell, Franklin I. *Beyond Preference: Liberal Theories of Independent Associations*. Chicago: University of Chicago Press, 1984.
Gansberg, Martin. "38 Who Saw Murder Didn't Call Police." Pp. 51–54 in *Vice and Virtue in Everyday Life*, 2d ed., edited by Christina Sommers and Fred Sommers. San Diego: Harcourt Brace Jovanovich, 1989.
Garland, Anne Witte, ed. *Women Activists*. New York: Feminist Press at CUNY, 1988.
Garrow, David J. *Bearing the Cross: Martin Luther King, Jr., and the Southern Christian Leadership Conference*. New York: Vintage Books, 1988.
Gauthier, David. *Morals by Agreement*. Oxford: Clarendon Press, 1986.
Gaylin, Willard, Ira Glasser, Steven Marcus, and David J. Rothman. *Doing Good: The Limits of Benevolence*. New York: Pantheon Books, 1981.
Geldof, Bob. *Is That It?* New York: Ballantine Books, 1986.
Gergen, Kenneth J., and Mary M. Gergen. "Foreign Aid that Works." *Psychology Today* (June 1974): 53–58.

———— "International Assistance from a Psychological Perspective." *Yearbook of World Affairs* 25. London: Institute of World Affairs, 1971.

Gert, Bernard. *Morality*. New York: Oxford University Press, 1988.

Gewirth, Alan. "The Golden Rule Rationalized." *Midwest Studies in Philosophy* 3 (1978): 133–147.

———— "Private Philanthropy and Positive Rights." Pp. 55–78 in *Beneficence, Philanthropy and the Public Good*, edited by Ellen Frankel Paul et al. New York: Basil Blackwell, 1987.

Gidron, Benjamin. "Sources of Job Satisfaction among Service Volunteers." *Journal of Voluntary Action Research* 12, no. 1 (1983): 20–35.

Gies, David L., J. Steven Ott, and Jay M. Shafritz, eds. *The Nonprofit Organization: Essential Readings*. Pacific Grove, CA: Brooks/Cole, 1990.

Gilligan, Carol. *In a Different Voice*. Cambridge: Harvard University Press, 1982.

Glaser, Myron Peretz, and Penina Migdal Glazer. *The Whistleblowers*. New York: Basic Books, 1989.

Godlovitch, Stanley. "On Wisdom." Pp. 262–284 in *Vice and Virtue in Everyday Life*, 2d ed., edited by Christina Sommers and Fred Sommers. San Diego: Harcourt Brace Jovanovich, 1989.

Gold, Doris B. "Women and Voluntarism." Pp. 533–554 in *Woman in Sexist Society*, edited by Vivian Gornick and Barbara K. Moran. New York: New American Library, 1971.

Gorman, Robert F. *Private Voluntary Organizations as Agents of Development*. Boulder: Westview Press, 1984.

Gouldner, Alvin. "The Norm of Reciprocity." *American Sociological Review* 25 (1960): 161–178.

Gowans, Christopher W., ed. *Moral Dilemmas*. New York: Oxford University Press, 1987.

Green, Ronald M. "Altruism in Health Care." Pp. 239–254 in *Beneficence and Health Care*, edited by Earl E. Shelp. Dordrecht, Holland: D. Reidel, 1982.

Greene, Graham. *A Burnt-Out Case*. New York: Penguin, 1977.

Grice, Russell. *The Grounds of Moral Judgement*. Cambridge: Cambridge University Press, 1967.

Griffin, James. *Well-Being*. Oxford: Clarendon Press, 1986.

Griggs, John, ed. *Simple Acts of Kindness: Volunteering in the Age of AIDS*. New York: United Hospital Fund of New York, 1989.

Grimshaw, Jean. *Philosophy and Feminist Thinking*. Minneapolis: University of Minnesota Press, 1986.

Hall, Peter Dobkin. "A Historical Overview of the Private Nonprofit Sector." Pp. 3–27 in *The Nonprofit Sector: A Research Handbook*, edited by Walter W. Powell. New Haven: Yale University Press, 1987.

Hallette, Garth L. *Christian Moral Reasoning: An Analytic Guide*. Notre Dame: University of Notre Dame, 1983.

Hallie, Philip. *Lest Innocent Blood Be Shed*. New York: Harper and Row, 1985.

Hammarskjold, Dag. *Markings*, translated by Leif Sjoberg and W. H. Auden. New York: Alfred A. Knopf, 1965.

Hammer, Armand. *Hammer*. New York: G. T. Putman's Sons, 1987.

Hampshire, Stuart. *Morality and Conflict*. Cambridge: Harvard University Press, 1983.

—— "Sincerity and Single-Mindedness." Pp. 232–256 in *Freedom of Mind and Other Essays*. Princeton: Princeton University Press, 1971.

Handy, Charles. "The Language of Leadership." Pp. 235–241 in *Contemporary Issues in Leadership*, 2d ed., edited by William E. Rosenbach and Robert L. Taylor. Boulder: Westview Press, 1989.

Hanfling, Oswald, ed. *Life and Meaning*. New York: Basil Blackwell, 1987.

Hardin, Garrett. *The Limits of Altruism*. Bloomington: Indiana University Press, 1977.

Hare, R. M. *Freedom and Reason*. New York: Oxford University Press, 1963.

Harman, John D., ed. *Volunteerism in the Eighties*. Lanham, MD: University Press of America, 1982.

Hart, H. L. A. "Are There Any Natural Rights?" *Philosophical Review* 64 (1955): 175–191.

Hawley, John Stratton, ed. *Saints and Virtues*. Berkeley: University of California Press, 1987.

Haworth, Lawrence. *Autonomy*. New Haven: Yale University Press, 1986.

Hawthorne, Nathaniel. *The Blithedale Romance*. Edited by Seymour Gross and Rosalie Murphy. New York: W. W. Norton, 1978.

—— *The House of the Seven Gables*. In *The Complete Novels and Selected Tales of Nathaniel Hawthorne*, edited by Norman Holmes Pearson. New York: Modern Library, 1937.

Held, Virginia. "The Grounds for Social Trust." Pp. 62–85 in *Rights and Goods*. Chicago: University of Chicago Press, 1984.

Hersey, John. *The Call*. New York: Penguin, 1986.

Heyd, David. *Supererogation*. Cambridge: Cambridge University Press, 1982.

Hill, Thomas E., Jr. *Autonomy and Self-Respect*. Cambridge: Cambridge University Press, 1991.

Hobbes, Thomas. *Leviathan*. London: Molesworth, 1841.

—— *On Human Nature*. Chapter 9, parts 9 and 17, in *The English Works of Thomas Hobbes*, edited by W. Molesworth. London: John Bohn, 1945.

Hodgkinson, Virginia A., Richard W. Lyman, and Associates. *The Future of the Nonprofit Sector*. San Francisco: Jossey-Bass, 1989.

Holloman, Charles R. "Leadership and Headship: There Is a Difference." In *Contemporary Issues in Leadership*, edited by Robert L. Taylor. Boulder: Westview Press, 1984.

Holt, J. C. *Robin Hood*. New York: Thames and Hudson, 1982.

Hooker, Michael. "Moral Values and Private Philanthropy." Pp. 128–141 in *Beneficence, Philanthropy and the Public Good*, edited by Ellen Frankel Paul et al. New York: Basil Blackwell, 1987.

Horwitt, Sanford D. *Let Them Call Me Rebel: Saul Alinsky, His Life and Legacy*. New York: Alfred A. Knopf, 1989.

Hughes, M. W. "Our Concern with Others." Pp. 83–112 in *Philosophy and Personal Relations*, edited by Alan Montefiore. London: Routledge and Kegan Paul, 1973.

Hunt, Lester H. "Generosity and the Diversity of the Virtues." Pp. 216–228 in *The Virtues*, edited by Robert B. Kruschwitz and Robert C. Roberts. Belmont, CA: Wadsworth, 1987.

Hunt, Morton. *The Compassionate Beast*. New York: William Morrow, 1990.

Huntington, James O. S. "Philanthropy—Its Success and Failure." Pp. 98–156 in Jane Addams et al., *Philanthropy and Social Progress*. Montclair, NJ: Patterson Smith, 1970. First published 1893.

Huxley, Julian. *Religion without Revelation*. New York: New American Library, 1957.

Ignatieff, Michael. *The Needs of Strangers*. New York: Penguin, 1986.

Irwin, T. H. "Generosity and Property in Aristotle's Politics." Pp. 37–54 in *Beneficence, Philanthropy and the Public Good*, edited by Ellen Frankel Paul et al. New York: Basil Blackwell, 1987.

Iyer, Raghavan, ed. *The Moral and Political Writings of Mahatma Gandhi*. Vols. 1–3. New York: Oxford University Press, 1986.

James, Susan. "The Duty to Relieve Suffering." Pp. 261–278 in *Feminism and Political Theory*, edited by Cass R. Sunstein. Chicago: University of Chicago Press, 1990.

James, William. "The Moral Equivalent of War." Pp. 311–328 in *Essays on Faith and Morals*, edited by Ralph Barton Perry. New York: Meridian Books, 1962.

——— *The Varieties of Religious Experience*. New York: Modern Library, 1902.

——— "The Will to Believe." Pp. 32–62 in *Essays on Faith and Morals*, edited by Ralph Barton Perry. New York: Meridian Books, 1962.

Jeavons, Thomas. "Giving, Getting, Grace, and Greed: An Historical and Moral Analysis of Fund Raising." Paper read at the 1990 Symposium of the Indiana University Center on Philanthropy, Indianapolis, June 6–8, 1990.

——— *Learning for the Common Good: Liberal Education, Civic Education, and Teaching about Philanthropy*. Washington, DC: Association of American Colleges, 1991.

Jencks, Christopher. "Varieties of Altruism." Pp. 53–67 in *Beyond Self-Interest*, edited by Jane J. Mansbridge. Chicago: University of Chicago Press, 1990.

Jenner, Jessica Reynolds. "Participation, Leadership, and the Role of Volunteerism among Selected Women Volunteers." *Journal of Voluntary Action Research* 11, no. 4 (October-December 1982): 27–38.

Jewett, Sarah Orne. "The Town Poor." Pp. 981–991 in *The Norton Anthology of Literature by Women*, edited by Sandra M. Gilbert and Susan Gubar. New York: W. W. Norton, 1985.

Johnson, Robert Matthews. *The First Charity: How Philanthropy Can Contribute to Democracy in America*. Cabin John, MD: Seven Locks Press, 1988.

Jonas, Hans. "Philosophical Reflections on Experimenting with Human Subjects." In *Experimentation with Human Subjects*, edited by Paul A. Freund. New York: George Braziller, 1970.

Kagan, Shelly. *The Limits of Morality*. Oxford: Clarendon Press, 1989.

Kamenka, Eugene, ed. *Community as a Social Ideal* New York: St. Martin's Press, 1982.

Kaminer, Wendy. *Women Volunteering*. Garden City, NY: Anchor, 1984.

Kant, Immanuel. *The Doctrine of Virtue*. Translated by Mary J. Gregor. Philadelphia: University of Pennsylvania Press, 1964.

——— *Foundations of the Metaphysics of Morals*. Translated by Lewis White Beck. Reprinted pp. 317–366 in *Ethical Theories*, edited by A. I. Melden. Englewood Cliffs, NJ: Prentice Hall, 1967.

Karl, Barry D., and Stanley N. Katz. "Foundations and Ruling Class Elites." *Daedalus*, Special Issue on *Philanthropy, Patronage, Politics* 116 (Winter 1987): 1–40.

Katz, Harvey. *Give! Who Gets Your Charity Dollar?* Garden City, NY: Anchor, 1974.

Katz, William Loren. *The Invisible Empire: The Ku Klux Klan Impact on History*. Washington, DC: Open Hand, 1986.

Kauber, Peter, and Peter H. Hare. "The Right and Duty to Will to Believe." *Canadian Journal of Philosophy* 4 (1974): 327–343.

Kavka, Gregory S. *Hobbesian Moral and Political Theory*. Princeton: Princeton University Press, 1986.

———— "The Futurity Problem." Pp. 109–122 in *Responsibilities to Future Generations*, edited by Ernest Partridge. Buffalo: Prometheus Books, 1981.

Keith-Lucas, Alan. *Giving and Taking Help*. Chapel Hill: University of North Carolina Press, 1972.

Kekes, John. "Benevolence: A Minor Virtue." Pp. 21–36 in *Beneficence, Philanthropy and the Public Good*, edited by Ellen Frankel Paul et al. New York: Basil Blackwell, 1987.

———— "Constancy and Purity." *Mind* 92 (1983): 499–518.

———— *The Examined Life*. Lewisburg: Bucknell University Press, 1988.

———— "Happiness." *Mind* 91 (1982): 358–376.

———— *Moral Tradition and Individuality*. Princeton: Princeton University Press, 1989.

Kellerman, Barbara. "Leadership as a Political Act." Pp. 63–89 in *Leadership*, edited by Barbara Kellerman. Englewood Cliffs, NJ: Prentice Hall, 1984.

Keneally, Thomas. *Schindler's List*. New York: Penguin, 1983.

Kennedy, Gail. "Pragmatism, Pragmaticism, and the Will to Believe—A Reconsideration." *Journal of Philosophy* 55 (1958): 578–588.

Kidder, Tracy. *Among Schoolchildren*. Boston: Houghton Mifflin, 1989.

Kierkegaard, Søren. *Purity of Heart Is to Will One Thing*. Translated by Douglas V. Steere. New York: Harper and Row, 1956.

King, Martin Luther, Jr. *Strength to Love*. Philadelphia: Fortress Press, 1963.

Kipnis, Kenneth. "Professional Responsibility and the Distribution of Legal Services." Pp. 130–142 in *Economic Justice*, edited by Kenneth Kipnis and Diana T. Meyers. Totowa, NJ: Rowman and Allanheld, 1985.

Kittay, Eva Feder. "On Hypocrisy." *Metaphilosophy* 13, nos. 3 and 4 (1982): 277–289.

Kittay, Eva Feder, and Diana T. Meyers, eds. *Women and Moral Theory*. Totowa, NJ: Rowman and Littlefield, 1987.

Kleinig, John. "Good Samaritanism." *Philosophy and Public Affairs* 5 (1976–77): 382–407.

Klemke, E. D., ed. *The Meaning of Life*. New York: Oxford University Press, 1981.

Kohn, Alfie. *The Brighter Side of Human Nature*. New York: Basic Books, 1990.

Kozol, Jonathan. *Rachel and Her Children: Homeless Families in America*. New York: Crown, 1988.

Kruschwitz, Robert B., and Robert C. Roberts, eds. *The Virtues: Contemporary Essays on Moral Character*. Belmont, CA: Wadsworth, 1987.

Kultgen, John. *Ethics and Professionalism*. Philadelphia: University of Pennsylvania Press, 1988.

Kupperman, Joel. "Character and Ethical Theory." *Midwest Studies in Philosophy* 13 (1988): 115–125.

La Rochefoucauld, François, duc de. *Maxims*. Translated by Leonard Tancock. New York: Penguin, 1986.

Ladd, John. "Loyalty." Pp. 97–98 in *The Encyclopedia of Philosophy*, Vol. 5, edited by Paul Edwards. New York: Macmillan, 1967.

La Follette, Hugh. "The Truth in Psychological Egoism." Pp. 500–507 in *Reason and Responsibility*, 7th ed., edited by Joel Feinberg. Belmont, CA: Wadsworth, 1989.

Lapierre, Dominique. *The City of Joy*. Translated by Kathryn Spink. New York: Warner Books, 1985.

Lappé, Frances Moore, and Joseph Collins. *World Hunger*. New York: Grove Press, 1986.

Lash, Joseph P. *Eleanor and Franklin*. New York: Signet, 1973.

Latane, Bibb, and John M. Darley. *The Unresponsive Bystander*. New York: Appleton-Century-Crofts, 1970.

Layton, Daphne Niobe. *Philanthropy and Voluntarism: An Annotated Bibliography*. New York: Foundation Center, 1987.

Lewis, Norman. *The Missionaries: God against the Indians*. New York: Penguin, 1990.

Loch, Charles S. "Charity and Charities." Pp. 860–891 in *Encyclopaedia Britannica*, vol. V. New York: Cambridge University Press, 1910.

Loeser, Herta. *Women, Work, and Volunteering*. Boston: Beacon Press, 1974.

Luther, Martin. *The Freedom of a Christian*. In *Martin Luther: Selections from His Writings*, edited by John Dillenberger. Garden City, NY: Anchor, 1961.

Lyons, Daniel. "Welcome Threats and Coercive Offers." *Philosophy* 50 (1975): 425–436.

Maas, Peter. *Serpico*. New York: Bantam, 1974.

Macaulay, J., and L. Berkowitz, eds. *Altruism and Helping Behavior: Social Psychological Studies of Some Antecedents and Consequences*. New York: Academic Press, 1970.

MacIntyre, Alasdair. *After Virtue*. 2d ed. Notre Dame: University of Notre Dame Press, 1984.

——— "Egoism and Altruism." Pp. 462–466 in *The Encyclopedia of Philosophy*, vol. 2, edited by Paul Edwards. New York: Macmillan, 1967.

——— *Whose Justice? Which Rationality?* Notre Dame: University of Notre Dame Press, 1988.

Mack, Eric. "Bad Samaritanism and the Causation of Harm." *Philosophy and Public Affairs* 9 (1979–80): 230–259.

Mackey, Philip English. *The Giver's Guide: Making Your Charity Dollars Count*. Highland Park, NJ: Catbird Press, 1990.

Magat, Richard, ed. *Philanthropic Giving* New York: Oxford University Press, 1989.

Maimonides, Moses. *The World of Moses Maimonides*, edited by Jacob S. Minkin. New York: Thomas Yoseloff Press, 1957.

Mansbridge, Jane J., ed. *Beyond Self-Interest*. Chicago: University of Chicago Press, 1990.

Manser, Gordon, and Rosemary Higgins Cass. *Voluntarism at the Crossroads*. New York: Family Service of America, 1976.

Margolis, Howard. *Selfishness, Altruism, and Rationality: A Theory of Social Choice*. Chicago: University of Chicago Press, 1982.

Martin, Mike W. *Everyday Morality: An Introduction to Applied Ethics*. Belmont, CA: Wadsworth, 1989.

——— "Love's Constancy." *Philosophy* 68 (1993): 63–77.

——— "Honesty with Oneself." Pp. 115–136 in *Rules, Rituals, and Responsibility: Essays Dedicated to Herbert Fingarette*, edited by Mary I. Bockover. La Salle, IL: Open Court, 1991.

——— Review of *Beneficence, Philanthropy and the Public Good. Nonprofit and Voluntary Sector Quarterly* 20 (Spring 1991): 118–120.

——— *Self-Deception and Morality*. Lawrence: University Press of Kansas, 1986.

Martz, Larry, et al. "God and Money." *Newsweek* (April 6, 1987): 16–22.

Mather, Cotton. *Bonifacius: An Essay upon the Good*. Cambridge: Harvard University Press, 1966. First published 1710.

Mathews, Jay. *Escalante*. New York: Henry Holt, 1988.

Mauss, Marcel. *The Gift*. New York: W. W. Norton, 1967.

Mayeroff, Milton. *On Caring*. New York: Harper and Row, 1971.

McCarthy, Kathleen D., ed. *Lady Bountiful Revisited: Women, Philanthropy, and Power.* New Brunswick, NJ: Rutgers University Press, 1990.

—— *Noblesse Oblige: Charity and Cultural Philanthropy in Chicago, 1849–1929.* Chicago: University of Chicago Press, 1982.

McConnell, Terrance. *Gratitude.* Philadelphia: Temple University Press, 1993.

McCormick, Pat. "NOW Task Force on Volunteerism" (November 1973). Reprinted in *Ms.* 3, part 2 (1975): 73.

McDowell, John. "Virtue and Reason." Pp. 87–109 in *Anti-Theory in Ethics and Moral Conservatism*, edited by Stanley G. Clarke and Evan Simpson. Albany: State University of New York Press, 1989.

McFall, Lynne. "Integrity." *Ethics* 98 (1987): 5–20.

McGoldrick, Patricia M. "Saints and Heroes: A Plea for the Supererogatory." *Philosophy* 59 (1984): 523–528.

Mead, George H. "Philanthropy from the Point of View of Ethics." Pp. 133–148 in *Intelligent Philanthropy*, edited by Ellsworth Faris, Ferris Laune, and Arthur J. Todd. Montclair, NJ: Patterson Smith, 1969. First published 1930.

Meilaender, Gilbert C. "The Virtue of Gratitude." Pp. 152–175 in *The Theory and Practice of Virtue.* Notre Dame: University of Notre Dame Press, 1984.

Melden, A. I. *Rights and Persons.* Berkeley: University of California Press, 1977.

—— *Rights in Moral Lives.* Berkeley: University of California Press, 1988.

—— "Saints and Supererogation." Pp. 61–81 in *Philosophy and Life: Essays on John Wisdom*, edited by Ilham Dilman. The Hague: Martinus Nijhoff, 1984.

Mellema, Gregory. *Beyond the Call of Duty: Supererogation, Obligation, and Offence.* Albany: State University of New York Press, 1991.

Mercer, Philip. *Sympathy and Ethics: A Study of the Relationship between Sympathy and Morality with Special Reference to Hume's Treatise.* Oxford: Clarendon Press, 1972.

Merrill, Charles. *The Checkbook: The Politics and Ethics of Foundation Philanthropy.* Boston: Oelgeschlager, Gunn and Hain, 1986.

Meyers, Diana T. *Self, Society, and Personal Choice.* New York: Columbia University Press, 1989.

Midgley, Mary. *Beast and Man: The Roots of Human Nature.* New York: New American Library, 1980.

—— "Creation and Originality." Pp. 43–58 in *Heart and Mind.* New York: St. Martin's Press, 1981.

—— *Evolution as a Religion.* New York: Methuen, 1985.

—— *Wisdom, Information, and Wonder.* New York: Routledge, 1989.

Mill, John Stuart. *The Autobiography of John Stuart Mill.* Garden City, NY: Doubleday.

—— *On Liberty.* Indianapolis: Hackett, 1978. First published 1859.

—— *Utilitarianism.* Indianapolis: Hackett, 1979.

Milo, Ronald D., ed. *Egoism and Altruism.* Belmont, CA: Wadsworth, 1973.

Molière. *The Critique of the School for Wives.* Translated by Donald M. Frame. Pp. 173–201 in *Tartuffe and Other Plays by Molière.* New York: New American Library, 1967.

Monroe, Kristen R., Michael C. Barton, and Ute Klingemann. "Altruism and the Theory of Rational Action: Rescuers of Jews in Nazi Europe." *Ethics* 101 (1990): 103–122.

Moore, Jennifer. "A Different Kind of Aid for the World's Poor." *Chronicle of Philanthropy* (October 16, 1990): 6–7, 14–15.

Moore, Larry F., ed. *Motivating Volunteers*. Vancouver, BC: Vancouver Volunteer Center, 1985.

Moskos, Charles C. *A Call to Civic Service*. New York: Free Press, 1988.

Mother Teresa of Calcutta. *My Life for the Poor*. Edited by Jose Luis Gonzalez-Balado and Janet N. Playfoot. New York: Ballantine Books, 1985.

Moyers, Bill. "Interview with Ernesto J. Cortes, Jr." In *A World of Ideas*, vol. 2. New York: Doubleday, 1990.

Muggeridge, Malcolm. *Something Beautiful for God: Mother Teresa of Calcutta*. New York: Harper and Row, 1971.

Muir, John. *To Yosemite and Beyond*. Edited by R. Engberg and Donald Wesling. Madison: University of Wisconsin Press, 1980.

Murdoch, Iris. *The Sovereignty of Good*. London: ARK Paperbacks, 1985.

Muyskens, James L. *The Sufficiency of Hope*. Philadelphia: Temple University Press, 1979.

Myrna, Frances. "Purity in Morals." *Monist* 66 (1983): 283–297.

Nagel, Thomas. *The View from Nowhere*. New York: Oxford University Press, 1986.

Narveson, Jan. *The Libertarian Idea*. Philadelphia: Temple University Press, 1988.

Newton, Lisa. "Inducement, Due and Otherwise." *IRB: A Review of Human Subjects Research* 4 (March 1982): 4–6.

Nichols, Bruce, and Gil Loescher, eds. *The Moral Nation: Humanitarianism and U.S. Foreign Policy Today*. Notre Dame: University of Notre Dame Press, 1989.

Niebuhr, Reinhold. "Man's Selfhood in Its Self-Seeking and Self-Giving." Pp. 106–125 in *Man's Nature and His Communities*. New York: Charles Scribner's Sons, 1965.

Nielsen, Waldemar A. *The Golden Donors: A New Anatomy of the Great Foundations*. New York: E. P. Dutton, 1989.

Nietzche, Friedrich. *Thus Spoke Zarathustra*. Translated by Walter Kaufmann. New York: Penguin, 1978.

Nightingale, Benedict. *Charities*. London: Allen Lane, 1973.

Noddings, Nel. *Caring: A Feminine Approach to Ethics and Moral Education*. Berkeley: University of California Press, 1984.

Norman, Richard. *The Moral Philosophers*. Oxford: Clarendon Press, 1983.

Nozick, Robert. *Anarchy, State, and Utopia*. New York: Basic Books, 1974.

———. *The Examined Life*. New York: Simon and Schuster, 1989.

Nygren, Anders. *Agape and Eros*. Translated by Philip S. Watson. Chicago: University of Chicago Press, 1982.

O'Connell, Brian, ed. *America's Voluntary Spirit*. New York: Foundation Center, 1983.

———. *Philanthropy in Action*. New York: Foundation Center, 1987.

———. "What Colleges Ought to Do to Instill a Voluntary Spirit in Young Adults." *Chronicle of Higher Education* (April 15, 1987): 104.

O'Connell, Robert J. *William James on the Courage to Believe*. New York: Fordham University Press, 1984.

O'Connor, John. "Philanthropy and Selfishness." Pp. 113–127 in *Beneficence, Philanthropy and the Public Good*, edited by Ellen Frankel Paul et al. New York: Basil Blackwell, 1987.

Odendahl, Teresa. *Charity Begins at Home: Generosity and Self-Interest among the Philanthropic Elite*. New York: Basic Books, 1990.

Oldenquist, Andrew. "Loyalties." *Journal of Philosophy* 79 (1982): 173–193.

———. *The Non-Suicidal Society*. Bloomington: Indiana University Press, 1986.

Oliner, Samuel P., and Pearl M. Oliner. *The Altruistic Personality*. New York: Free Press, 1988.

O'Neill, Michael. *The Third America: The Emergence of the Nonprofit Sector in the United States*. San Francisco: Jossey-Bass, 1989.

O'Neill, Onora. *Faces of Hunger: An Essay on Poverty, Justice and Development*. Boston: Allen and Unwin, 1986.

Oppenheimer, Helen. "Christian Flourishing." *Religious Studies* 5 (1969): 163–171.

Ortega y Gasset, José. *The Revolt of the Masses*. New York: W. W. Norton, 1932.

Ostrander, Susan A. *Women of the Upper Class*. Philadelphia: Temple University Press, 1984.

Ostrander, Susan A., Stuart Langton, and Jon Van Til. *Shifting the Debate: Public/Private Sector Relations in the Modern Welfare State*. New Brunswick, NJ: Transaction Books, 1987.

Ostrander, Susan, and Paul G. Schervish. "Giving and Getting: Philanthropy as a Social Relation." Pp. 67–98 in *Critical Issues in American Philanthropy*, edited by Jon Van Til. San Francisco: Jossey-Bass, 1990.

Outka, Gene. *Agape: An Ethical Analysis*. New Haven: Yale University Press, 1972.

Overvold, Mark Carl. "Self-Interest and the Concept of Self-Sacrifice." *Canadian Journal of Philosophy* 10 (1980): 105–118.

Panas, Jerold. *Mega Gifts: Who Gives Them, Who Gets Them*. Chicago: Pluribus Press, 1984.

Paul, Ellen Frankel, Fred D. Miller, Jr., Jeffrey Paul, and John Ahrens, eds. *Beneficence, Philanthropy and the Public Good*. New York: Basil Blackwell, 1987. Simultaneously published as a special issue of *Social Philosophy and Policy* 4, no. 2 (Spring 1987).

Payton, Robert L. "American Values and Private Philanthropy." Pp. 3–20 in *Private Means, Public Ends*, edited by Kenneth W. Thompson. Lanham, MD: University Press of America, 1987.

——— "Morality, Polity, and Voluntary Initiative." Paper read at the International Conference on "Voluntarism, Non-Governmental Organizations and Public Policy," Jerusalem (May 1989).

——— "On Discovering Philanthropy: An Informal Guide to the Core Literature." *Change* (November/December 1988): 33–37.

——— "Philanthropic Values." Pp. 21–47 in *Private Means, Public Ends*, edited by Kenneth W. Thompson.

——— *Philanthropy: Voluntary Action for the Public Good*. New York: Macmillan, 1988.

Payton, Robert, Michael Novak, Brian O'Connell, and Peter Dobkin Hall. *Philanthropy: Four Views*. New Brunswick, NJ: Transaction Books, 1988.

Penelhum, Terence. "Human Nature and External Desires." *Monist* 62 (1979): 304–319.

Pennock, J. Roland. "Coercion: An Overview." Pp. 1–5 in *Coercion*, edited by J. Roland Pennock and John W. Chapman. New York: Atherton, 1972.

——— "The Problem of Responsibility." Pp. 3–27 in Carl J. Friedrich, ed. *Responsibility*. New York: Liberal Arts Press, 1960.

Pennock, J. Roland, and John W. Chapman, eds. *Voluntary Associations: Nomos XI*. New York: Atherton Press, 1969.

Petrovic, G. "Alienation." Pp. 76–81 in *The Encyclopedia of Philosophy*, vol. 1, edited by Paul Edwards. New York: Macmillan, 1967.

Phelps, Edmund S., ed. *Altruism, Morality, and Economic Theory*. New York: Russell Sage Foundation, 1975.

Pincoffs, Edmund L. *Quandaries and Virtues*. Lawrence: University Press of Kansas, 1986.

Plato. *The Republic*. Translated by F. M. Cornford. New York: Oxford University Press, 1945

Poe, Donald B. "The Giving of Gifts: Anthropological Data and Social Psychological Theory." *Cornell Journal of Social Relations* 12 (1977): 47–63.

Powell, Walter W., ed. *The Nonprofit Sector: A Research Handbook*. New Haven: Yale University Press, 1987.

Pritchard, Michael S. *On Becoming Responsible*. Lawrence: University Press of Kansas, 1991.

Prochaska, F. K. *Women and Philanthropy in Nineteenth-Century England*. Oxford: Clarendon Press, 1980.

Pugmire, David. "Altruism and Ethics." *American Philosophical Quarterly* 15, no. 1 (1978): 75–80.

Rachels, James. "Egoism and Moral Skepticism." Pp. 398–411 in *Vice and Virtue in Everyday Life*, 2d ed., edited by Christina Hoff Sommers and Fred Sommers. New York: Harcourt Brace Jovanovich, 1989.

Rader, Melvin. *The Right to Hope*. Seattle: University of Washington Press, 1981.

Railton, Peter. "Alienation, Consequentialism, and the Demands of Morality." *Philosophy and Public Affairs* 13 (1984): 134–171.

Ramsey, Paul. *The Patient as Person*. New Haven: Yale University Press, 1970.

Rand, Ayn. *The Virtue of Selfishness*. New York: New American Library, 1964.

Rashdall, Hastings. "Self-Realization and Self-Sacrifice." Pp. 61–106 in *The Theory of Good and Evil*. Vol. 2. Oxford: Clarendon Press, 1907.

Rawls, John. *A Theory of Justice*. Cambridge: Harvard University Press, 1971.

Reeder, John P. "Beneficence, Supererogation, and Role Duty." Pp. 83–108 in *Beneficence and Health Care*, edited by Earl E. Shelp. Boston: D. Reidel, 1982.

Reiterman, Tim. *Raven*. New York: E. P. Dutton, 1982.

Rescher Nicholas. *Ethical Idealism*. Berkeley: University of California Press, 1987.

——— *Unselfishness: The Role of Affects in Moral Philosophy and Social Theory*. Pittsburgh: University of Pittsburgh Press, 1975.

Reynolds, Charles H., and Ralph V. Norman, eds. *Community in America: The Challenge of Habits of the Heart*. Berkeley: University of California Press, 1988.

Richards, A. J. *A Theory of Reasons for Action*. New York: Oxford University Press, 1971.

Rorty, Amélie. "Virtues and Their Vicissitudes." Pp. 314–329 in *Mind in Action*. Boston: Beacon Press, 1988.

Rosenbach, William E., and Robert L. Taylor (eds.). *Contemporary Issues in Leadership*. 2d ed. Boulder: Westview Press, 1989.

Rosenfeld, Steven B. "Mandatory *Pro Bono*: Historical and Constitutional Perspectives." *Cardozo Law Review* 2 (1981): 255–297.

Rosenthal, A. M. *Thirty-Eight Witnesses*. New York: McGraw-Hill, 1964.

Ross, Angus. "The Status of Altruism." *Mind* 92 (1983): 204–218.

Ross, Edward Alsworth. "Philanthropy from the Viewpoint of the Sociologist." Pp. 225–242 in *Intelligent Philanthropy*, edited by Ellsworth Faris, Ferris Laune, and Arthur J. Todd. Montclair, NJ: Patterson Smith, 1969. First published 1930.

Ross, Ishbel. *Angel of the Battlefield: The Life of Clara Barton*. New York: Harper and Row, 1956.

Ross, W. D. *The Right and the Good.* New York: Oxford University Press, 1930.

Roth, John K. *American Dreams: Meditations on Life in the United States.* San Francisco: Chandler and Sharp, 1976.

Royce, Josiah. *The Philosophy of Loyalty.* New York: Macmillan, 1916.

———— *The Spirit of Modern Philosophy.* New York: W. W. Norton, 1967.

Russell, Bertrand. *The Conquest of Happiness.* New York: Liveright, 1971.

Sahlins, Marshall. *Stone Age Economics.* New York: Aldine, 1972.

Salzman, Jack, ed. *Philanthropy and American Society.* New York: Columbia University, Center for American Culture Studies, 1987.

Sanders, Steven, and David R. Cheney, eds. *The Meaning of Life.* Englewood Cliffs, NJ: Prentice Hall, 1980.

Santayana, George. "The Philanthropist." Pp. 124–161 in *Dialogues in Limbo.* New York: Scribners, 1925.

Sartorius, Rolf, ed. *Paternalism.* Minneapolis: University of Minnesota Press, 1983.

Sartre, Jean-Paul. *Anti-Semite and Jew.* Translated by George J. Becker. New York: Schocken Books, 1965.

———— "Existentialism Is a Humanism." Pp. 345–369 in *Existentialism from Dostoevsky to Sartre*, rev. ed., edited by Walter Kaufmann. New York: New American Library, 1975.

Scanlon, T. M. "Preference and Urgency." *Journal of Philosophy* 72 (1975): 655–669.

Schacht, Richard. *Alienation.* New York: Anchor, 1971.

Scheffler, Israel. *Of Human Potential: An Essay in the Philosophy of Education.* Boston: Routledge and Kegan Paul, 1985.

Scheffler, Samuel, ed. *Consequentialism and Its Critics.* New York: Oxford University Press, 1988.

Scheman, Naomi. "On Sympathy." *Monist* 62 (1979): 320–330.

Schneiter, Paul H. *The Art of Asking: A Handbook for Successful Fund Raising.* New York: Walker and Company, 1978.

Schulweis, Harold M. Foreword to Samuel P. Oliner and Pearl M. Oliner, *The Altruistic Personality.* New York: Free Press, 1988.

Schweitzer, Albert. *Memoirs of Childhood and Youth.* Translated by C. T. Campion. New York: Macmillan, 1961.

———— *Out of My Life and Thought.* Translated by C. T. Campion. New York: A Mentor Book, 1949.

Shalev, Carmel. *Birth Power: The Case for Surrogacy.* New Haven: Yale University Press, 1989.

Shapiro, David L. "The Enigma of the Lawyer's Duty to Serve." *New York University Law Review* 55 (1980): 735–792.

Shaw, Bernard. *Major Barbara.* Northbrook, IL: AHM Publishing, 1971. First produced 1905.

Shepard, Charles E. *Forgiven: The Rise and Fall of Jim Bakker and the PTL Ministry.* New York: Atlantic Monthly Press, 1989.

Shklar, Judith N. "Let Us Not Be Hypocritical." *Daedalus* 108 (Summer 1979): 1–25.

———— "What Is Wrong with Snobbery?" Pp. 87–137 in *Ordinary Vices.* Cambridge: Harvard University Press, 1984.

Shue, Henry. *Basic Rights.* Princeton: Princeton University Press, 1980.

Sidorsky, David. "Moral Pluralism and Philanthropy." Pp. 93–112 in *Beneficence, Phi-*

lanthropy and the Public Good, edited by Ellen Frankel Paul et al. New York: Basil Blackwell, 1987.

Simmons, John A. *Moral Principles and Political Obligations*. Princeton: Princeton University Press, 1979.

Singer, Irving. *The Nature of Love*. Vol. 1, 2d ed. Chicago: University of Chicago Press, 1984.

Singer, Peter. "Famine, Affluence, and Morality." Pp. 22–36 in *World Hunger and Moral Obligation*, edited by William Aiken and Hugh La Follette. Englewood Cliffs, NJ: Prentice Hall, 1977.

—— *Practical Ethics*. Cambridge: Cambridge University Press, 1979.

Slote, Michael A. "An Empirical Basis for Psychological Egoism." Pp. 100–107 in *Egoism and Altruism*, edited by Ronald D. Milo. Belmont, CA: Wadsworth, 1973.

Smart, J. J. C. "Utilitarianism." Pp. 3–74 in J. C. C. Smart and Bernard Williams, *Utilitarianism: For and Against*. Cambridge: Cambridge University Press, 1973.

Smith, Chesterfield H. "A Mandatory *Pro Bono* Service Standard—Its Time Has Come." *University of Miami Law Review* 35 (1981): 727–737.

Smith, David Horton. "Altruism, Volunteers and Volunteerism." Pp. 23–44 in *Volunteerism in the Eighties*, edited by John D. Harman. Lanham, MD: University Press of America, 1982.

Smith, Jane S. *Patenting the Sun: Polio and the Salk Vaccine*. New York: William Morrow, 1990.

Smith, Michael D. "The Virtuous Organization." Pp. 172–175 in *Professional Ideals*, edited by Albert Flores. Belmont, CA: Wadsworth, 1988.

Smithson, Michael, Paul R. Amato, and Philip Pearce. *Dimensions of Helping Behavoir*. New York: Pergamon Press, 1983.

Snyder, C. R., Raymond L. Higgins, and Rita J. Sticky. *Excuses*. New York: John Wiley and Sons, 1983.

Solomon, Robert C. *A Passion for Justice*. New York: Addison-Wesley, 1990.

Sommers, Christina, and Fred Sommers, eds. *Vice and Virtue in Everyday Life*. 2d ed. San Diego: Harcourt Brace Jovanovich, 1989.

Stanton, Elizabeth Cady, and the Revision Committee. *The Woman's Bible*. Seattle: Coalition on Women and Religion, 1974. First published 1895.

Staub, Ervin, et al., eds. *Development and Maintenance of Prosocial Behavior*. New York: Plenum Press, 1984.

Stehle, Vince. "Prospect Researchers, Who Collect Confidential Information about Potential Donors, Are Divided over Ethical Questions." *Chronicle of Philanthropy* (September 5, 1989): 5, 11.

Stern-Gillet, Suzanne. "The Rhetoric of Suicide." Pp. 93–103 in *Suicide*, edited by John Donnelly. Buffalo: Prometheus Press, 1990.

Stevenson, Charles L. "Persuasive Definitions." *Mind* 47 (1938): 331–350.

Storr, Anthony. *Solitude: A Return to the Self*. New York: Free Press, 1988.

Stout, Jeffrey. *Ethics after Babel: The Languages of Morals and Their Discontents*. Boston: Beacon Press, 1988.

Strawson, P. F. "Social Morality and Individual Ideal." Pp. 26–44 in *Freedom and Resentment and Other Essays*. New York: Harper and Row, 1974.

Suckiel, Ellen Kappy. *The Pragmatic Philosophy of William James*. Notre Dame: University of Notre Dame Press, 1982.

Sullivan, Roger J. *Immanuel Kant's Moral Theory*. Cambridge: Cambridge University Press, 1989.

Sullivan, William M. *Reconstructing Public Philosophy*. Berkeley: University of California Press, 1986.

Sutherland, John. Introduction to William Makepeace Thackeray, *The Book of Snobs*. New York: St. Martin's Press, 1978.

Szabados, Béla. "Hypocrisy." *Canadian Journal of Philosophy* 9, no. 2 (1979): 195–210.

Taylor, A. E. "Self-Realization—A Criticism." *International Journal of Ethics* 6 (1896): 356–371.

Taylor, Charles. *The Ethics of Authenticity*. Cambridge: Harvard University Press, 1992.

Taylor, Gabriele. "Integrity." Pp. 108–141 in *Pride, Shame, and Guilt*. Oxford: Clarendon Press 1985.

Taylor, Richard. *Ethics, Faith, and Reason*. Englewood Cliffs, NJ: Prentice Hall, 1985.

Telfer, Elizabeth. *Happiness*. New York: St. Martin's Press, 1980.

Thagard, Paul, and Richard E. Nisbett. "Rationality and Charity." *Philosophy of Science* 50 (1983): 250–267.

Thomas, Laurence. *Living Morally: A Psychology of Moral Character*. Philadelphia: Temple University Press, 1989.

Thompson, Kenneth W. (ed.). *Philanthropy: Private Means, Public Ends*. Lanham, MD: University Press of America, 1987.

Thoreau, Henry David. *Walden and Civil Disobedience*. New York: Penguin, 1983.

Titmuss, Richard M. *The Gift Relationship: From Human Blood to Social Policy*. New York: Vintage Books, 1971.

Tocqueville, Alexis de. *Democracy in America*, edited by Thomas Bender. New York: Random House, 1981. First published 1840.

Tolstoy, Leo. *Anna Karenina*. Translated by David Magarshack. New York: New American Library, 1960.

Tormey, Judith Farr. "Exploitation, Oppression and Self-Sacrifice." Pp. 206–221 in *Women and Philosophy*, edited by Carol C. Gould and Marx W. Wartofsky. New York: G. P. Putnam's Sons, 1976.

Toufexis, Anastasia. "Creating a Child to Save Another." *Time* (March 5, 1990): 56.

Tournier, Paul. *The Meaning of Gifts*. Translated by John S. Gilmour. Richmond, VA: John Knox Press, 1963.

Trollope, Anthony. *The Warden*. Oxford: Oxford University Press, 1980.

Urmson, J. O. "Saints and Heroes." Pp. 198–216 in *Essays in Moral Philosophy*, edited by A. I. Melden. Seattle: University of Washington Press, 1958.

Useem, Michael. "Corporate Philanthropy." Pp. 340–359 in *The Nonprofit Sector*, edited by Walter W. Powell. New Haven: Yale University Press, 1987.

Uyl, Douglas Den, and Tibor R. Machan. "Recent Work on the Concept of Happiness." *American Philosophical Quarterly* 20 (April 1983): 115–134.

Van Til, Jon. *Mapping the Third Sector: Voluntarism in a Changing Social Economy*. New York: Foundation Center, 1988.

Van Til, Jon, and Associates. *Critical Issues in American Philanthropy*. San Francisco: Jossey-Bass, 1990.

Vonnegut, Kurt. *God Bless You, Mr. Rosewater*. New York: Dell, 1965.

Wade, Wyn. *The Fiery Cross: The Ku Klux Klan in America*. New York: Simon and Schuster, 1987.

Walker, A. D. M. "Political Obligation and the Argument from Gratitude." *Philosophy and Public Affairs* 17 (1988): 191–211.

Wall, Joseph Frazier. *Andrew Carnegie*. Pittsburgh: University of Pittsburgh Press, 1989.

Wallace, James D. *Moral Relevance and Moral Conflict*. Ithaca: Cornell University Press, 1988.

—— *Virtues and Vices*. Ithaca: Cornell University Press, 1978.

Walton, Douglas N. *Courage*. Berkeley: University of California Press, 1986.

Wartofsky, Marx. "On Doing It for Money." Pp. 187–195 in *Biomedical Ethics*, edited by Thomas A. Mappes and Jane S. Zembaty. New York: McGraw-Hill, 1981.

Weisbrod, Burton A. *The Nonprofit Economy*. Cambridge: Harvard University Press, 1988.

Weitman, Sasha R. "Prosocial Behavior and Its Discontents." Pp. 229–246 in *Altruism, Sympathy, and Helping: Psychological and Sociological Principles*, edited by Lauren Wispé. New York: Academic Press, 1978.

Welty, Eudora. *The Ponder Heart*. New York: Harcourt Brace Jovanovich, 1953.

Wernham, James C. S. *James's Will-to-Believe Doctrine*. Kingston: McGill-Queen's University Press, 1987.

Wertheimer, Alan. *Coercion*. Princeton: Princeton University Press, 1987.

Wheatley, Steven C. *The Politics of Philanthropy*. Madison: University of Wisconsin Press, 1988.

Wilhelm, Richard, and Cary F. Baynes, eds. and trans. *The I Ching*. Princeton: Princeton University Press, 1967.

Williams, Bernard. "A Critique of Utilitarianism." Pp. 77–150 in J. J. C. Smart and Bernard Williams, *Utilitarianism: For and Against*. Cambridge: Cambridge University Press, 1973.

—— *Ethics and the Limits of Philosophy*. Cambridge: Harvard University Press, 1985.

—— "Persons, Character, and Morality." Pp. 1–19 in *Moral Luck*. Cambridge: Cambridge University Press, 1981.

Williams, Daniel Day. *The Spirit and the Forms of Love*. Lanham, MD: University Press of America, 1981.

Wilson, Edward O. *On Human Nature*. Now York: Bantam, 1979.

Wispé, Lauren, ed. *Altruism, Sympathy, and Helping: Psychological and Sociological Principles*. New York: Academic Press, 1978.

Wittgenstein, Ludwig. *Culture and Value*. Translated by Peter Winch. Chicago: University of Chicago Press, 1980.

—— *Philosophical Investigations*. Translated by G. E. M. Anscombe. New York: Macmillan, 1953.

Wolf, Susan. "Above and Below the Line of Duty." *Philosophical Topics* 13 (Fall 1986): 131–148.

Wolff, Robert Paul. *The Poverty of Liberalism*. Boston: Beacon Press, 1968.

Wong, David B. "On Flourishing and Finding One's Identity in Community." *Midwest Studies in Philosophy* 13 (1988): 324–341.

Woolf, Virginia. *Three Guineas*. New York: Harcourt Brace Jovanovich, 1938.

Worchel, Stephen. "The Darker Side of Helping." Pp. 379–395 in *Development and Maintenance of Prosocial Behavior*, edited by Ervin Staub et al. New York: Plenum Press, 1984.

Wuthnow, Robert. *Acts of Compassion*. Princeton: Princeton University Press, 1991.

Young, Dennis R. "Executive Leadership in Nonprofit Organizations." Pp. 167–179 in *The Nonprofit Sector: A Research Handbook*, edited by Walter W. Powell. New Haven: Yale University Press, 1987.

Young, Robert. *Personal Autonomy*. London: Croom Helm, 1986.

Zwiebach, Burton. *The Common Life: Ambiguity, Agreement, and the Structure of Morals*. Philadelphia: Temple University Press. 1988.

Index

Abortion, 96

Adams, Robert, 179n42, 181n97, 193n67

Addams, Jane, 1, 112, 154–55

Aesthetic appreciation, sense of, 30, 43–44

AIDS: and compassion, 32; and perseverance of volunteers, 55; and priorities in philanthropy, 86

Aiken, William, 183n18

Alinsky, Saul, 59

Altruism: defined, 123; and ideals of purity, 149; in mixed motives, 123–31 *passim*; sociobiology of, 138; and women, 113

Alumni giving: and internal goods of education, 16; responsibilities in, 73

Alvarado, Elvia, 179n50

Ambiguity, moral: of philanthropy, 1, 100, 169–72

American Civil Liberties Union, 95

American Red Cross, 116, 160. *See also* Barton, Clara

Anguiano, Lupe, 98

Animals: caring for, 23; caring among, 137; rescue of, 16; welfare of, 25–26

Applied ethics, 3–4

Argyros, Judie, 58

Aristotle: on generosity, 29; on happiness, 196n45; on moral vagueness, 85; on philanthropy, 174n19; on philosophy, 5

Authenticity: moral, 132, 149; Sartre on, 148–49

Authority, responsible, 31, 59

Autonomy: as freedom, 157–60; respect for, 30, 48–50, 94–122 *passim*; three aspects of, 94–95; and women, 113–14

Ayala, Abe and Mary, 110

Baier, Annette, 178n35, 198n78

Bakker, Jim and Tammy Faye, 48

Barton, Clara, 112, 160–61

Battin, Margaret P., 187n24

Baum, Robert J., 185n55

Beauvoir, Simone de, 113, 151–52, 172

Becker, Lawrence C., 70, 178n22, 178n27, 179n60, 182n1, 183n21

Beckman, Arnold, 44–45

Bellah, Robert, 27–28, 195n36

Benevolence: connection with justice, 36; as a philanthropic virtue, 24, 31–35; as a self-reported motive, 124

Benjamin, Martin, 180n66, 187n18

Benn, S. I., 176n49

Bentham, Jeremy, 3

Berger, Fred R., 178n23

Berger, Peter L., 176n50

Big Brothers and Sisters, 25

Bingham, Sallie, 44

Blee, Kathleen M., 173n2

Blood donations: as recent practice, 15; symbolism of, 25; voluntary versus paid, 116

Blum, Lawrence A., 130, 177n4, 177n7

Bradley, F. H., 151, 197n64

Braybrooke, David, 182n4

Bremner, Robert, 175n28, 175n36

Broudy, Harry S., 39

Buckley, William F., Jr., 120–21

Buddha, 50

Bullard, Edward P., 97

Butler, Joseph: on duties, 62; on paradox of happiness, 163

Camenisch, Paul F., 38

Camus, Albert, 143–44

Care, Norman, 186n62

Caring: good will and judgment, ix, 1; as generic virtue, 24; and resolving dilemmas, 91; and volitional necessity, 76, 159; wholehearted, 159–60; within communities, 22–28; as worrying, 158

Carnegie, Andrew: encouraged self-reliance, 97; funding libraries, 59, 73; funding medical schools, 104–105; motives of, 47

Carter, Jimmy and Rosalynn, 99

Cass, Rosemary Higgins, 123–24

Catholic Workers Movement, 43

Character, dimensions of, 4–5

Charity: meanings of, 8; as philosophical topic, 2; in religions, 43

Chavez, Cesar, 59

Cherishing, enlightened, 39–45

Civil disobedience, 60

MIKE W. MARTIN is Professor of Philosophy at Chapman University. He is author of *Everyday Morality* and *Self-Deception and Morality*, coauthor of *Ethics in Engineering*, and editor of *Self-Deception and Self-Understanding*, and has written numerous articles on applied ethics.

MIKE W. MARTIN is Professor of Philosophy at Chapman University. He is author of *Everyday Morality* and *Self-Deception and Morality*, coauthor of *Ethics in Engineering*, and editor of *Self-Deception and Self-Understanding*, and has written numerous articles on applied ethics.